WWII: Marine Fighting Squadron Nine (VF-9M)

by Jess C. Barrow

MODERN AVIATION SERIES

TAB BOOKS Inc.

BLUE RIDGE SUMMIT, PA. 17214

FIRST EDITION

FIRST PRINTING

MARCH 1981

Copyright © 1981 by TAB BOOKS Inc.

Printed in the United States of America

Library of Congress Cataloging in Publication Data

Barrow, Jess C
    WWII Marine Fighting Squadron Nine (VF-9M)

    Includes index.
    1. World War, 1939-1945—Aerial operations, American. 2. United States, Marine Corps. Fighting Squadron Nine—History. I. Title.
D790.B29   940.54'4973   80-28357
ISBN 0-8306-2289-6 (pbk.)

Front & back cover illustrations by B.W. Campbell

Preface

Fighting Squadron Nine-M, United States Marine Corps, was without doubt one of the most colorful squadrons in the history of Marine Aviation—and in some ways, one of the most controversial. Based at Brown Field, Quantico, Virginia, during the 1920's and 1930's, it performed before millions of people. It was seen at almost every important civil and military function in the United States in the promotion of Marine Aviation. For reasons unknown, its accomplishments and extraordinary flying skills have never been told. With the passing of years former squadron members cannot remember or agree on all of the details, but they *are* sure of one thing: *"It was the best damn squadron that I ever flew with."*

After World War I, Marine Aviation was fighting for its very existence. At one time in the early 1920's there were only 43 pilots in the *entire* Marine Corps. It was largely through the efforts of such men as Colonel Thomas C. Turner and Major Roy S. Geiger—men who could forsee the future—that Marine Aviation survived.

Various methods were used to promote Marine Aviation during the 1920's and 30's and this story of Fighting Squadron Nine-M is about one such way. It is a story of a few dedicated men who took it upon themselves to promote the cause of Marine Aviation by selling it directly to the public. During one period, this squadron was promoting Marine Aviation almost on a full-time basis.

It is not the intent to suggest that Marine Aviators were the best or most skillful, or to bring out all of the details of the political struggle that the Corps was engaged in for recognition. This is documented elsewhere. The main intent is to record—for historical purposes—facts about its activities, places it performed, dates, its airplanes and squadron markings—and possibly a few humorous stories on its personnel to make the reading more pleasurable.

Jess C. Barrow

Acknowledgements

The writing of history—almost always—is a never-ending task and one with many problems. Not the least among them is where it should end. Years of research, interviewing, sorting over old documents and photos, and travel ultimately must end.

My original intention was to record the history of VF-9M from 1930 through 1937. These were the years in which the squadron was most active in its promotion of Marine Aviation and carried the designation of VF-9M used in the title. However, certain people prevailed upon me to start with squadron's inception and continue to the start of World War II. This I tried to do, but the task proved too great and reluctantly, I decided to terminate the history as of 31 December 1938.

There will be those who will disagree with portions of the text, and a few may feel slighted because of the omission of their names. But in writing any history, there are facts that come to light too late to be included in the final draft.

The vast majority of material and information for this history came from former squadron members through correspondence and interviews. They were generous in supplying many documents, especially old photo albums that contained many photos heretofore unpublished. Further, I am indebted to these fine people for their wonderful cooperation and very good memories. So glamorous were their careers that a book could be written about each and every one of these fine gentlemen. I have come to know many personally and will value their friendship always. Their names are listed according to rank and not to their contribution.

General Christian F. Schilt, USMC (ret)
General Vernon E. Megee, USMC (ret)
Lieutenant General Carson A. Roberts, USMC (ret)
Major General Lawson H. M. Sanderson, USMC (ret)

Major General Ford O. Rogers, USMC (ret)
Major General Alexander W. Kreiser, USMC (ret)
Rear Admiral Ralph Sperry Clarke, USN (ret)
Brigadier General Boeker C. Batterton, USMC (ret)
Brigadier General Clarence J. Chappell, USMC (ret)
Brigadier General Frank G. Dailey, USMC (ret)
Brigadier General John F. Dobbin, USMC (ret)
Brigadier General Harold R. Lee, USMC (ret)
Brigadier General William L. McKittrick, USMC (ret)
Brigadier General Ivan W. Miller, USMC (ret)
Brigadier General Edward A. Montgomery, USMC (ret)
Brigadier General Perry O. Parmelee, USMC (ret)
Brigadier General Frank H. Schwable, USMC (ret)
Brigadier General Wilford H. Stiles, USMC (ret)
Brigadier General Daniel W. Torrey, USMC (ret)
Brigadier General Edward L. Pugh, USMC (ret)
Brigadier General Frank H. Wirsig, USMC (ret)
Colonel Charles C. Campbell, USMC (ret)
Colonel Harold R. Jordan, USMC (ret)
Colonel Theodore A. Petras, USMC (ret)
Colonel Joseph N. Renner, USMC (ret)
Colonel Millard T. Shepard, USMC (ret)
Lieutenant Colonel Leonard I. Beatty, USMC (ret)
Lieutenant Colonel Joseph P. Fuchs, USMC (ret)
Lieutenant Colonel Burnette A. Kempson, Jr., USMC (ret)
Lieutenant Colonel Robert E. Lillie, USMC (ret)
Lieutenant Colonel Lee E. Roberts, USMC (ret)
Lieutenant Colonel Carl E. Volter, USMCR (ret)
Captain James J. Bradley, USMC (ret)
Captain Alexander A. Case, USMC (ret)
Captain Richard E. Gilmore, USMC (ret)
First Lieutenant Tom J. Griffis, USMC (ret)
Chief Warrant Officer John E. Curtis, USMC (ret)
Chief Warrant Officer Joseph W. Wheeler, USMC (ret)
Master Sergeant Earle J. Zalanka, USMC (ret)

Others who provided assistance and useful data were Colonel David E. Schwulst and Master Sergeant Clyde W. Gillespie of the Marine Corps Museum; Mr. Louis Casey, Curator of Flight Craft, National Air and Space Museum; Mr. Lee Pearson, Bureau of Naval Weapons Historian; Mr. William T. Larkins, American Aviation Historical Society; Mr. Gordan S. Williams of the Boeing Company; Mrs. Edward L. Pugh and Ms. Annis Walker.

Special mention is due Mr. Boyd Campbell for his beautiful drawings of the squadron airplanes and illustrations of squadron maneuvers; to Mr. Tom George for his drawing of the Squirrel Cage maneuver; and to Mr.

Stephen J. Hudek for his fine reproductions of numerous faded photographs from old picture albums.

I wish to express my appreciation and gratitude to Major John M. Elliott, USMCR (ret), who gave freely of his time in my behalf. He toiled untold hours in the National Archives and Marine Corps Headquarters Historical Section, checking offical documents and verifying important dates and events. His help is without parallel.

Last and perhaps of equal importance is the patience and support given by my wife Elnora, during the several years of research and writing. Without it, I might have given up.

Dedication

FOR:

Major General Lawson H. M. "Sandy" Sanderson, USMC
(1895-1979)

Contents

Chapter 1

In The Beginning

A significant event occurred for Marine Aviation in 1925 when, on 3 May, Rear Admiral William A. Moffett, Chief of the Navy Bureau of Aeronautics, issued a directive authorizing three Fighting Squadrons within the Marine Corps. They were to be listed officially as Fighting Plane Squadron One (VF-1), Fighting Plane Squadron Two (VF-2) and Fighting Plane Squadron Three (VF-3). The directive was the result of constant pressure from Lieutenant Colonel Thomas C. Turner, who during his first tour of duty as Officer-in-Charge of Marine Aviation never let pass an opportunity to badger his Navy superiors for due recognition of Marine Aviation. Admiral Moffett, long in sympathy with Col. Turner, finally issued the directive establishing the three squadrons, but failed in his attempt to secure the necessary funds from Congress and the Navy Department to provide them with new airplanes. Nevertheless, Turner was satisfied and greatly relieved with the Navy's authorization; with fighter squadrons assured, he would worry about funds, equipment and manpower later. After all, a big step had been taken in the right direction. Until 1925, Marine Aviation did not appear at all in the Navy's Aeronautical Organization, even though Naval Aviation—in its early development— owed much to its Marine members.

The Marines were, of course, elated over their new status. Speculation among aviation personnel was soon running wild as to when the new squadrons were to be formed. With Colonel Turner driving hard, they didn't have long to wait.

On 6 June a letter was issued by the Commandant of the Marine Corps indicating how the three squadrons were to be organized, together with dates they were to be formed and their primary duties and base of operations. Also named were three squadron commanders selected by Colonel Turner.

This was the official approval Turner had been waiting for. It was from those three squadrons that Marine Fighting Squadrons developed and grew through the years as we know them today.

Of the three squadrons VF-2, (later carrying designations VF-5M, VF-9M and VMF-1) was destined in the next 12 years to become the greatest fighter squadron in the history of the Marine Corps. It provided the principal source for the Corps' outstanding aviators and, moreover, laid the foundation from which emerged the highest echelon in Marine Aviation at the start of World War Two.

The Squadron is Born

Its meager beginning was on 1 September 1925, when it was officially commissioned as Fighting Plane Squadron Two (VF-2), with First Lieutenant Lawson H.M. "Sandy" Sanderson as its first Commanding Officer.

The headquarters directive authorizing formation of the squadron said in part: *"The primary mission of this squadron will be the training and perfecting of pursuit pilots and the testing and development of pursuit aircraft."* As will be seen, that they did against almost insurmountable odds.

When Lieutenant Sandy Sanderson reported in at Brown Field, Quantico, Virginia (Fig. 1-1), he found his new squadron to be mostly on paper. Observation Plane Squadron Four (VO-4) had been disbanded the year before so its funds, enlisted personnel, and possibly an airplane or two could be used to form the nucleus of the new fighter squadron.

Unhappy with his lot, Sandy submitted a request for ten pilots and twelve airplanes. He received exactly *one* pilot, however a very capable one: First Lieutenant Franklin G. Cowie. After much "cussin" and "discussin" he managed to acquire seven airplanes from various sources within the Corps. All were in questionable flying condition. There were four Vought VE-7 trainers, one Vought VE-7SF scout fighter and one Vought VE-9 observation plane. Also included was old Martin MT Bomber. He didn't have the faintest idea what he would do with the old bomber in a fighter squadron, but he accepted any and everything that was offered.

Actually, Sandy knew he had fared exceedingly well. At this time there were only 56 pilots and slightly more than 80 aircraft of all types in the entire Marine Corps, and they were thinly spread halfway around the world.

The poor condition of the airplanes led Sandy to be determined in his selection of crew chiefs. He wanted the best men and would settle for no less. In those days, a crew chief was measured by his ability to improvise, get things done, and keep the airplanes flying. If spare parts were unavailable, the chiefs knew how to make them. With the help of Lt. Cowie, Sandy presented a list of men from within the First Aviation Group to Col. Turner, who recently had taken over as group commander at Quantico.

It is not known for sure *how* Sandy was able to rob other squadrons of choice men, but, importantly, he *did*. Perhaps the answer lies in the fact that Sanderson and Turner were old friends, and that Turner considered

Fig. 1-1. Flying Fields, Quantico, Virginia in 1925. Brown Field One is on the right side (east) of the railroad tracks and Brown Field Two on the left (west) side (courtesy Marine Corps).

Sanderson the top fighter pilot in Marine Aviation. It was Turner along with Sanderson, Lt. B. G. Bradley and Gunnery Sgt. C. W. Rucker who, four years previously, had led a fight of two DH-4's from Washington, D.C. to Santo Domingo and back-the longest unguarded flight of its kind over land *or* water up to that time. For this the four were awarded the Distinguished Flying Cross.

Sandy, who possessed a naturally aggresive spirit, viewed his new assignment as a real challenge. Since World War I, Marine Aviation had been looking forward to the day when it would have fighter squadrons similar to the Army and Navy. The time was here and now. It was Sandy's intention from this time forward to see that Marine Aviation *remained* on the Navy's Organizational Chart. In fact, he vowed that pilots sent to his squadron would become well trained and indoctrinated in the latest known fighter tactics.

At the end of the first thirty days of VF-2's existance, its small crew of mechanics were well on their way toward repairing the airplanes assigned to them. Three Vought VE's requiring only minor repairs were now in good operating condition. Another three Voughts removed from storage were being restored to flying status. Any parts that crew chiefs were unable to "scrounge" were made by hand or modified from similar parts. The old Martin MT Bomber was operating too, but only after the first of the month when a new supply of gasoline was allocated to Brown Field. The roster of pilots in the squadron was still exactly two: Sanderson and Cowie. It was to remain so for some time to come.

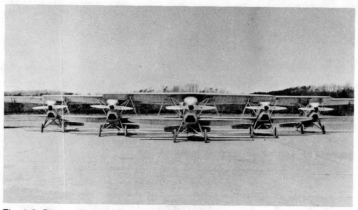

Fig. 1-2. Six new Boeing FB-1 Fighters for Squadrons VF-1 and VF-2 in March 1926 (courtesy Marine Corps).

During the remainder of 1925, the squadron was used as a staging area for personnel waiting for reassignment or enroute to other areas or squadrons. Sometimes as many as 100 men were temporarily attached to VF-2 while awaiting orders. Further adding to Sandy's woes, an epidemic of influenza swept through Quantico in January 1926 and immobilized the squadron for thirty days.

First Fighters Arrive

Returning to duty on 9 February, Sandy learned that six Boeing FB-1's had been assigned to Quantico and were enroute from San Diego, California. This called for rejoicing. They were to be the first actual airplanes specifically designed as fighters to be received by VF-2 and would most certainly be welcomed.

Four of the Boeings were received by rail on 23 February. The remaining two arrived on 2 March. Three were assigned to VF-2 and three to Squadron VF-1 (Fig. 1-2).

The new FB-1's were immediately pressed into service for advanced combat instruction. Sandy worked with these planes to further improve the fighter tactics used within the Corps. Until this time few such tactics existed for Marine fighter planes and pilots, mainly due to lack of suitable equipment.

Sandy quickly ordered that his three FB-1's were to carry full ordnance gear on all flights and that at every opportunity bombing and gunnery were to be practiced. Of the six FB-1's, VF-2's three were the only ones to be so equipped while based at Quantico.

In addition to running an advanced fighter school for pilots, VF-2 was giving primary training to several enlisted men. The first man to receive his wings from VF-2 was First Sergeant Joseph I. Hockman. Designated a Naval Aviation Pilot (NAP), Hockman also became the first pilot added to the squadron as Sandy was allowed to keep his first graduate. The roster of pilots now totaled three.

On 4 April, 1926, Lt. Frank Cowie, who had been with the squadron since its inception, was transferred to Service Squadron One. Cowie, a man of many talents, was reassigned as Engineering Officer for the First Aviation Group at Quantico. During his seven months as Executive Officer of VF-2, he had worn many hats including those of gunnery, personnel, morale, and training officers, to name a few. He would be missed.

On 5 April 1st Lt. Christian F. Schilt (Fig. 1-3) joined the squadron as Cowie's replacement. Schilt, also a man of many talents, proved to be an excellent replacement and immediately took over the many squadron administrative duties vacated by Cowie.

Fig. 1-3. 1st Lt. Christian F. Schilt beside his FB-1 at Brown Field in May 1926. Schilt later won the Medal of Honor for his bravery at Quilali, Nicaragua in 1927 (courtesy Marine Corps).

From the first, Sanderson and Schilt made an excellent team. Both were highly talented pilots and each believed strongly in Marine Aviation, devoting many hours both on and off duty to its promotion.

Sandy learned that the Army Air Service was to hold an aerial machine gun and bombing competition during 10-15 May at Langley Field, Virginia. He felt that the contest, which was open to all military pilots, was a fine opportunity to test one's skills against aviators of the Army and Navy, who were flying better equipment and had more diversified experience.

Sandy immediately submitted a request to Col. Turner for himself and Schilt to enter the competition. Turner, who never passed up an opportunity to help his aviators sharpen their competitive spirit, gave permission pending confirmation from Headquarters. To make up a three-plane team, Sandy urged 1st Lt. Harmon J. Norton, of Fighting Squadron One (VF-1), to participate.

Within a few days, targets for bomb dropping and machine gun firing were placed in the Potomac River east of the field. Each day, people from Brown Field and Quantico lined the river to watch the practice flights and to cheer them on.

Three days before the competition team was to leave, practice flights were terminated to allow the crew chiefs to make the FB-1's as near perfect as possible (Fig. 1-4). It was their responsibility, among many other things, to see that the armament functioned perfectly. Sandy didn't want any of the machine guns jamming, or any nicks or bullet holes through the propellers during the competition. After bore-sighting, the guns were harmonized to each pilot's satisfaction.

The three-plane squadron arrived at Langley Field the day before the contest, and the three officers were invited to a party that evening hosted by the commanding officer of the station. Throughout the evening, the three men were on the receiving end of many jokes and remarks about the Marines and their "big air force." No one expected the Marines to make a decent showing.

On opening day and each day during the matches, the three crew chiefs were always at the flight line ahead of Sandy and his "big air force." It seems they were having more fun than the pilots, as some big money had been bet among the crew chiefs of the other services.

As the competition became keener, a holiday atmosphere seemed to take over the matches. Some top brass was present from the various services, and this made each of the competing pilots more determined to win. As the final day of the eliminations drew near, it became evident that it was going to be a very close contest between the Army and the Marines. When the final score was tallied, Sanderson captured second place, missing first by a very narrow margin. Schilt and Harmon won third and fourth place respectively. Further, Marine Captain R. C. Archibald won second place in the observation contest.

The Marines were jubilant. However, to say that the Army was unhappy would be putting it mildly. Unofficial score keepers insisted that

Fig. 1-4. FB-1, A-6891 of VF-2 at Brown Field Two on 4 April 1926 (courtesy Marine Corps).

15

Fig. 1-5. Boeing FB-1's from Squadrons VF-1 and VF-2 at the Philadelphia Sesquicentennial Exposition in 1926 (courtesy Marine Corps).

some form of collusion took place to prevent the Marines from sweeping the entire matches, but it was never proven.

On 21 May each contestant received a letter of commendation from Major General John A. Lejeune, Commandant of the Marine Corps, for their outstanding performance at Langley Field. Further, on 9 June they were advised that the following letter was received by the Secretary of the Navy from the Secretary of War.

WAR DEPARTMENT
Washington   *3 June, 1926*
SUBJECT: Annual Machine Gun and Bombing Matches
TO: The Secretary of the Navy

The Chief of the Air Service has advised me of the splendid scores made during the Annual Machine Gun and Bombing Matches recently completed at Langley Field, Virginia, by First Lieutenants L. H. Sanderson, C. F. Schilt and H. J. Norton of the Marine Corps, who won second, third and fourth places respectively, in the events for pursuit pilots; and Captain R. C. Archibald also of the Marine Corps, who won second place in the observer's course. Such splendid performance by these officers most highly for the efficiency of their Corps.

The Executive Officer in charge of the conduct of the matches stated in his report that the officers reflected credit and honor upon the Marine Corps both by their skillful shooting and by their sportsmanlike conduct.

I wish to offer my personal congratulations to these officers, and I trust that these matches, which are to be held annually, will result in bringing the flying personnel of all services into closer relationship and in increasing the interest in these important subjects.

(Signed) DWIGHT F. DAVIS
Secretary of War

The First Airshow

On 14 and 15 June, VF-2 teamed with three airplanes of VF-1 to perform its first major airshow before the public at the Sesquicentennial Exposition at Philadelphia, Pennsylvania (Fig. 1-5). Sandy, a great showman, welcomed this opportunity to show the public what they could do. However, at the last minute he was unable to attend and Captain James T. Moore volunteered to lead the two squadrons through their routine (Fig. 1-6). The show's success resulted in the Marines being asked to return for the Exposition's Fourth of July celebration.

Due to the shortage of funds, it was designated that only VF-2 would attend the Fourth of July show. Sandy decided to use a three-plane stunt team for the occasion. He, Frank Schilt, and 2nd Lt. Thomas J. Walker, who temporarily was assigned to the squadron, made up the team. Second Lt. William G. Manley, also temporarily attached to VF-2 for the summer, was assigned to fly all support personnel to the show in the old Martin bomber. Sandy figured the old bomber would make a good "attention getter," as it probably would be the largest airplane there.

Instead of the usual military formation flying, Sandy presented a 20-minute show of three-plane loops, rolls, upside—down flying, and dive bombing that thrilled the crowd and established beyond doubt that Marine Aviation did exist.

That evening, Sandy and his men were treated to a large dinner party and afterward, an all-night tour of the local "speakeasy" clubs. Before departing for home the following afternoon, the Mayor of Philadelphia received a promise from the Officer-in-Charge of Marine Aviation that

Fig. 1-6. Cap. James T. Moore flying Vought VE-7, Serial No. A-5969, west of Brown Field on 3 June 1926 (courtesy Marine Corps).

Fig. 1-7. VF-2's Martin Bomber on its nose after sliding into hedge-row during the 1926 National Air Races in Philadelphia. Cpl. Harold R. Jordan in front cockpit was slightly injured (courtesy Marine Corps).

VF-2 would be allowed to return for the National Air Races to be held there in September.

The 1926 National Air Races opened on 4 September at Model Farms Field, Philadelphia, southwest and adjacent to the Sesquicentennial Exposition Grounds. Originally scheduled for one week, it lasted nine days because of heavy rains. There were 215 entrants signed up for the 19 racing events, plus many other contests such as spot landing and parachute jumping. As usual, the military was also well represented.

Because the show was a national event, Squadron VF-1 was again allowed to participate with VF-2. Each day, the two squadrons, acting as one, took their FB-1's aloft to present a daring aerial display of tactical formations, dogfighting, loops in line, loops in "V", and dive bombing. After each performance, a tremendous round of applause and cheering were given the two squadrons when they taxied up and shut down their engines in front of the crowd.

Two days of rain turned the field into one large mudhole that caused concern for the pilots during take off and landing. It also added a few extra thrills for the spectators. Master Sgt. Harry L. "Doc" Blackwell, flying the squadron's old Martin Bomber, was among the concerned pilots when he volunteered the use of the bomber to take the parachutists up for their jump. When landing, Blackwell was unable to bring the big bomber to a stop because of the slippery mud and it ended up on its nose in a hedgerow at one end of the field (Fig. 1-7). Luckily, no one was seriously hurt.

On Saturday, 11 September, the Kansas City Rotary Club sponsored a trophy race open to all military pilots (Fig. 1-8). Sandy decided to enter with a Boeing FB-3 loaned to him by the Navy. Shortly after the race was underway, his engine began to lose power, forcing him to fall behind. He thus ended up in seventh place with an average speed of 163.36 miles per hour. The race was won by Lt. Cuddihy, USN, in a Boeing FB-3, who also established a new world's speed record for pursuit planes of 180.50 miles per hour.

At least Sandy was able to finish this one. For several years he had entered numerous races around the country but always had some kind of trouble. Two years previously at the St. Louis Air Meet he had run out of fuel at the end of the race. Rather than attempt a dead-stick landing on the airport and possibly endanger the lives of the spectators, he deliberately crashed his plane in a haystack near one side of the field. He came out with only a sprained ankle and a few bruises. For some time it had been the talk among Marine Aviators that Sandy had walked away from more airplane crashes than anyone in the Marine Corps. Some said he was lucky and others said it was because he was an expert pilot. When asked about this, Sandy remarked, "Whatever it is, I'm damn glad I've got it!"

Returning to home base at Brown Field, Sandy and his squadron were pleased with their wonderful acceptance by the public. If air races and air shows were to be the salvation of the flying Marines, then that is what they would continue to do. This view was shared by officers in the top echelon as well.

The excitement of the past summer made the squadron's regular duties seem dull (Fig. 1-9). Sanderson and Schilt continued primary and secondary flight instruction for four crew chiefs assigned as student Naval Aviation Pilots (NAP's). Also, advanced tactical training flights were resumed for regular and reserve officers on active duty. As of 1 October 1926, the status of VF-2 was as follows:

Fig. 1-8. FB-1, A-6888 of VF-2 was entered in one of the races at the 1926 Nationals. Note race number on the nose (courtesy U.S. Navy).

aircraft

3 Boeing FB-1 fighters	1 Dayton-Wright TW-3
6 Vought VE-7 trainers	1 Martin MT bomber
1 Boeing NB-2 trainer	

personnel

2 Officers (Sanderson, C.O., Schilt, Exec).
74 Enlisted Men (1 Naval Aviation Pilot)
76 Total

One VE-7 was under repair because of minor damage by a student, and the Martin bomber was in storage indefinately awaiting repair after its damage at the National Air Races. Sandy hated to see the bomber out of commission. Of late, he and Schilt used it to experiment with new bombing techniques. It was also an excellent flight-time builder for pilots and crew members entitled to flight pay but unable to get it any other way.

On 22 October, Lt. Frank Schilt was detached from VF-2 and assigned as a member of the United States Racing Team for the famed Schneider Trophy Race to be held 13 November at Hampton Roads, Virginia. The United States was counting heavily on winning this international event, and Schilt was an excellent choice. Flying a Curtiss R3C-2, he won second place for the United States with an average speed of 231.4 mph. For this, Schilt received a letter of commendation from the Commandant of the Marine Corps.

Meanwhile, Sandy Sanderson was selected to attend the Company Officers Course at Marine Corps Schools in Quantico. All senior lieutenants were required to graduate from this course before becoming eligible for promotion to captain. He was detached from VF-2 on 1 November and assigned to VF-1 for the duration of his schooling. Though pleased over his school assignment, he was nevertheless reluctant to leave his first command. During his tenure as commanding officer, he shaped the squadron along ideas of his own and introduced several new variations to the method of flying tactical formations, both attack and defensive.

In the first 14 months of VF-2's existence, it made first—rate fighter pilots of all personnel able to finish the course. Several skilled mechanics, unable to qualify for flight training at Pensacola because of educational requirements, were taught to fly and received their wings as Naval Aviation Pilots. Further, as a requisite for graduation, nine student Naval Aviators assigned to the Marine Corps were transferred from Pensacola to VF-2 for their final training under the expert guidance of Sandy. Time permitting, he taught students an up-to-date version of the art of glide-bombing he invented in Haiti. For this outstanding record of accomplishment, he and his squadron were awarded a letter of commendation from the Commandant of the Marine Corps.

In regard to Sandy's glide-bombing, it was over the Haitian jungles in 1919 that he made the first successful glide-bombing attacks. To effectively assist ground troops in their efforts to stem the overthrow of

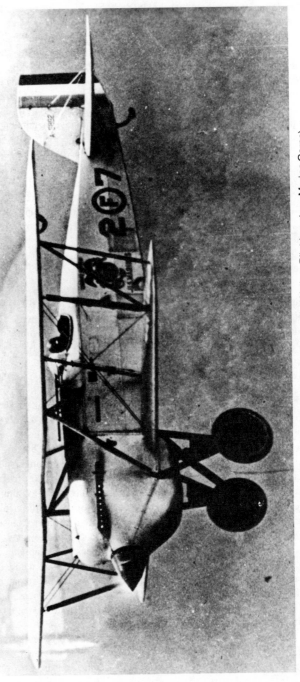

Fig. 1-9. FB-1, A-6892 flying south of Quantico, July 1926. 2nd Lt. Thomas J. Walker, Pilot (courtesy Marine Corps).

the Haitian government by rebel leaders, Sandy put his ingenuity to work and came up with a new bomb delivery system. In lieu of a bomb rack, he fastened a heavy mail bag to the underside of the airplane's fuselage with the open end facing forward. A bomb was then slipped inside the bag and the open end was closed with one end of a long rope that extended to the cockpit. When ready to attack, he nosed the plane down steeply and aimed directly at the target. At the right instant the rope was pulled, the mail bag opened, and the bomb fell on its way to the target. It was a crude operation when judged by today's standards, but an effective beginning of a new technique.

Sandy's departure proved to be somewhat of a setback for VF-2's morale. It was his influence that had taken the squadron from its meager beginning and transformed it into one of recognition, and he had done it mostly with two ingredients: discipline and perfection. Actually, that was about all Marine Aviation had to offer at that time except hope. However, it was those ingredients in years to come that payed tremendous dividends in the future of Marine Aviation.

New Commander—Jay Swartwout

First Lieutenant Jay D. Swartwout took command of VF-2 from Sanderson on 1 November 1926. Within hours he learned he was to be a busy man; also assigned to VF-2 on this date for training were 16 student pilots (nine officers and seven enlisted men). All but the enlisted men had previous training and required only a refresher course in fighter tactics to receive their wings. This was allowed under a ruling from the Navy Department if certain conditions were met, thus reducing the work load at Pensacola.

Swartwout's orders were: "Graduate as many men as possible *within 30 days!*" A few days later he learned why the rush! On 1 December the three Boeing FB-1 Fighters in his squadron, along with those in VF-1, were to be transferred to the West Coast for shipment to China.

Swartwout, along with Doc Blackwell, the only remaining pilot in the squadron, took their work seriously. Many days they worked from dawn to dusk to make up flying time lost to weather. On cold days, training flights were short. The weather had no respect for open-cockpit airplanes. At times freakish weather turned the dirt field into a quagmire, closing down operations. The Marines had no such luxuries as paved runways.

Nevertheless, within 30 days six officers (one captain, one first lieutenant and four second lieutenants) received their designations as Naval Aviators. Due to the loss of the FB-1 fighters, the remaining three officers (second lieutenants) returned to Pensacola to complete their training. The seven crew chiefs, in their dual-instruction stage, remained with VF-2.

The departure of the Boeing fighters forced VF-2 to revise its training syllabus to primary and secondary training only. Two new Consolidated NY-1 trainers (Fig. 1-10) were assigned to the squadron to relieve the

Fig. 1-10. Consolidated NY-1 (A-7192) used for training by VF-2 (courtesy Glen J. Carter).

work load on the two old Boeing NB-2 trainers that had seen better days. VF-2's morale was shaken further in December when its rival squadron, VF-1, received eight new Curtiss Hawk F6C-3 fighters. It looked as though VF-2 was destined for obscurity.

This didn't sit too well with Swartwout. At the risk of a reprimand for bypassing the chain of command, he dispatched a letter to Major Edward H. "Chief" Brainard, Officer-in-Charge of Marine Aviation, tactfully pointing out the situation. Brainard, who knew all of his 65 aviators, replied with assurance that any new fighters delivered to Quantico in the future would go to VF-2.

A String of Leaders

From this point onward, the future of VF-2 looked bleak. A succession of commanding officers tended to suggest the squadron's existence was questionable.

On 6 January 1927, Chief Marine Gunner Elmo Reagan replaced Jay Swartwout as commanding officer of VF-2. On 2 March, "Socko" Reagan was transferred to Haiti and 2nd Lt. Wilson S. Trundle, attached to VF-2 for training, became its commanding officer until 27 March.

On 28 March, Capt. William T. Evans became the "skipper" of VF-2. At his takeover, VF-2 was composed of 11 aircraft, one pilot (NAP) and 51 enlisted men. Of the 11 airplanes, only six were flyable—three Vought VE-7's, two Consolidated NY-1 trainers and one Boeing NB-2 trainer. Of the remaining five, one NB-2 was under extensive repair, having been demolished by one of the students. Two VE-7's that were no longer repairable were in storage, awaiting an official letter from the Bureau of Aeronautics authorizing that they be stricken (scrapped) from the list of

Fig. 1-11. Gunnery Sgt. George W. "Dick" Bransom (left) after taxing his Vought VE-7, 2-F-2, into Boeing NB-2, 2-F-7, at Brown Field, February 1927. Friend is Jim Knowlan (courtesy Colonel Harold Jordan).

Naval aircraft (Fig. 1-11). The old Martin MT Bomber was still in storage but the letter authorizing that it be scrapped arrived on 28 March. Also awaiting action on its disposition was the old Dayton-Wright TW-3; its letter had already been received. Incidentally, it was this airplane, modified by 1st Lt. F. G. Cowie, that pioneered aerial dusting in the Marines' efforts to control the Anopheles mosquitos. The first experiments were conducted in the Chopawamsic Swamp near Quantico and eventually lead the Marines to adopt aerial dusting in the control of malaria.

Chapter 2

The Hawks Arrive

The first important event in the VF-2 under Bill Evans' reign was the arrival on 6 April 1927, of four Curtiss Hawk F6C-4 Fighters. The new Hawks had air-cooled radial engines and proved to be lighter and more maneuverable than the F6C-3's delivered to VF-1. Their arrival was well timed. During the previous week, accidents had reduced the number of flyable airplanes to two Vought VE-7's.

Evans, elated over the new airplanes, immediately ordered the training syllabus returned to advanced fighter tactics. On orders from Major Lutz, commanding officer of all East Coast squadrons, the training of fledgling pilots was delegated to Observation Squadron Three (VO-3). VF-2's four primary trainers were gladly turned over to their command.

Prior to delivery of the new Hawks, VF-2 was forced to bow out of the Army-Navy maneuvers scheduled for 13-21 May at Naragansett Bay, Rhode Island. Knowing that a substantial portion of the Navy's tactical air support was committed to Marine Aviation, Evans requested that VF-2 be reinstated. He further requested two additional pilots. At that moment, only he and Doc Blackwell filled the pilot roster.

Headquarters responded to Evans' request barely in time. Two officers from the Marine Reserve, Capt. A.N. Parker and 1st Lt. S.A. McClellan, reported to VF-2 on 2 May for 30 days active duty.

F6C-4 Flaw Discovered

The first training flight following checkout of the two Reserve Officers in the F6C-4's almost proved disastrous. However, it brought out a design flaw in the landing gear. Evans scheduled a four-plane Battle Practice Exercise and the four Hawks taxied to the south end of the field for a formation takeoff. When all were in position, Evans gave the usual hand signal and the airplanes started their takeoff roll. When the formation was approximately 15 feet in the air, the engine in McClellan's F6C-4 quit without warning. He set the airplane back down on the field, but to avoid

Fig. 2-1. Curtiss F6C-4, serial No. A-7397, flown by Lt. McClellan, upside-down on Brown Field after wheel spokes gave way during forced landing (courtesy Marine Corps).

ending up in the creek bordering the north end of the field, he groundlooped the airplane to the right. Halfway through the groundloop, the wire spokes in the left wheel began to snap, causing the wheel to collapse completely. McClellan and his airplane came to rest upside down (Fig. 2-1). He was unhurt. With cooperation from the Assembly and Repair Shop the airplane was returned to service in three days.

At the conclusion of the Army-Navy maneuvers, the referees awarded Marine Aviation a "well done" for its overall performance. Evans was proud of VF-2. He invited the two reserve pilots to stay on. Both had to decline because of their civilian jobs.

At 0800 on 6 June, Captain Evans relinquished command of VF-2 to 1st Lt. Vernon M. "Red" Guymon, with the usual good-luck wish and handshake. Guymon was a relatively new aviator, having received his wings in VF-2 under Sanderson slightly more than six months previously.

It was Guymon's first command and he wanted to make an impression. He did! In the afternoon of his first day during checkout in an F6C-4 (S/N A-7397), the right wheel gave way during landing. The airplane ended up on its nose, bending both propeller blades and breaking the forward front spar in the right lower wing. The wheel failure was the same type experienced by Lt. McClellan.

Five days later A-7397 was returned to the flight line. Guymon took her up for a test hop. During his landing roll the left wheel collapsed, tearing the left landing gear off, breaking the forward spar in the left lower wing and again bending both propeller blades. A-7397 went back to the repair shop, seemingly its home since arriving at Brown Field.

A New Name—VF-9M

On 1 July 1927 the squadron designation of VF-2 was changed to Fighting Squadron Nine-M, (VF-9M). The renumbering of Marine squadrons plus the addition of the suffix "M" (Marines) was ordered by the Chief of Naval Operations to eliminate confusion that existed among Navy and Marine squadrons with identical designations.

Guymon hoped the new designation would somehow end the run of bad luck. It didn't. His remaining months as commanding officer were filled with turmoil. VF-9M's airplanes kept the Assembly and Repair Shop on a 24-hour schedule.

Two more accidents involving wheel spokes occurred before a fix was authorized. A Marine trouble board recommended that all F6C-4's in Naval service be refitted with 32″ × 6″ wheels and tires. VF-9M didn't like the idea. They solved the problem by installing wire spokes of larger diameter.

A major accident involved 1st Lt. Horace C. Busbey, assigned to VF-9M for training. He ditched F6C-4 A-7397 in the Potomac River, sending it to the A&R Shop this time for two months. It was during aerobatic practice over the Widewater area, south of Brown Field, that Busbey nosed over into a steep dive. As his speed built up, he closed the throttle. Making his pullout at 1500 feet, he found the throttle was stuck in the closed position. With the engine idling, he realized it would be impossible to make it to shore. Not knowing what might happen during ditching, he decided it was best to unfasten his safety belt. On impact with the water, he was thrown clear of the airplane as it flipped over. A few

Fig. 2-2. In trouble again! F6C-4, A-7397 ditched in Potomac River at Widewater, Virginia, by Lt. Horace C. Busbey after throttle stuck in closed position (courtesy Marine Corps).

minutes later he was plucked from the water by nearby fishermen, unhurt but very wet (Fig. 2-2). A-7397 was also recovered and eventually repaired (Fig. 2-3).

Another accident involved a former squadron commander of VF-2, 1st Lt. Swartwout. He departed Brown Field in an F6C-4, S/N A-7394, on an authorized cross-country training flight to New York. As he approached Staten Island, the auxiliary fuel tank ran dry. He turned the fuel selector valve to the main tank. However, after several attempts, he was unable to restart his engine. Spotting the beach at Great Kills, he set up his glide and landing approach for a deadstick landing. When a short distance away, he realized there were many sunbathers lying on the beach. He quickly turned inland and made a rough landing into heavy sand. The airplane flipped over on its back, causing major structural damage. There were no injuries. A trouble board found Swartwout guilty of negligence and recommended that he be grounded for 10 days without pay.

Actually, an overdose of accidents had plagued Marine Aviation since the early twenties. Most were the result of our involvement in small "brush wars" in the countries of Nicaragua and Haiti. No less a contributing factor were the old derelict airplanes left over from WWI they were forced to fly in those areas. Crew chiefs who over the years learned the art of keeping old relics flying now put their skills to tests that payed off many times over. Almost every day they performed miracles in making and swapping parts among various types of airplanes. One crew chief was heard to remark, "If Headquarters knew how many bastard parts this plane was made of, they would insist on giving it a new serial number."

Because of a pilot shortage, two and sometimes three duty tours were required of pilots in those countries. Fighting disease as well as bandits, they performed acts of heroism during years of bombing, strafing, dropping supplies, flying out wounded, and just about any other operation one can name. It was here that Marines really pioneered the use of close air support that proved its worth many times over in World War II, Korea and Viet Nam.

There is a story often told in Marine Aviation circles about a young officer wanting to sign-up in 1924 for aviation duty. He was asked if he wanted a three, four, or five-year term. "What's the casualty rate?" he inquired. "About 25 percent a year," he was told. "In that case," the young officer said, "put me down for five years and I'll be 125 percent dead when my tour of duty is up."

On 3 October, four months after assuming command of VF-9M, Red Guymon departed for Managua, Nicaragua. In Nicaragua for 17 months, Guymon's luck changed. He flew 1,021 hours over the jungles, fighting the bandits and removing the sick and wounded from the forward battle areas. For his outstanding devotion to duty under hazardous conditions, he was awarded the Navy Cross.

On 6 October 1927, 1st Lt. George H. Towner Jr. was awarded the dubious honor of commanding VF-9M. There were six airplanes when he

Fig. 2-3. A-7397 at Brown Field on 10 November 1927. Lt. Williamson, pilot (courtesy Marine Corps).

arrived: three F6C-4's, three VE-7's (two flyable) and one MT Bomber. Personnel had diminished to a total of 30.

Towner was aware this assignment was only temporary, so he decided not to rock the boat and made do with what he had. Advanced training continued for pilots from both regular and reserve areas. He was good at the art of instructing formation flying and gunnery. At the close of his tenure, the record of VF-9M showed improvement: there were no airplanes in the A&R shop attributed to accidents.

At 0800, 21 January 1928, 1st Lt. William O. Brice relieved George Towner. Having just returned from China, Brice was a rough and ready Marine. He had served his military career mostly in overseas assignments; first in World War I with the Army, then in Haiti, Guam and China with the Marines. He was used to getting along without and knew how to get the most from what he had. In his younger days his capacity for out-drinking his friends had earned him the nickname of "Whisky Bill".

At that time of year the weather was anything but good, sometimes curtailing flight operations for days. Brice took advantage of this time to bring all airplanes to top condition. Earlier, VF-9M had received three old Curtiss Hawk F6C-1 fighters from the West Coast, but Brice refused to fly them until all were given a major overhaul and equipped with full ordinance gear. This irked the group engineering officer but Brice stood his ground.

By 1 May, VF-9M had six operational fighters—three F6C-1's and three F6C-4's, each equipped with bomb racks and two .30 caliber machine guns. Flight operations were increasing daily as reserve aviators began arriving for their annual two weeks of active-duty training.

On 1 July 1928, VF-9M's designation was changed to Fighting Squadron Five-M (VF-5M) by order of the Chief of Naval Operations. This order affected all Marine squadrons. Also on this date the squadron's personnel was reduced to a grand total of 14 men. Brice was *very* unhappy about the loss of more men, but realized the Marines' committments in Haiti and Nicaragua were responsible. Nevertheless, he voiced loud complaints and was given eight additional men as mechanics helpers.

In August a rumor began circulating that the Navy was unhappy with the performance of the new Curtiss F7C-1 Seahawk fighter, then undergoing tests at Anacostia. Rumor also said: "In all probability the Navy may turn them over to the Marines." No one could substantiate the rumor, but Brice had it on good authority that it was true.

On 4 September everyone knew it *was* true. On this date the commandant issued a directive authorizing the group commander at Quantico to send selected enlisted men to the Pratt-Whitney engine factory for schooling in the assembly and maintenance of the R-1340 air-cooled radial engines supplied on the new Seahawks.

On 8 October 1st Lt. William R. Hughs replaced Brice. Hughs, like all former C. O.'s, was plagued with the same old problems. When he asked, "How many pilots will I have in my squadron?", he was told: "You're it!"

Luckily, flying had slowed somewhat. Three aviators from headquarters were taking refresher training in advanced fighter tactics and two student NAP's were within a few hours of receiving their wings. However, as the only pilot in the squadron, Hughs was flying his butt off, drilling his students in section tactics and dogfighting. On the ground he was stuck with blackboard sessions before and after each flight. A one-man operation was not easy.

The Seahawks

On 28 December 1928, VF-5M received another commanding officer. He was 1st Lt. Horace D. "Hoke" Palmer, from headquarters in Washington. Also on this date, two new Curtiss F7C-1 Seahawks arrived at Brown Field from the factory. VF-5M was authorized to receive nine of the new airplanes: six to be operational and three for spares.

Two days later, Palmer was notified that three additional F7C-1's were at the factory awaiting delivery. Losing no time, he collected two of his fellow pilots from VF-4M and flew the new airplanes to Brown Field on New Years Eve. By 4 January 1929, all were in the hands of VF-5M (Fig. 2-4).

The new Curtiss F7C-1's were well liked even though it was felt their overall performance did not quite equal that of the F6C-4 (Fig. 2-5). Pilots from other squadrons at Brown Field were invited to fly the fighters, and it was soon discovered that its dogfighting ability was superior to other airplanes then in service.

Palmer, happy over the new airplanes, readily saw this as an opportunity to make VF-5M into a top-notch organization. He promptly

Fig. 2-4. Three of VF-5M's new Curtiss F7C-1 "Seahawk" Fighters at Brown Field in April 1929 (courtesy Marine Corps).

contacted old friends at headquarters for help. He accomplished what no other C.O. had since Sanderson—he was given two pilots from VF-4M. They were 1st Lt. Frank D. Weir and the notable 2nd Lt. Thomas J. "Jocko" McQuade. Because of his zest for living, McQuade seemed to get into trouble on occasion. Palmer thought he could take care of that. He made McQuade squadron Engineering Officer for the new F7C-1's. New airplanes just becoming operational usually pose many problems that keep a normal man busy—but not Jocko! Palmer enlisted the aid of the Group Commander, and Jocko was given additional duties as Officer-in-Charge of the Erection Shop, Officer-in-Charge of the Electrical Shop, assistant Field Engineering Officer and Guard Officer of Brown Field. The added duties seemed to have little effect on Jocko's behavior. He somehow managed at least three nights a week to tour the hot spots between Quantico and Washington, adding to his reputation. Palmer gave up!

On 26 April it happened to VF-5M again. Hoke Palmer was transferred to Managua, Nicaragua. Frank Weir was temporarily placed in charge. Commanding officers came and went faster than their names could be added to the roster. At a symposium in Washington, Palmer had his say about the constant turnover of personnel and commanding officers and stressed that something had to be done to bring this to an end; otherwise morale in aviation would continue to decline. Even so, it was agreed that the quality of training was never sacrificed, and where possible, squadron commanders had been chosen very carefully to keep it that way.

Col. Thomas Turner—Patron of Marine Aviation

On 10 May 1929 Colonel Thomas C. Turner, who previously was Officer-in-Charge of Marine Aviation in the early 1920's, again took over this all-important command. To the small, overworked force in aviation, this was the best thing that could possibly have happened to them. His appointment would have far-reaching results in years to come. Turner was a real champion of Marine Aviation, a hard-driving man and a strict disciplinarian. His love of aviation constantly kept him on the lookout for ways in which to focus the nation's attention on the flying "Leathernecks." And where possible, he never allowed anything or anyone to stand in his way for long. Several times during his career he had locked horns with personnel of flag rank both in the Navy and Marine Corps and had somehow managed to keep the respect of everyone, including his superiors. Admiral Moffett consistently marked Turner's fitness report 4.0 in all categories. In his previous efforts to build up Marine Aviation, Turner persistantly talked with influential men both in the Navy Department and Congress and often stated that, with any sizable appropriation of funds to relieve its shortage of pilots and equipment, Marine Aviation would make history. Actually, the Marines were already making history around the world *without* the help of Congress or funds from the Navy Department. In fact, nowhere did the taxpayer get more value for his dollar in defense spending than in Marine Aviation.

On 11 May, 1st Lt. Hayne D. "Cuckoo" Boyden reported to VF-5M as its new skipper. Boyden had been in aviation a long time and had earned his nickname because of his daring and somewhat unorthodox methods of doing things. At his arrival there were nine F7C-1's (two under repair), and 26 men, including two pilots: Jocko McQuade and Gunnery Sergeant Millard T. Shepard. Shepard two days previously had received a citation from the Commandant of the Marine Corps for his outstanding ability as a pilot during a recent tour of duty in Nicaragua. One paragraph of the citation read: His courage and ability played a vital part in organizing and keeping an incredible passenger and freight system operating that saved untold lives and will bring about an early end to the conflict there."

Now that VF-5M had airplanes, it had a shortage of pilots. Nevertheless, Boyden decided they should be represented at the annual Bombing and Gunnery Exercises at Hampton Roads, Virginia from June 1-11. Unable to procure additional pilots, Cuckoo Boyden said, "To hell with them. We'll take three planes as Sanderson did in 1926 and we'll skin the hell out of 'em." Unfortunately, it was not to be. Malfunctions occurred in the guns of the three planes often enough to keep the Marines from making the top. However, they didn't return home without having made an impression. When his guns failed to fire, McQuade engaged in a little comedy flying that wasn't appreciated by the brass.

Boyden kept up his pressure for more pilots. Each week he submitted a letter on the subject and each week it was turned down. Finally, on 27 August, Gunnery Sgt. Joseph I. Hockman rejoined VF-5M. He had been the first man to receive wings from the squadron in 1926. When he reported aboard, Boyden was heard to remark sarcastically, "We just had a twenty-five percent increase in pilot strength."

At Marine Corps Headquarters, Col. Turner was working hard on this very problem. He noted that the officer-pilot strength was considerably below that recommended by the Commandant in his annual report, but

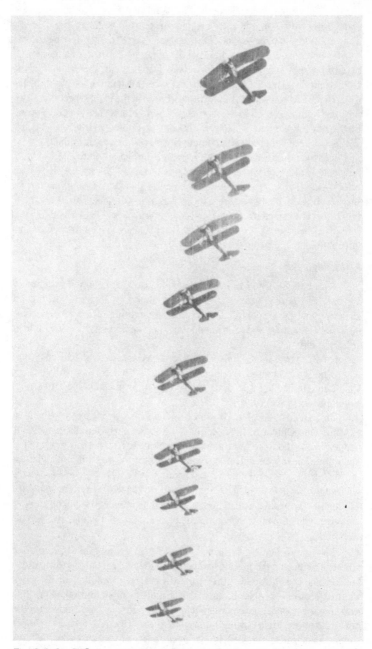

Fig. 2-5. Six F7C-1's of VF-5M and three F6C-3's of VF-4M in flyover during
Sunset Parade at Quantico in May 1929 (courtesy Marine Corps).

until Turner took over, no one had pressed the point. He hoped to get enough new pilots to end the alarming turnover in commanding officers. The problem had to be solved if the Marines were to build for the future. Turner had asked for a hundred-percent increase, but it was an overall twenty-percent increase that the Navy Department agreed to for the 1929-1930 fiscal year. This would increase the number of pilots in the Corps from 85 to a total of 102. It was a big step in the right direction.

In October VF-5M received three new pilots. They were Second Lieutenants Raymond E. Hopper, Joseph L. Wolfe, and John S. Young. Wolfe and Young were newly commissioned and fresh out of flight school at Pensacola. Hopper came from Observation Squadron Six-M (VO-6M) and had some experience in squadron tactics. This gave VF-5M six pilots—its largest number ever permanently assigned pilots. Further, for the first time since its inception in 1925 as a fighter squadron, it was up to full authorized strength in *both* pilots and airplanes. To Boyden's way of thinking, this called for a celebration. Headaches and hangovers were not uncommon the following day.

A New Beginning

With a foundation from which to build, Boyden commenced to mold VF-5M into a real squadron. Each day found them aloft, drilling in squadron tactics, bombing, gunnery, and dogfighting. They were becoming sharper each day and soon joined the other squadrons at Brown Field in aerial parades.

On 27 November, Cuckoo Boyden was transferred to Pensacola, where he was assigned as a flight instructor. Boyden was well liked at Quantico. He had brought the squadron a long way and helped it earn an excellent safety record.

On 1 December 1929 1st Lt. Christian Frank Schilt became the new Commanding Officer of VF-5M. He was its eleventh Commander. Schilt had just returned from Nicaragua where he had won the nation's highest decoration, the Medal of Honor (Fig. 2-6). It was awarded for ten flights he made there from 6-8 January, 1928 into the besieged town of Quilali, where two Marine patrols had been ambushed and cut-off by rebel bandits. During the three days he had evacuated 18 wounded, carried badly needed supplies, and flown in a replacement commander to lead the ground fighting.

To make a landing strip from the village's rough and rolling main street, Marines on the ground had to burn and level part of the town; since the airplanes had no brakes, they had to help stop it by pulling on its wings when it slowed enough. Enemy fire during landings and takeoffs, plus low-hanging clouds, mountains, and tricky air currents added to the difficulty of the flights, which the citation described as feats of "almost superhuman skill combined with personal courage of the highest order."

As it will be remembered, Schilt previously served in the squadron under Sanderson during its first year of operation. He, too, believed in

Fig. 2-6. President Calvin Coolidge presented the Medal of Honor to 1st Lt. Christian F. Schilt at White House ceremonies for his daring flights at Quilalie, Nicaragua, in 1927 (courtesy U.S. Navy).

discipline, which he administered quietly but firmly. In line with Turner's new policy, Schilt was to promote Marine Aviation any way and anywhere possible.

In January 1930, two additional pilots came aboard to boost the total to eight—four officers and four NAP's. The total squadron personnel now numbered 35 men. Things were looking better all the time.

In Washington, Colonel Turner was working on Admiral Moffett to provide the remaining nine Curtiss F7C-1's. Four were in Navy use for various tests and the remaining five were being used at Pensacola for advanced training. Turner's argument was, "If there are no funds available to the Marines for new fighters, then logically the remaining nine F7C-1's should go to the Marines, where they would be put to good use." Besides, Turner pointed out, they had been rejected by the Navy, and Pensacola at that moment had all the fighter trainers it needed. Possibly to get Turner off his back more than for any other reason, Admiral Moffett agreed to Turner's request—but in due time.

With the enlargement of VF-5M, it began to take on a new status. Training schedules were stepped up and provisions were made to bring in additional reserves for advanced training. Each month, flying hours of the previous month were surpassed. Six-plane formations, three-plane section tactics, dive bombing, gunnery, and single-aircraft battle practice were engaged in every day, weather permitting.

With the increased activity, Schilt began having operational problems. Two airplanes were laid up with major damages from ground accidents because of poor pilot technique, and one pilot was placed under arrest for 10 days for reckless flying. As can be expected, increased flying operations, especially training, always bring additional risks. This squadron was no exception. However, what the squadron wasn't ready for was the death of three of its pilots within a short time.

Second Lieutenants Joseph L. Wolfe and William R. Ostertag were killed in what should have been an avoidable accident. In the afternoon of 20 February 1930, the two men took off from Brown Field to conduct Single Aircraft Battle Practice in F7C-1's. After sparring a while for position, Ostertag got on the tail of Wolfe's airplane. Wolfe, unable to outmaneuver his opponent, dove his airplane almost straight down, trying to pull away and shake him off, but Ostertag kept following close behind. As people watched in horror, both airplanes dove into the Potomac River, just off the mouth of Chopawomsic Creek, which formed the north border of Brown Field. It was the opinion of witnesses that, in all probability, Wolfe was looking backward at Ostertag, trying to shake him from his tail and because of the glassy surface of the river, misjudged his altitude and dove straight into the water. Ostertag, following close behind Wolfe and concentrating on getting a "kill," was unable to pull up in time and also dove into the river beside Wolfe (Fig. 2-7).

The deaths of these two young pilots had a sobering effect on everyone at Quantico and resulted in an investigation that called for stricter flying regulations governing battle practice.

On 11 June, the third fatal accident occurred when 2nd Lt. Guy D. Chappell crashed during a test flight in an F7C-1. The airplane had been used for touch-and-go landings on East Field the night before and was reported by its pilot as being "out of rig," with the left wing having a tendency to be heavy. A thorough inspection of the rigging indicated a definite shift had taken place and the airplane was grounded. The next morning the crew chief made the necessary rigging adjustments, and Lt. Chappel volunteered to test fly the airplane.

Fig. 2-7. Remains of the two Curtiss F7C-1's in which Lieutenants Joseph L. Wolfe and William R. Ostertag were killed during dogfight near Quantico on 20 February 1930 (courtesy Marine Corps).

As part of the test he decided to power-dive the airplane. During his wide-open dive from 10,000 feet, the lower fuselage fitting, where the left wing flying wires are attached to fuselage, severed and the aircraft completely broke up, crashing into the woods just west of the field. All F7C-1's in service were immediately grounded for inspection. An investigation by a Marine trouble board recommended that all wing and fuselage fittings be modified and made stronger on the remaining airplanes of this type. It also ordered that all terminal-velocity dives be prohibited until the modification was completed.

Chapter 3

The Sanderson Era

In the spring of 1930, Colonel Turner accepted an invitation for a Marine squadron to participate in the upcoming National Air Races at Chicago from 23 August through 1 September. Turner, always looking for ways to promote Marine Aviation, could think of no other squadron better qualified to represent the Marines than VF-5M. He immediately phoned Maj. Roy S. Geiger, the group commander at Quantico, to discuss the possibilities. From this conversation began one of the most intense publicity campaigns in the history of Marine Aviation. It was decided that the Marines not only would be represented at Chicago but, in the forseeable future, they would accept *all* invitations to perform at public affairs.

The Chicago 10-day "spectacular" would attract the world's best pilots, and fierce competition was assured among them for the large prize money offered to winners of various races. Aside from the Marines, the Army and Navy were also invited to perform with their best squadrons to add additional color and thrills for the public. Prior to this, Marine Corps participation in national events—with one or two exceptions—had been limited mostly to individual pilots competing for speed records.

However, Geiger informed Turner that a squadron commander of outstanding qualities was required if this type of promotion was to be pursued. He reminded Turner that Schilt, a few days previously, had received orders from the Bureau of Aeronautics for his transfer to the Naval Aircraft Factory in Philadelphia as its chief test pilot.

Both Turner and Geiger had no problem agreeing on who Schilt's replacement should be. Turner quickly issued orders assigning Lieutenant Sanderson, who was commanding Observation Squadron Seven-M (VO-7M), in Nicaragua, to take command of VF-5M.

Sandy Takes Over

On Sunday, 15 June, First Lieutenant Lawson H.M. "Sandy" Sanderson became the skipper of VF-5M (Fig. 3-1). To Sandy it was like old home week to be back at Quantico and in command of his old squadron again. It had been almost five years and many old friends were there for the occasion. After Schilt officially turned the squadron over to Sandy, the two officers and several friends retired to the squadron office to talk over old times. In short order a bottle and glasses mysteriously appeared. After a drink all around, Sandy remarked, "I have a feeling this is a new era for Marine Aviation and if I have my way, I intend to build this squadron into the finest in the Marine Corps." All raised their glasses as someone said "I'll drink to that!"

Fig. 3-1. Steel-eyed 1st Lt. "Sandy" Sanderson shortly after his takeover as Commanding Officer of VF-5M (courtesy Marine Corps).

Two days after assuming command, Sandy was summoned to an all-day conference in Washington with Col. Turner and Maj. Geiger to discuss the details of the upcoming show. It was decided that Sandy would be given a free hand to do whatever he deemed necessary.

He was to take a six-plane formation to Chicago. This would be rough without a spare airplane to fall back on. Two F7C's were received in April to replace the two lost in the crashes of Lieutenants Wolfe and Ostertag, but as yet a replacement for the aircraft lost in the crash of Lt. Chappell had not been received. Sandy asked that the F7C-1 stationed at Anacostia for the use of pilots at Headquarters, Marine Corps, be returned to Quantico for use as a spare. This was agreed to. Further, it was brought to the attention of the group commander that two of the squadron's airplanes were in the Assembly and Repair shop with an estimate of 25 days working time to repair them. Geiger ordered that work on all other projects be stopped and that VF-5M's airplanes be given priority over everything in the repair shop, unless authorized by him personally.

Next, Sandy turned his attention to the pilot shortage. Presently, only four remained. To get the caliber he wanted, he had to have several from which to choose. At Sandy's request, five second lieutenants from the Marine Corps Volunteer Reserve were hastily called to active duty from the Eastern Reserve Area at Philadelphia. Four additional pilots—two reserve and two regular—were transferred from VO-6M. Sandy now had 13 pilots to work with. All but two had reported for duty by 7 July.

Things were beginning to fall in place. If the two airplanes under repair could be ready in a few days, he estimated he would have about three weeks to get ready. As it actually worked out, he had slightly more than two weeks.

On 18 August, by authority of the Chief of Naval Operations, VF-5M was ordered to revert to its former squadron designation of VF-9M. However, with only four days remaining until their departure for Chicago, Sandy got approval to delay adding the new squadron markings to the airplanes until after their return.

Being somewhat of a showman, Sandy wanted something out of the ordinary for the Chicago show. He had no intention of duplicating the usual tactical maneuvers and formations usually performed by military squadrons. He intended that the audience would remember the Marines long after the show was over.

For several days he had thought about an idea for an act that was indeed different and approached Major Geiger for approval. Geiger, not one to restrain his officers, thought it was great—*provided* it could be accomplished without spending too much time. Two things the Marines were in short supply of were time and money.

Sandy's idea was to perform night aerobatics, using a three plane stunt team composed of himself, Second Lieutenant Dave Cloud and Master Sergeant Millard Shepard. He made a sketch of what he wanted and gave it to Sergeant Earl Zalanka, of the Assembly and Repair Shop, to work

work out the details. Within two days each of the three airplanes was fitted with eight lights along the underside of the lower wings and six lights along the underside of the fuselage, forming a "T" when they were switched on. Sandy, the leader, had red lights; the other airplanes had white and blue, making a very colorful sight when seen at night from the ground.

To add a little "esprit de corps" within the squadron, Sandy had the crew chiefs paint the nose, wheels, headrest and the cowling around the engine compartment of each airplane with bright red paint. He then named the squadron "Rojo Diablos" (Red Devils). Even though it was nonregulation, it had the approval of the group commander.

As the time grew near for their departure to Chicago, Sandy thought it best to increase the daily flying schedule to four hours, with approximately two hours devoted to the show. After flying was secured for the day, the crew chiefs worked most of the night to have the airplanes ready for the next day's flying. Friendly rivalry had developed among them and none wanted *his* airplane to be the one to return to the flight line because of faulty maintenance.

Remembering the old cliche "All work and no play," Sandy decided to secure all operations two days before they were to leave. He knew it was important to allow the pilots time to rest and unwind. For the previous two weeks everyone had worked hard and deserved some relaxation. Several of the pilots and crew chiefs were beginning to show signs of strain; even so, many of the latter insisted on using this time to give their airplanes a final check.

Sandy had a tough decision to make. Of the seven reservists, he had to choose three to fill out the squadron. All were first class pilots. His final selection was Second Lieutenants Kerr, Brewster and Burchard.

On Friday morning, 22 August at 0800 hours, Sandy gave the hand signal for the six-plane formation to start its take-off roll. Making a

Fig. 3-2. F7C-1's of VF-5M at 1930 Chicago National Air Races. Boeing F4B-1's of Navy Squadron VF-5B are in the background (courtesy Steve Hudek).

climbing turn to the right and circling the field, the formation set course for Cleveland, Ohio as its first fuel stop. The mechanics had departed earlier in a Ford JR-2 Trimotor transport plane with the necessary parts, tools and equipment to maintain the six Curtiss F7C-1 Seahawks in top condition throughout the ten-day meet. After a one-hour refueling stop at Cleveland, the squadron arrived over the Curtiss-Reynolds Airport, just north of Chicago, at shortly after 1500 hours (Fig. 3-2). That evening everyone was invited to a big hangar party to get acquainted. There were a few headaches in order the next morning.

1930 National Air Races

Saturday, 23 August, was opening day and promised to be the start of the greatest exhibition of airplanes and pilots ever. A total of 34 closed-course races were scheduled during the next ten days, including—for the first time—closed-course races for women. The Navy sent one of its crack squadrons, Fighting Squadron Five (VF-5B), flying its new Boeing F4B-1 fighters all the way from San Diego. This long flight was a feat in itself. The Army Air Corps was represented by an 18 plane squadron that would be hard to beat. Numerous other entries were there, such as Al Williams and his famous "Gulfhawk," an act that was tops in acrobatic flying.

When it came time for the Marines to perform, a voice from the field stand announced: "We now have the United States Marine Corps Red Devil Squadron from Quantico, Virginia, under the command of First Lieutenant Sandy Sanderson, who will demonstrate six-plane tactical maneuvers".

After viewing the Army and Navy squadrons, a six-plane squadron seemed rather small to many people, but they didn't know Sandy. He loved competition and a challenge. On signal from the field controller, Sandy lead the squadron in a close six-wedge formation take-off. From that moment on there was no doubt about the quality of the Marines' contribution to the show. With only six planes, Sandy was able to fly at a lower altitude and keep all maneuvers in close and low enough so that the people could see them well.

Loops in line, loops in vees, tailchasing, dive bombing, and low-altitude rolls recovering only a few feet off the ground gave the audience much more than it expected to see. Admiral Moffett, who was Colonel Turner's guest at the races, thought the squadron's show was too dangerous and should be toned down somewhat. However, Turner, while assuring the Admiral that Sandy knew what he was doing, promised to have a talk with him.

Their formations were so close at times that they actually touched wing tips. This caused some consternation among the crew chiefs because patching of the fabric was frequently necessary. Each day at the finish of their 30-minute show, the audience gave them a standing ovation. For the crowds who stayed for the evening events such as aircraft displays, fireworks, and grand prize drawing, Sandy put on his three-plane specialty act and completely captivated them. He went through a 20-minute routine similar to their daytime show and had everyone amazed at the "daring" Marines. Night flying was not generally done in those days, especially not stunt flying, and the planes with their red, white and blue "T" lights were very thrilling. The people left the airshow with a new appreciation for the Marine Corps.

The squadron's popularity grew with each day's performance. During its 10-day stay it thrilled more than a half-million people with precision formation flying and unusual low-altitude maneuvers. Sandy, unable to stay away from racing, entered his Seahawk in the Curtiss Marine Trophy race and won with a speed of 142.4 mph.

The 10-day meet was not without its tragic side. On the last day of the show Captain Author Page, in his highly modified Curtiss Hawk, was way out front in the Thompson Trophy Race when, in the seventeenth lap of the 20-lap race, he was overcome by carbon monoxide fumes from his engine and crashed near the home pylon. He died the next day.

Chicago was a wonderful host to Sandy and the squadron. They received praise from almost everyone and a special invitation to return from the mayor. There were flattering stories in the newspapers and on radio.

Following their success at Chicago, Sandy and his squadron were immediately asked to attend the All-American Air Maneuvers to be held 8-10 January 1931, at Miami, Florida. They were especially invited to compete with the Army and Navy for the "Sir Charles Orr" Trophy. It was to be presented by the Governor of the Bahama Islands to the most outstanding aerobatic team during the three-day meet. This was especially to Sandy's liking. As an ex-football player, he loved a challenge and never backed away from competition, no matter what the odds. He decided then and there to bring the trophy home to Quantico.

But first, it became evident that mountains of work were going to be necessary. The first complete airframe inspection on the F7C's after returning from Chicago revealed that four of the six aircraft had broken engine mounts near the top of the engine mounting ring. This was a serious defect and resulted in grounding all airplanes until the Engineering Department could come up with an approved fix. One of the reserve officers remarked, "Its a damn good thing we didn't have one more show to perform at Chicago or we may have given the airshow fans a *real* thrill with engines falling out of the sky!"

To further complicate things, Dave Cloud, the squadron engineering officer, was in receipt of a letter from the Navy Department recommending that the F7C's be limited to shallow dives. This could put VF-9M out of business. It will be remembered that, after Chappell's death, orders had been issued forbidding terminal velocity dives with this type airplane until all had been modified. The letter from the Navy was a report on tests conducted with an F7C-1 at the Naval Proving Grounds, Dahlgren,

Virginia, following Chappell's crash. During subsequent meetings, enough engineering data was analyzed by the Navy Department to allow Sandy to return to unrestricted operations by 1 October. However, he agreed to a complete airframe inspection of the planes after each 25 hours of flying time.

By 1 November Sandy had the personnel for his Miami show secured, and flying was scheduled almost every day, weather permitting. By the middle of December it became increasingly more difficult to complete the flying assignments. Flying several hours a day in open cockpit planes can be very chilling in winter time, to say the least.

After recovering from a gala New Years Eve party, where Sandy pledged to bring home the Sir Charles Orr trophy from Miami, the squadron began making preparations to leave. All F7C's were in first-class condition and were not to be flown until time to leave. Sandy wasn't taking any chances.

All-American Air Maneuvers—Miami 1931

The squadron's take-off was scheduled for 0800 hours Tuesday morning January 6th, and despite the cold weather a large crowd turned out for their departure. They wanted to wish them well and especially to let them know that all Quantico was behind them.

The squadron's Ford Trimotor transport plane, piloted by Master Sgt. Shepard, was the first to depart. It carried the crew chiefs and all the equipment needed for the trip.

After farewells all around, the six-plane squadron finally got under way at 0830 hours. The first section consisted of Sanderson, with Second Lieutenants Frank H. Wirsig and Warren E. Sweester Jr. flying left and right wing respectively. The second section was composed of Second Lieutenants: David L. Cloud Jr., section leader, with William D. Saunders and Willard Reed Jr. flying left and right wing respectively.

The flight plan called for an overnight stop at Jacksonville, Florida, with a refueling stop at Ft. Bragg, North Carolina. By the time they reached Ft. Bragg they were bucking such strong headwinds that it was questionable if they could make Jacksonville without refueling. Sandy, remembering the beautiful Cloister Resort Hotel on Sea Island, near Brunswick, Georgia, decided to give his men a real treat and stop there overnight. Circling the island just before dark, he brought the squadron into Redfern Field on nearby St. Simons Island shortly after 1730 hours, with just barely enough daylight left to see the ground.

The Cloister was about 65 miles north of Jacksonville, and in those days was one of the most beautiful resorts on the east coast. Sandy had stayed there before, was friendly with the management, and knew he could give his men a well-deserved treat.

The hotel manager told Sandy that if they won the Governor's Trophy at Miami, they were invited to stop enroute home as guests of the hotel for several days. Sandy assured him they would be back. He also hinted they might put on an airshow for both the island and the nearby city of Brunswick, Georgia.

It was 0930 the next day before the squadron could get under way. The planes attracted a large number of the island residents to the field to watch them take off. An article in the *Brunswick News* said:

> *A Marine Air Squadron of Curtiss Hawks landed at Redfern Field at 5:30 yesterday afternoon after combatting headwinds in their flight from Quantico, Virginia. Under the command of Lieutenant L.H. Sanderson, the squadron is enroute to Miami where it is scheduled to be one of the leading attractions. The group is accredited with being one of the most spectacular and efficient in government service. Lieutenant Sanderson, who visited Sea Island last year, expressed a desire to return on his way from Miami and the following day stage an exhibition. If the squadron presents itself, residents of this section are assured of a most interesting and thrilling demonstration of aviation maneuvers.*
>
> *Their departure from Redfern Field this morning brought out a large number of the island residents who admired the ability of the aviators in handling their small pursuit planes. Taking off in threes, the planes lifted from Redfern Field in perfect formation and was one of the prettiest sights ever presented at the island airport.*

After a brief stop at Jackonsville, Florida, for refueling and a weather check, VF-9M continued on to Miami, arriving there at 1600.

The Marines loved Miami and the city fathers quickly took charge of their every need. Each day they were guests of dignitaries at luncheons and attended lavish parties in the evening. There were plenty of girls, too! A local socialite arranged for dates and escorts. Sandy told his men to have a "hell of a good time" but warned them their flying had better stay sharp because the stakes were high—the Governor's Trophy plus the honor of the Marine Corps. He closed with: "We *will* win that trophy! Is that understood?" One squadron member, remembering the incident, said, "Even though Sandy never said 'that's an order,' we knew damn well he meant it to be."

During the squadron's three-day stay at Miami, it demonstrated the Marine Corps brand of precision to more than 125,000 people. Its six-plane loops, snap rolls, inverted flying, dive-bombing, and other low-altitude maneuvers were flown with such flawless precision that, needless to say, they were awarded the Sir Charles Orr Trophy for the most outstanding aerobatic team to visit Miami (Fig. 3-3). Second place was won by a Navy Team lead by Lieutenant John G. Crommelin.

It was just what Marine Aviation needed to bolster its sagging morale. Colonel Turner, who witnessed the performance, accepted the trophy in behalf of the Marine Corps at an Aviation Banquet at the Biltmore Country Club of Miami. In his acceptance speech he vowed to continue with this type of promotion in hopes of winning additional support for Marine

Fig. 3-3. VF-9M pilots with the Sir Charles Orr Trophy won in competition at the 1931 Miami All-American Air Maneuvers as the most outstanding aerobatic squadron. Left/right: 2nd Lt. Willard Reed, Jr.; Master Sgt. Millard Shepard; 2nd Lt. Frank Wirsig; 2nd Lt. William Saunders; 1st Lt. Sandy Sanderson, C.O.; 2nd Lt. William Sweetser; 2nd Lt. Dave Cloud, Jr (courtesy Marine Corps).

Aviation from the Navy and Congress. Admiral Moffett and the Assistant Secretary of the Navy, also present at the Banquet, gave approving smiles.

Sandy was very proud of his pilots and told them so many times. He praised the crew chiefs for their untiring efforts in keeping the three-year old F7C-1's in top condition. He would see that they were rewarded by including them in the stop-over at St. Simons Island on the way home.

After celebrating most of the night, VF-9M departed Miami at 1130 hours on Sunday morning, January 11th, for St. Simons Island, Georgia. Sandy fully intended to collect on the invitation from the manager of the hotel. After a brief stop at Jacksonville for fuel, the squadron arrived over the island at 1530 hours. The next day the *Brunswick News* said:

> *Enroute to the Marine Base at Quantico, Virginia, from the All-American Air Maneuvers at Miami, Florida, where they captured the Sir Charles Orr Trophy for formation maneuvers, seven United States Marine Corps planes landed at Redfern Field, Saint Simons Island, at 4:00 yesterday afternoon. Upon reaching Sea Island, the planes circled low over the Cloister Hotel and then went into numerous*

difficult maneuvers, for the entertainment of the scores who had gathered to watch their arrival. Later they performed over Redfern Field some of the most thrilling and dangerous movements known in the profession. The demonstration had been promised the local residents by the fliers during their stop-over at the island last week. A special show for the city of Brunswick is planned for tomorrow.

From stories that are told, an outstanding holiday was enjoyed by the Marines. A special-dinner dance was arranged in their honor Sunday evening and a number of Brunswick's young ladies were invited.

At 1000 hours Tuesday morning, VF-9M departed Redfern Field for Quantico. Sandy brought the squadron around in a very low pass over the field and the hotel to salute their host in appreciation for the wonderful hospitality they had received. It was something they would not forget.

The Heroes Return

Refueling at Fort Bragg, the seven airplanes circled Quantico at 1700 hours, and noticed a large crowd gathered at Brown Field. It was a welcoming committee awaiting their arrival to show its appreciation for their performance at Miami. After shutting down the engines, Sandy and his men were immediately surrounded by well-wishers and several news reporters. That evening a large celebration was held in their honor at

Fig. 3-4. Three pilots of the famed "Rojo Diablos" (Red Devils) at Brown Field in March 1931. L/R: Second Lieutenants Frank Dailey, William Saunders and Frank Wirsig (courtesy BGen. Frank H. Wirsig).

Fig. 3-5. A new and much larger airfield under construction at mouth of Chopawamsic Creek in April 1931 (courtesy Marine Corps).

Quantico and one of the pilots was heard to remark, "I don't think I can take much more of being famous."

The next day, much to his surprise, Sandy found that the Navy had turned another F7C-1 over to the squadron with a promise that he would receive the remaining six soon. This was indeed good news. They needed a spare airplane badly to ease the workload on the crew chiefs.

The following morning several reporters arrived to interview Sandy and take pictures of the squadron with their trophy (Figs. 3-4, 3-5). At the conclusion Major Geiger informed Sandy that, due to the publicity they had received, a special Navy camera plane would be at Quantico on the 29th of January to record the squadron's maneuvers in the air. This was welcome news and Colonel Turner hoped the films would be released for public showing across the nation. It would be splendid publicity for Marine Aviation.

Chapter 4

The Squirrel Cage

On Thursday morning, 29 January, the movie plane arrived from Washington to film the "Red Nosed" aerobatic team of VF-9M. The camera operators and their pilot spent considerable time with Sandy explaining variations in maneuvers that would have to be made in order to look right on film. Sandy didn't take to this very kindly and informed them that it was they who would have to work around the squadron, *not* the other way around. However, before the day ended, enough footage had been filmed to put together a 20-minute movie of the "Red Devils" of Quantico, Virginia.

In the last week in April, VF-9M began preparing for the annual gunnery and bombing exercises at Cape May, New Jersey, on 13-22 May. Sandy wanted very much for the squadron to win several "E" awards (E for excellence) in both gunnery and bombing. Major Geiger reminded him that he and the squadron had better look good at Cape May. During the following two weeks considerable time was used sharpening the skills of each pilot towards this end.

Only eight of the squadron's twelve pilots were allowed to participate in the exercises. The seven Reserve pilots called to active duty the previous July were still with Sandy, and he decided to include six of them in his try for excellence. As only six F7C-1's were available, Sandy asked for the one in use at Headquarters; to his surprise it was flown down to him the next day. With one airplane short, two of the pilots hopefully could complete the exercises by using the same airplane.

VF-9M departed Brown Field at 0700 hours on the 18th for Cape May with seven F7C-1's and a Curtiss XOC-3. The XOC-3 was flown by one of the pilots for transportation only. A Curtiss RC-1 "Kingbird" transport plane, flown by Sgt. Jack Church, did the ferrying of all mechanics and other equipment.

The squadron made a first-class showing and possibly could have been the top scorer at the meet had not two of the airplanes developed problems which kept the team from completing all of the exercises.

However, a total of ten "E" awards was earned, which placed the squadron near the top. Pilots and their awards are as follows:

Lt. L. H. Sanderson, two E's (1 for gunnery - 1 for bombing),
Lt. R. H. Kerr, two E's (bombing and gunnery),
Lt. R. B. Burchard, two E's (bombing and gunnery),
Lt. T. O. Brewster, one E, (gunnery),
Lt. D. L. Cloud, one E (gunnery),
Lt. T. J. Noon, one E, (bombing),
Lt. W. Reed, one E (bombing),

Major Geiger was indeed pleased with VF-9M's performance and was happy to inform Sandy of good news. His squadron had been invited to the National Air Races scheduled for 10 days starting 29 August through 7 September at Cleveland. This was what Sandy had hoped for, but his reaction was, "Damn-it-all, I need and *must* have more airplanes! What happened to the remaining F7C-1's promised by the Navy several months ago?"

"I don't know", said Geiger, "but I'll find out." After a lengthy conversation with Col. Turner, Geiger was promised that the remaining six Seahawks would be delivered for certain before start of the Cleveland races. Turner had somehow convinced Admiral Moffett he *must* have them immediately.

On 5 June, Sandy was informed that three airplanes were ready for delivery at his convenience. Not one to waste time, he, Dave Cloud, Tom Noon and Johnny Carter took off on 8 June in the Curtiss Kingbird for Pensacola to pick up the three F7C-1's. Sandy, Cloud and Noon returned to Quantico on the 10th. That was *superb* time in those days. Five days later a dispatch from the Navy informed Geiger's office that another F7C-1 was awaiting pickup at Hampton Roads, Virginia. Cloud flew it home on the 17th, giving VF-9M a total of 11 airplanes. Colonel Turner was keeping his promise.

Returning from thirty days leave in July, Sandy was informed that he was assigned to the Marine Corps Schools for the next ten months and was to report on 27 August—two days before the start of the National Air Races. First Lieutenant Clayton C. Jerome, who had recently joined the squadron, was slated to take over command. This was bad news to Sandy. However, Turner informed him that he would continue as commanding officer until after the air races and said further, "Keep up the good work and dazzle the hell out of the public at Clevelend." What Turner could not know at the time was, that was *exactly* what they would do!

Sandy's plans were to use nine airplanes for the show and leave two for spares. He requested that Roy Geiger assign several of the Corps' best pilots. Five Reserve officers reported for duty in July, plus 1st Lt. William O. "Bill" Brice. Brice was an outstanding pilot and had commanded VF-9M three years previously in 1928.

A New Stunt

The next few weeks were busy as Sandy drilled the formation on a maneuver he called the "Squirrel Cage." Basically, it was a tail-chasing loop with all nine airplanes going around at the same time, then ending up as a "Snake Dance," or follow the leader.

Most every day, residents of the nearby Virginia countryside could be seen looking skyward and shaking their heads in disbelief as they watched "those crazy boys from Quantico" rolling around the sky, perfecting their routine.

The Navy delivered its last two F7C-1's to the Marines in July and August. There were no more. VF-9M had received the 18 that were built. Sandy had 14 airplanes to work with now and decided to fly them all to Cleveland for use in formation flying. He still intended to use only nine airplanes in the main portion of his show.

On Friday morning, 28 August, VF-9M departed Quantico with 13 Curtiss F7C-1's and three transports for Cleveland (Fig. 4-1). Flying the three transports were Sgt. Robert E. "Bob" Lillie in the RC-1 Kingbird, Sgt. John S. "Johnny" Carter in the Ford Trimotor, and Maj. Roy S. Geiger

Fig. 4-1. Pilots of 12-plane formation of VF-9M prior to going to the Cleveland Air Races in August 1931. L/R: 2nd. Lt. Frank H. Schwable; 1st Lt. David L. Cloud; 2nd Lt. John G. Adams; 1st Lt. Edward L. Pugh; 2nd Lt. Warren E. Sweetser; 1st Lt. Lawson H.M. Sanderson, CO.; 1st Lt. William O. Brice; 2nd Lt. Allen C. Koonce; 2nd Lt. Joel D. Nott; Staff Sgt. Fred H. Smith; 1st Lt. Clayton C. Jerome, 1st Lt. Alexander W. Kreiser (courtesy Marine Corps).

in the RS-3 Sikorsky. Geiger was going by way of Anacostia to take Col. Turner, Adm. Moffett, and several high-ranking officers of the Navy Department to Cleveland for the weekend. Sergeant Shepard was flying the spare F7C-1 and would accompany Geiger in the RS-3.

Everything seemed to be going well when, about 20 miles from Cleveland, Lt. Adams switched the fuel valve in his F7C from main to reserve. Shortly afterwards, the engine suddenly quit. Working the wobble pump, he was able to restart the engine and pull up into the formation again. After he had gone through this procedure several times, the engine quit for good. By this time considerable altitude had been lost and he set his ship down in the only place available, through several fences and a large ditch. The airplane was almost a complete washout but Adams escaped with only a few minor cuts and bruises. Ed Pugh stayed behind and circled until he was sure that Adams was alright. The National Guard at Cleveland sent a car for Adams and posted a guard over the plane until it could be hauled away. That evening the National Guard played host to the squadron, and a very good time was had by all, including Adams, who was none the worse for his experience.

1931 National Air Races

The 1931 National Air Races opened up with a tremendous fanfare. Many notables and important people were in attendence, including many Hollywood stars. Will Rogers, the noted humorist, labeled the air races "the greatest of all shows."

The first part of VF-9M's performance consisted of close tactical formations using 12 planes (Fig. 4-2). After several intricate maneuvers and the conclusion of the dive bombing sequence, Sandy finished his performance using nine planes as planned. This included section and squadron loops, snap rolls, and his first public performance of the Squirrel Cage. After breaking out of the Squirrel Cage, Sandy lead the squadron in a series of crazy power spirals, rolls and loops that gave the impression of a tangled-up snake as he led the squadron downward. The show ended with a pass at wide-open throttle across the field in front of the stands, at about 50 feet above the ground. The show was well received and the newspapers called them the "devil-may-care Marines."

Actually, the routine Sandy had worked out for entering into the Squirrel Cage was the most interesting part of the maneuver and demanded the utmost in pilot skill. They all formed a line to the right of the squadron leader's plane, then slid under each other-one by one-into a nine-plane vertical stack (pancake fashion), with 10 to 12 feet between planes. They held this formation by each pilot looking up and carefully holding his plane *precisely* under the plane directly above, just keeping clear of the landing gear and propeller. The entire stack of planes was then dived, gently at first, but increasing in steepness and dive speed until the "stack" was doing more than 225 miles an hour. At that point the squadron leader—at the top of the stack—pulled upward into the sky in a wide easy

Fig. 4-2. Nine of VF-9M's F7C-1's enroute to 1931 Cleveland Air Races. Note grass on tailskid of number three airplane (courtesy Marine Corps).

loop, then each succeeding plane followed his off the top of the stack in similar fashion at timed intervals. With all nine planes spaced perfectly around in a single large loop, it was a spectacular maneuver to watch as the cage was completed. The formation was held for a few minutes, then, before landing, the leader dove and entered into a Snake Dance on the way down to end the show.

Mid-Air!

If the audience thought Fighting Nine's performance was good on opening day, they only had to be there on the second day of the show to witness their grand finale. It provided the air-race fans with a Roman Holiday-type of show that almost cost Sanderson and Brice their lives.

It was very gusty day with a strong northwest wind blowing, a situation that makes close-formation flying almost impossible. However, Sandy continued with the show, and on occasion the planes bumped wing tips because of the turbulent air. He then took the squadron to 6,000 feet, seeking smooth air to commence the Squirrel Cage. After some difficulty getting into the Squirrel Cage, things began to happen. Fred Smith, who was flying the number three position, remembers that eventful day this way:

"After we formed the stack good enough to suit Sandy's experienced eye, I saw him peel off and up into the sky, with number two following three seconds thereafter. As my turn came to follow I eased my plane upwards and over into the loop, keeping number two between my cabane struts as I reached the top, as was our method to avoid flying through the prop wash of the preceeding planes in the circuit."

"I can remember looking back over my shoulder and downward toward the green Ohio prairie as I went over the top. Sandy had, as usual, stretched his first loop at the top to allow entry room for the planes following him off the top of the stack, and in order to cooperate with him and plane number two, I had to fly flat upside down for a few seconds. This gave me my daily facewash of 80 octane gasoline mixed with a few drops of engine oil, but having learned to inhale and digest this mixture during weeks of practice, it didn't bother me too much.

"Looking backward again as I came down the backside of the loop, all nine aircraft were in their proper places around the loop, with Sandy just about to reach the top of his second one. Everything was okay now, and we continued this chase for several minutes.

"Since we were losing some altitude in the chase, we soon ran into some of the worst turbulent air I had ever flown in. We must have gone around 10 or 12 loops when Sandy's plane got blown out of line just enough to put him in the turbulent propwash and slipstream of plane number nine just ahead. His plane did a reeling flipflop, rolled onto its side, then back again and started to spin downward upside down.

"Fascinated, still rounding the top of the same loop myself, I watched him as my plane went by him, both of us on our backs, though he was out of control. It was necessary that I stay in position and watch the number two plane in front of me, though I wanted so badly to see how Sandy was making out. As I came down the back side of the loop again, I saw him struggling to recover from the upside down spin. At the last split-second he recovered, but the resulting dive was in such a position that he dove through the wings of Bill Brice's plane at the bottom of the squirrel cage. Both planes disintegrated instantly. By now I was diving at around 250 miles per hour, which was very fast in the turbulent air, as pieces of wings, cowling and miscellaneous parts from the two planes came flying by. I pulled out and over to the side of full throttle and climbed into the biggest stretch of blue sky that I could find."

The crowd was horrified, as only one parachute was seen to open. Brice had gotten out of his plane all right, but Sandy was having his problems. The impact of the mid-air collision had forced the center-section of the upper wing down and backward partially over the cockpit, just enough to block Sandy's exit. Through what seemed like superhuman effort, he managed to push the wing structure forward enough to free himself and jump, pulling the ripcord of his chute as he went over the side. But this wasn't the end of Sandy's troubles. As his chute began to open, several of its shroud lines caught on the tail of his spinning plane and once again within a few seconds he was fighting for his life. By this time the crowd was standing paralyzed as it watched the drama unfolding above.

For Sandy, time was precious as he tried desperately to free his chute lines from the falling plane. With death now staring him in the face, he somehow pulled himself upward and yanked the lines free. As he fell away, his chute blossomed open just barely in time to save his life.

Fire trucks, ambulances, photographers, and spectators by the thousands were now running towards the two pilots and the wreckage of their planes. Both planes had fallen just outside of the airport boundary—Brice's on top of the Brook Park school house (Fig. 4-3); Sandy's in a nearby field on Wilson road that had just moments before been cleared of spectators by police (Fig. 4-4). Both pilots landed a short distance from each other, ran up, shook hands, and congratulated themselves on their narrow escapes from death. Although a bit shaken up, both were all right.

Fig. 4-3. Brice's plane fell on the Brook Park School House adjacent to the airport boundry (courtesy MGen. L.H. Sanderson).

Fig. 4-4. Remains of Sanderson's F7C-1 after mid-air collision with Bill Brice, during the squadron's Squirrel Cage manuever at the 1931 Cleveland Air Races. Sanderson, a veteran of many airplane crashes, managed to parachute safely with only seconds to spare (courtesy MGen. L.H. Sanderson).

Because the show was being broadcast on radio, thousands of motorists from around the Cleveland area heard of the accident and came speeding to the airport. The resulting traffic jam took hours to clear.

When the crowd in the stands was informed that the two Marines were all right, it began settling down. In approximately 20 minutes Sanderson and Brice arrived at the announcers stand, where Admiral Moffett and Colonel Turner were waiting to congratulate them on their narrow escape (Fig. 4-5). When asked to say a few words to the crowd, Sandy stepped to the mike. "I sure hope everyone here liked our show," he said. Brice then stepped forward and added, "That goes for me too!" When the cheering subsided, the announcer remarked: "These Marine lads are not noted for making long-winded speeches." As the two Marines walked from the stand, the crowd stood up and applauded.

Later it was announced over the local news that the Marines were performing again during the evening program. The newscaster said: "The two Marine flyers who flirted with death this afternoon will go aloft again to demonstrate to the people how the Marines carry on in the face of disaster." A crowd of more than 10,000 looked on as Sanderson, Brice and Cloud performed their three-plane night show with only the red, white and blue lights visible in the darkened sky as they rolled around in perfect formation. On landing, the audience gave the three pilots a tremendous round of applause, and honking horns could be heard from hundreds of cars around the airport boundary, where people parked to watch the show.

At the show's end, the National Guard hosted an impromptu party for the Marines, and it can truthfully be said that much whisky was consumed in honor of their afternoon show.

An article in a Cleveland newspaper the following day said of the Marines' show:

Fig. 4-5. Brice and Sanderson moments after parachuting to safety from mid-air collision on 30 August 1931 (courtesy Col. R.E. Lillie).

'Red Devil Sanderson treated 12 U.S. Marine flyers, here for the air races, to the finest meal in Cleveland today. All because he forgot to save the 'ring' from his parachute that safely brought him to earth yesterday after his Curtiss Seahawk had been put out of control during the Marines' maneuvers at the airport. It's an old air-service custom to save the ring from your chute when making a jump. If you don't, it's a meal for everyone in the outfit.

First Lieutenant Lawson H. Sanderson, leader and commander of the famous 'Rojo Diablos' (Red Devil) Fighting Squadron of the Marines, had too many other things to think about yesterday, other than saving his parachute ring, after crashing into the plane of First Lieutenant William O. Brice, leader of the squadron's second section. For instance, he had plenty to think about when his chute caught on the tail of his falling plane and was dragging him through space while he untangled it.

Sanderson has been flying for 13 years and is considered the most expert aerobatic pilot in the Marine Corps. He has earned many decorations for his accomplishments and bravery.

The squadron's spectacular performance kept attendance at a maximum during the remaining days of the air show and earned for it the title: "The greatest exhibition squadron in the world!"

On VF-9M's return to Quantico, Major Geiger ordered that a trouble board be convened to determine, if possible, the cause of the collision. Also, there was the matter of Lieutenant Adams' forced landing enroute to Cleveland, resulting in extensive damage to yet a third airplane.

The Navy Department said in rather strong words that it—and *especially* the Marine Corps—could not afford the loss of any more aircraft during stunting exhibitions and it warned Colonel Turner to tone down the squadron's shows. He was further reminded that he had been advised about this previously at Chicago. Nevertheless, it was Turner's belief that the loss of three aircraft was part of the overall price that Marine Aviation had to pay for recognition. He continued to badger his superiors and those having some control over military spending to allocate funds for its overall improvement.

Chapter 5

Turner is Killed

On 9 September 1931, as previously ordered, Sanderson relinquished command of VF-9M to Lieutenant Jerome and reported to the Marine Corps Schools at Quantico for its 10 month command course.

The same day, VF-9M, under the command of its new skipper, departed Quantico with seven F7C-1's for Sioux Falls, North Dakota, to compete in the air races scheduled on 11 through 13 September. Geiger reminded Jerry of the Navy's warning about the destruction of any more airplanes, and Jerry told him not to worry.

The trip out was uneventful. At the conclusion of their first show, Lt. Sweetser ground-looped his plane while landing in a strong gusty wind and broke the spar and several ribs in the left lower wing. Remembering the Navy's stern warning, Jerry knew the damage had to be kept quiet. Working day and night, the crew chiefs repaired the airplane in time for Sweetser to fly it home after the three-day meet, and no one was the wiser.

Arriving home on Tuesday, the 15th, Jerry was informed that two additional airshows were scheduled for the remainder of the year. The first in October at Valley Stream, Long Island; the other in November at New Berne, North Carolina. Obviously the squadron's popularity was increasing at a rapid pace, as Turner had hoped it would.

Valley Stream Airshow

At noon, 16 October, VF-9M departed Quantico with nine Curtiss F7C-1's for Valley Stream, Long Island. The Valley Stream Airshow was part of a giant four-field air-pageant organized by the Mayor of New York to raise $12,000,000 for the Unemployment Relief Fund. The United States at this time was in the middle of the Great Depression, and everyone in aviation was asked to donate their talent for the cause.

Four shows daily were to be carried on simultaneously at four different airports in the New York area—the Glen H. Curtiss Field at North Beach in Queens; Floyd Bennett Field at Barren Island, Brooklyn

Fig. 5-1. Red-nosed Seahawk of VF-9M at Floyd Bennett Field in October 1931 (courtesy BGen. E.L. Pugh).

(Fig. 5-1); the Curtiss-Wright Airport at Valley Stream, Long Island; and Roosevelt Field on Long Island. To make it possible for those who might want to see *all* of the shows, a special airline connected the four fields on the closest schedule ever attempted. Every six minutes and forty seconds a fully loaded transport plane took off from each field for a circuit of the four. The fees collected from the passengers were contributed to the fund. It turned out to be the single most successful fund-raising item of the show.

A New York newspaper said: "Scarcely had the reserve squadrons from New York completed their performance when the slight lull beneath the darkened sky of clouds was broken by a terrific roar. Nine airplanes swooped down in so tight a formation that they seemed like one. The Marines had arrived! Sweeping the runway once, the squadron leader, Lieutenant Clayton C. Jerome, waggled his wings and the squadron pulled straight up to start its wonderful show."

The Army and Navy were well represented at the show, and after the first day a contest developed between the three services. Lieutenant John Griffiths, of the First Pursuit Group, Selfridge Field, Michigan, led a stunt formation of Boeing P-12's known as "The Turtles" through a series of aerobatics that thrilled the large crowd.

The Navy, not to be outdone, had Lieutenant Commander John E. Ostrander lead his twelve Boeing F4B-1's from the aircraft carrier *Langley* through an exciting show that just about carried away the honors. He even tried VF-9M's Squirrel Cage but didn't quite pull it off as Sanderson had. An officer from the Navy Bureau of Aeronautics was heard to remark, "With the rivalry between them, its a damn good thing the show lasted only three days or, sure as hell, someone would have been court martialed or even killed!"

The air pageant was a huge success and attracted many prominent people and just about everyone who could afford the price of admission. The Mayor of New York said of VF-9M's performance: "It was one of the outstanding highlights of this great Air Pageant."

Tragic Accident

On 26 October a terrible tragedy descended on Marine Aviation and left its mark from top to bottom. Colonel Thomas C. Turner was struck by a whirling propeller and died two days later in a hospital at Port-au-Prince, Haiti. Marine Aviation's champion was dead. Turner was, without a doubt, its most ambitious man and had fought harder for his chosen service than any man up to that time (Fig. 5-2). From the moment he first assumed command of Marine Aviation, he ruled it with an iron hand and never let his men get the idea that the best aviators are those without strict discipline. The only time he may have ever relaxed this role somewhat was in the case of VF-9M and its promotion of Marine Aviation.

Gunnery Sergeant Robert E. A. "Bob" Lillie, (now a retired Colonel) who was flying the big Sikorsky RS-1 transport (Fig. 5-3) whose propellers struck him on that fateful day recalls:

Fig. 5-2. Col. Thomas C. Turner, Officer-in-Charge of Marine Aviation. At his death, he was about to be promoted to brigadier general, a rank no other Marine Aviator attained until eight years later (courtesy National Archives).

61

Fig. 5-3. Sikorsky RS-1 (A-8842) at Bowen Field, Port-Au-Prince, Haiti, on 25 November 1931. Col. Turner died two days later after walking into the left propeller of this airplane at Gonaives Beach on 26 October 1931 (courtesy BGen. Frank H. Schwable).

"Joe Ed Davis, Commanding Officer at Haiti, was in the copilot's seat. Colonel Turner, Mrs. Davis, Gunnery Sergeant Jesse Towles and Sergeant Curtiss Goehring were in the cabin. We left Port-au-Prince on the afternoon of October 26 for Gonaives on an inspection trip. It was my expressed desire to land in the bay and discharge the passengers because there was no field at Gonaives, and I started to make a pass to do so. Small planes with balloon tires regularly landed on this beach, which was hard, salt-encrusted sand. I felt the Sikorsky RS-1 wheel loading was much too high for the beach. However, Davis directed me to land on the beach, which we did.

"The landing was okay and as we were approaching the shack on the beach, we were moving about five mph when the left wheel dropped through the salt crust. The keel touched the sand, causing the left side to be considerably lower than usual. Colonel Turner pulled the rear cabin hatch cover, dashed up front around the left side, looked under the hull from well up front, indicated no damage was done and I cut the engines. Turner then walked toward the plane and continued on into the left propeller. It made less than one turn after striking him. He was not knocked off his feet nor did he lose consciousness, although a significant portion of his jaw and skull had been cut-off. In fact he remained conscious until his death two days later.

"After being treated at a Marine Corps field medical facility, where Sergeant Towles and I had taken him in an open carry-all, Turner was returned on the 27th aboard the Coast Guard cutter *Woodcock* to Port-au-Prince where he died the next day in the hospital.

"He was held in high esteem by all who knew him, and he had a devotion to Marine Aviation not found in many since. My personal experience with him can best be summed up by saying that he treated me like his son, and I had the greatest respect for him."

At the time of Turner's death he was about to be promoted to the rank of brigadier general, a rank no other aviator had ever attained—and would not—until just before World War II. He was the 104th Marine Aviator to meet a violent death.

Leadership Passed On

Major Geiger succeeded Turner as Officer-in-Charge of Marine Aviation on 6 November 1931 and pledged to continue Turner's policies. He assured everyone in aviation that there was only one way to go and that was forward. Several congressmen sympathetic to the Marines' cause and saddened by Turner's death renewed promises to do their utmost to provide funds for more men and equipment. Further, Admiral Moffett, whose respect for Turner knew no bounds, agreed that the Marines would get new aircraft under the next fiscal appropriation awaiting passage in Congress.

Major Ralph J. Mitchell took over the job vacated by Geiger on 16 November 1931. Mitchell was an excellent choice to command the East Coast Squadrons. In seniority he was the number two aviator, second only to Geiger. He was under consideration for a Distinguished Flying Cross, which had been recommended by the Commanding General in Nicaragua, for his outstanding service while commanding squadrons there.

On 20 November, Cloud departed Brown Field with six F7C-1's for New Berne, North Carolina, to take part in the dedication of the city's new airport. Because of other assignments, Jerome and two squadron pilots were unable to take part. Cloud borrowed three pilots from squadron VO-6M to complete the assignment.

As usual VF-9M was well received on its arrival at New Berne and were the guests of the city during its three-day stay. Saturday afternoon, Cloud led the squadron through its exciting performance and, just before preparing to land, gave the hand signal for the squadron to form a Lufberry circle.

It was Cloud's intention to lose altitude gradually and, at the same time, tighten the circle. When low enough, he would break out of the circle into a dive, with each airplane following to form a line; then, with throttles wide open, to dive past the grandstand at less than 50 feet off the ground. This was always a crowd pleaser.

The six-plane formation was getting lower and the circle was getting tighter. Cloud was about to give the signal to follow him down when Lt. Joel Nott, flying the number two position behind Cloud, suddenly flipped over into a spin, and before he could possibly recover, crashed to his death

Fig. 5-4. Crash of F7C-1 that killed 2nd Lt. Joel D. Nott during airshow at New Berne, North Carolina, on 21 November 1931 (courtesy Marine Corps).

on the airport to the horror of the spectators (Fig. 5-4). In all probability the fatal spin was the result of two things: the near-stalled attitude of the airplane as Nott tried to stay in the tight formation, and the turbulent prop-wash created by the other airplanes in the continuous tight circle.

It was a terrible blow to Cloud, who somehow blamed himself. Nott was the least experienced of the six pilots, and it was for this reason that Cloud has assigned him as his number one wingman where he could keep an eye on him. His death marked the eighth violent Marine fatality of the year.

In a telephone call to Major Mitchell at Quantico, Cloud was instructed to complete the assignment as scheduled and continue with the show on Sunday. Lieutenant Ed Pugh flew a replacement aircraft to New Berne on Sunday morning for this purpose.

The F7C-1's continued to be plagued from time to time with engine-mount ring problems. Major Mitchell decided that all air shows should be cancelled pending the results of further structural tests under investigation at this time. The squadron settled down to regular routine duties of flying tactical formation, but the aircraft were limited to shallow dives and low G loads in all maneuvers.

More Engine Mount Problems

Meanwhile the Naval Aircraft Factory at Philadelphia, working on a verbal agreement with the Engineering officer at Quantico, modified several of the Hawks with a new steel engine mount designed by the

Curtiss Company. According to Curtiss, this was a cure-all for the problem. However, after it was installed in all airplanes, a very embarrassing situation was discovered. The impulse generator which ran the trigger motor and fired the machine guns would not fit behind the new mounts. Jerome immediately wrote the following letter to his Commanding Officer.

VF SQUADRON 9M, AIRCRAFT SQUADRONS, ECEF,
MARINE BARRACKS, QUANTICO, VA.

5 January 1932

From: The Comanding Officer, VF-9M
To: The Commanding Officer, Aircraft
Squadrons, E.C.E.F.
Subject: Installation of gunnery gear on F7C-1
airplanes

1. The new steel engine mounts recently supplied this squadron do not permit the installation of the Nelson generators. The generator cannot be put in place due to the location of the upper diagonal brace members in the mount. The E-4 generator can be slipped in place before the engine is mounted, but there is not sufficient clearance for the impulse assembly. The specifications on the cable of this assembly require that it be bent with a radius not less than six inches and in this instance it must be bent to a radius of 1 to 1% inches. With this abrupt bend, the armament section reports that transmission of impulses from the generator to trigger motor will be dampened out by friction, thereby causing such an installation to be useless.

2. There is no way this gunnery gear can be made to function without alteration of the engine mounts. Since these airplanes are nearing the end of their useful existance and nearly all of the mounts for this squadron have been completed at the Naval Aircraft Factory, it is recommended that this squadron not participate in the annual gunnery practices this year.

Clayton C. Jerome

From Jerome's letter, a series of letters were written back and forth between the Bureau of Aeronautics, the Chief of Naval Operations, the manager of the Naval Aircraft Factory, the Curtiss Aeroplane Company, and the engineering officer at Quantico. An investigation determined that the Curtiss Company was at fault due to lack of proper information on the new engine mount drawings. However, the whole controversy was forgotten when the following letter was received from the Chief of Naval Operations.

23 January 1932

From: Chief of Naval Operations
To: Commanding Officer, Aircraft Squadrons, ECEF. Marine
            Barracks, Quantico, Va.
Subject: Gunnery Exercises—VF Squadron 9M

1. Aircraft gunnery and bombing exercises as prescribed for VF Squadron 9M will not be conducted with F7C-1 type airplanes.

2. VF Squadron 9M will conduct the prescribed gunnery exercises when F4B-4 type airplanes are delivered to that squadron.

Frank H. Clark

(by
direction)

That letter had to be about the best news received by the Marines at Quantico for some time. It's easy to imagine the rejoicing that went on over the last paragraph. Rumors had been circulating for months that Turner, before his death, had made sure the Marines were to receive the new Boeing F4B-4's to replace the aging F7C-1's. Until this letter, no one expected it would happen.

In March the Marines were authorized 28 new Boeing F4B-4's. VF-9M was to receive 16; 12 to be operational and four as spares. The remaining 12 were allocated to Squadron VF-10M on the West Coast. Geiger assured Mitchell he would watch closely to make sure none became side-tracked into Navy channels.

Sandy Returns

On 11 June 1932, Lieutenant Sandy Sanderson, after completing the 10-month Command Course at Marine Corps Schools, again assumed command of Fighting Squadron Nine-M. The *Gazette*, a Quantico magazine, stated: "Now that 'Red Devil' Sanderson is back as skipper of Fighting Nine, look out, for big things are sure to happen." It was true that Sandy was a very colorful Marine and had acquired quite a reputation as a hot-shot pilot. His love and zest for flying knew no bounds, and he could always be counted on to liven up any air meet and to do the impossible. Of course, on occasion this got him into a little trouble, but he always managed to come out looking better than before.

Born in Sheldon, Washington, on 22 July 1895, Sanderson came into the Marines from the University of Montana, where he had been a football star. After graduating in 1917, he enlisted in the Marines and rose to the rank of gunnery sergeant in the incredible time of only eight months. Following his assignment as an aviation cadet in 1918, he was transferred to the Marine Flying Field at Miami, Florida, where he received his wings and was designated a Naval Aviator on 14 January 1919.

After receiving his wings, it didn't take long for Sandy to become well-known throughout the Marine Corps. It was only a few months later, over the jungles of Haiti, that he was dive-bombing bandits with the "mailsack" routine he invented. According to Major Evans, who was Sandy's commanding officer in Haiti at the time, "Sandy wanted to drop larger bombs and directly on the target. The present wing racks didn't suit his purpose. The mailsack was a crude way to do it, but it showed real ingenuity on his part. And it sure scared hell out of the bandits."

One story told about Sandy when he was in Nicaragua fighting the bandits, was that he had a fear of being shot in the rear end while flying over the bandits' jungle hideouts. They were constantly shooting at the airplanes as they flew overhead. To Sandy the most embarrassing thing that could possibly happen to a pilot would be to get a bullet in the rear. To prevent this from happening, he secured an iron lid from an old cook stove and carried it between himself and his parachute. One day after a mission during which ground fire had been extremely heavy, the iron lid fell from under his parachute as he climbed out of the cockpit. A curious fellow pilot standing nearby was puzzled by the lid and asked about it. When told of its meaning, he practically rolled on the ground with laughter. It took some time for Sandy to live down his new nickname of "Ironbutt."

All pilots in Marine Aviation held Sandy in high esteem, and anytime a group of pilots got together to "shoot the breeze" or for some friendly hangar talk, Sanderson lore always managed to become part of the conversation. He was credited with walking away from more airplane accidents than anyone in Marine Aviation. And any former Marine Aviator will tell you: "With Sandy it wasn't luck. It took some damn fine flying to be able to accomplish that."

Meanwhile, on 30 May 1932, Major Ross E. "Rusty" Rowell arrived at Quantico to take over Mitchell's duties after the latter had been ordered to attend the War College. Rowell was a go-getter when it come to living and promoting Marine Aviation. He, Geiger, and Sanderson would prove to be an unbeatable trio. In 1927 Rowell had distinguished himself in Nicaragua when he led a flight of old DH's in relief of a Marine garrison surrounded by bandit forces at Ocotal. His tactics on that occasion are considered to be the first organized dive-bombing attack in combat.

After Sandy returned from his 10 months at Marine Corps Schools, VF-9M was scheduled at two important airshows: the Canadian Air Pageant at Montreal on 20-21 August, and the classic event of the year, the National Air Races on 27 August through 5 September. The F7C-1's were still barred from airshow work, so Sandy was naturally showing concern about delivery of new airplanes—especially as time was fast running out. A letter from Admiral Moffett stated that eight of the new Boeing F4B-4's were to be delivered in April and six in May. However, as of 1 July this had not materialized. Status of VF-9M on this date was:

Aircraft	Personnel
8 F7C-1 Curtiss Seahawks	3 Officers (pilots)
1 RR-2 Ford Trimoter Transport	3 Enlisted pilots (NAP's)
1 RC-1 Curtiss Kingbird Transport	39 Enlisted (all other)
10 Total	45 Total

Finally, on the morning of 2 August, Rowell telephoned Geiger at Headquarters to stress that VF-9M had less than three weeks to prepare for the Montreal show and still no new airplanes had arrived. Geiger, well aware of the situation, informed Rowell that the Navy had rescheduled delivery of the new planes for sometime in September. This angered Rowell, but Geiger suggested he quit worrying and said before hanging up, "Rusty, I've seen you do with a hell-of-a-lot less. From here on out I'm giving you a free hand to do what's necessary, and I'm sure you'll put on a good show."

As time was short, Rowell met with Sanderson and 1st Lt. Clarence J. "Buddy" Chappell, commanding officer of Observation Squadron Six-M (VO-6M), to finalize plans for the shows. Rowell informed the two officers that both the Montreal and Cleveland shows would have to be performed with Chappell's Curtiss 02C-1 Helldivers. A nine-plane formation was decided on, with Rowell to lead it. Sandy was to recruit the best pilots he could find and to have the airplanes repainted in special markings that he and Rowell quickly designed (Fig. 5-5).

The VO Squadron was a very busy place both in the air and on the ground during the next two weeks. In addition to repainting, each airplane was given a complete airframe and engine inspection. The work was mostly performed at night because of the squadron's stepped-up flying schedule, and crews and helpers from other squadrons pitched in to help.

Airshow in Montreal

The nine-plane formation of Curtiss Helldivers departed Brown Field at 0800 on 19 August for Montreal. Enroute stops were made at Floyd Bennett Field, and Albany, New York. Lieutenant Schilt flew the big Alantic RA-3 transport to carry supplies, mechanics tools and several dignitaries to the show. Total flight time to Montreal was six hours and forty minutes.

The Canadians loved the U.S. Marines show on Saturday, and the glorious accounts in the Sunday morning newspapers brought many people out on Sunday afternoon where they witnessed a special three-plane performance by Sandy, Pugh and Cloud. Flying their Helldivers like

Fig. 5-5. Lined up for inspection are pilots, mechanics and 02C-1 "Helldivers" in their new "Acey-Deucy" markings designed for the Canadian Air Races at Montreal (courtesy U.S. Navy).

Fig. 5-6. Nine of the 12 pilots that made up the formation for the 1932 Cleveland Air Races. L/R: Thomas J. Cushman, Sandy Sanderson, Dave Cloud, Frank Schilt, LCol. Ross E. Rowell, Edward Pugh, T.J. Walker, Glen Britt and Buddy Chappell (courtesy Marine Corps).

fighter planes, the three pilots flew upside-down formations, slow rolls, and both inside and outside loops in formation, making the Marines the hit of the two-day pageant.

That evening at a party given in their honor by the city, Rusty Rowell promised that the Marines would always honor any invitation by their Canadian neighbors.

Departing at 1000 hours on Monday morning, the squadron arrived at Quantico at 1800 after stops at Albandy and Floyd Bennett Field in New York.

1932 National Air Races

Five days later, on 27 August, VO-6M departed Brown Field with a 12-plane formation to perform at the National Air Races at Cleveland (Fig. 5-6). Three additional pilots making up the fourth section were First Lieutenants Schilt, Z.C. Hopkins and Staff Sergeant Fred Smith.

At Cleveland, the Marines were treated royally—especially Sanderson. Everyone remembered the show that he and Bill Brice had put on the previous year. He also came in for a bit of ribbing about flying with the observation squadron, but he informed his tormentors that next year, with the new Boeings, things would be different. "Just watch my smoke," was his only answer. He didn't know it, but it would be his last performance as a pilot at the famed Cleveland Air Races.

Returning to Quantico in the afternoon of 6 September, Sandy again took up the duties of C.O. of VF-9M. The next morning Rowell telephoned Sandy to say that he had received a letter from the Bureau: three F4B-4's had been shipped from the Boeing factory by rail on 3 September; three

Fig. 5-7. First of the new Boeing F4B-4 Fighters (serial no. 9010) on the flight line at Brown Field after test flight by Ed Pugh on 23 September 1932 (courtesy Tom J. Griffis).

more were scheduled for shipment on 10 December; and the remaining ten would be delivered before year's end. Sandy called out the good news to Ed Pugh, working in the next room. Both officers agreed that the occasion called for a toast. Without too much trouble, enough liquid was found to engage in several.

At Sandy's urging, Rowell wrote Geiger, requesting a minimum of 14 pilots to man the new airplanes. Presently, there were only five pilots remaining in VF-9M.

The F4B-4's Arrive

On 16 September the first three Boeing F4B-4's (serial numbers 9010, 9011 and 9012) arrived at Quantico by rail. Everyone from VF-9M turned out to help unload the airplanes from the boxcar. A Boeing representative was on hand to assist Master Sergeant Earl Zalanka and his crew from the Assembly and Repair Shop put the airplanes together.

On 23 September F4B-4 serial number 9010 (Fig. 5-7) was rolled to the flight line and started by Sgt. Tom J. Griffis. Ed Pugh, the squadron engineering officer, who supervised its assembly, was standing by to take it aloft on its first flight.

After sliding into the cockpit and waving to everyone, Ed taxied slowly to the north end of the field, where he completed his checklist and engine runup. With most of Brown Field watching, Ed opened the throttle slowly and was airborne almost before he knew it. After a twenty-minute familiarization flight, Ed landed and returned to the flight line, a big grin on his face. A few minor adjustments were made and Ed went up again for further tests. When he landed, he just couldn't say enough about its performance.

Sandy, anxiously awaiting his turn, hopped into 9010 for a thirty-minute checkout flight. He, too, returned to the flight line with warm praise for the new Boeing.

The day before, three additional F4B-4's (serial numbers 9013, 9014 and 9015) had arrived and were being assembled. All the talk at Brown Field was about the new Boeings. They were the most modern airplanes within the military, with an all-metal fuselage and tail assembly plus many items of new equipment, including provision for two-way radio. In addition, their performance was superb, showing in flight tests that they were 35 miles per hour faster than the F7C-1's. Incidentally, among Navy and Marine Corps pilots of the 1930's the Boeing F4B-4 became one of the best loved fighter planes, and the F4B series of aircraft had the distinction of remaining in Naval service longer than any other fighter design between the two World Wars.

Almost every day Sandy was aloft, putting one of the new planes through loops, snap-rolls and any other maneuver he could think of. If they had any bad habits, he wanted to discover them before new pilots came into the squadron. After each flight he became more enthusiastic with their performance and selected number 9010 as his personal plane.

The crew chiefs were very impressed with the airplane's ease of maintenance. However, the new Pratt-Whitney 550-horsepower engines required the addition of tetraethyl lead to the fuel, and Brown Field wasn't set-up for this as yet. Glen Carter, a former crew chief, said, "It was a mixture of three and one-half CC's of lead to a gallon of fuel. I used to fill my plane with regular aviation fuel and multiply the gallons added by three and one-half, pour the lead in the tank, and then rock hell out of the plane from the wing tip until I had it thoroughly mixed. We were supposed to wear rubber gloves because the lead was poison. I can attest to this as I almost lost a thumb because I didn't want to bother with gloves. It taught me something—follow rules."

Chapter 6

Britt Bails Out

By early November, Sandy was very disturbed because headquarters had made no move to assign pilots to VF-9M. He was committed to perform at the All-American Air Maneuvers at Miami in January and was fast running out of time. He obtained permission from Rusty Rowell to borrow four pilots of his choice, with the understanding they would be released from their regular duties to practice and attend the show. With himself and Ed Pugh, he now had a six-plane formation.

On 10 December, the remaining 10 new F4B-4's (serial numbers 9230 through 9239) arrived at Quantico—much too late for Sandy to take a 12-plane formation to Miami.

Special Markings

Sandy thought his new planes should have special markings, possibly on the order of the Red Devils. Rowell agreed. They finally agreed to paint the engine cowls and wheels of all planes bright red, similar to the Red Devil markings on the F7C-1's. Each three-plane section was to have solid color tails in red, white, or blue. The section leader's plane was to carry red; plane number two (left wing) had a white tail; number three plane (right wing) bore blue. The fuselage would remain Navy grey and the wings would stay all silver, with the top of the upper wing orange-yellow.

To help pilots quickly locate each other while rolling around the sky in wild maneuvers, Sandy suggested that regular squadron markings be eliminated and replaced with large numbers on each side of the fuselage. Also, inasmuch as the new planes' serial numbers were in sequence, the numbers would correspond to the last digit of the serial number. Thus, serial number 9011 would carry squadron number 1, serial number 9012 would be number 2, and so on. This would be an automatic cross check of side numbers versus serial numbers (Fig. 6-1).

One problem quickly popped up. The serial number of Sandy's F4B-4 was 9010. Sandy quipped, "Guess I'll have to put a big 0 on my plane."

Fig. 6-1. Lineup of F4B-4's at Brown Field showing their non-regulation show markings (courtesy Marine Corps).

Fig. 6-2. Sanderson in cockpit of his personal plane "O" (9010) at Floyd Bennett Field (courtesy BGen. E.L. Pugh).

Rowell replied, "Why not? It sure as hell will draw lots of attention and conversation." Sandy was hoping Rowell would say that when he made the suggestion, but didn't want to carry the non-regulation marking bit too far (Fig. 6-2).

As each airplane went to the paint shop, large individual squadron numbers 24 inches high were painted in black on each side of the fuselage and 30-inch numbers was added to the underside of the right lower wing panel. "U.S. MARINES" had been centered across the topside of the upper wing prior to this. By mid-December all F4B-4's were carrying the new markings and looked very flashy lined up on Brown Field for inspection.

By this time Sandy had decided to stay with a six-plane formation and give the people at Miami a show they would never forget. He had done it before, so why not again? And as usual, Sandy always made good on his promises.

Back To Miami

It was a very cold morning on 3 January 1933, when VF-9M departed Brown Field for Miami. The seven-plane formation, which got underway at 0800 hours, set down at Charleston, South Carolina, for fuel and to check the weather ahead. Sandy decided it was safe to continue on but at Savannah, Georgia, the weather deteriorated so badly that he decided to remain there overnight.

They arrived in Miami at 1430 the following afternoon and were invited to a pre-show party that evening sponsored by the promoters of the show. It was a typical Miami bash, with an ample supply of girls and booze.

The next morning it was rather easy to detect those who had over indulged in elbow bending the night before.

Opening day on Friday saw quite an array of civilian pilots entered in all categories of racing and stunting. As in the past, when it came time for the Marines' portion of the show, everyone gave them their undivided attention. Captain Harrison of the local Marine Reserve stepped to the microphone and said, "Next on our program is what you all have been waiting to see this afternoon. From Quantico, Virginia, comes the Marine's crack squadron—Fighting Squadron Nine, under the very able command of Lieutenant Sandy Sanderson, the Mad Marine, who will, as in the past, lead his squadron through a thrilling show; that I can assure you."

As predicted, VF-9M (Fig. 6-3) kept everyone on the edge of his seat throughout the performance especially during its last few minutes, when 1st Lt. Glen M. "Jimmy" Britt gave the huge crowd an unexpected thrill during a low-level pass across the field. Less than a minute before, Sandy had given the signal to break out of a Lufbery circle and dive across the field in trail formation past the stands in a final salute to the audience. Britt was flying the number five position in line, and as he passed in front of the grandstand, his airplane suddenly rolled on its right side and seemed to go completely out of control. To the horror of the spectators, it dived straight for the ground. At the last split-second, Britt was seen to fall from his

Fig. 6-3. VF-9M at Miami All-American Air Maneuvers on 5 January 1933. Kneeling L/R: Elmer Saltzman, Jimmy Britt, Dave Cloud, and Buddy Chappell. Standing L/R: Lt. Schultz of Miami Marine Reserve, Rusty Rowell, Sandy Sanderson and Ed Pugh (courtesy G.W. Romer).

Fig. 6-4. Crash of Britt's F4B-4 (9015) at Miami. Britt wearing helmet and goggles is in center of photo (courtesy G.W. Romer).

plane, with his parachute opening just a few feet before he hit the ground, cheating death by a second or so. Except for a sprained ankle, he was unhurt.

As Sandy pulled up from his run he looked back in time to see Britt's chute pop open. Not knowing what happened, he quickly turned around and flew over the wreckage. "I determined only one airplane was involved," said Sanderson, "however, on my second pass over the wreckage, which landed just behind the stands and across Le Jeune road, I saw Britt jumping around on one foot and thought he was clowning around again. He was a great actor and clown, and you never knew when he was or wasn't kidding."

A police cordon was quickly thrown around Britt and the wreckage of his plane to keep away the souvenir hunters and the large crowd of onlookers that always seem to gather so fast at accidents (Fig. 6-4). Those still left in the stands were going wild with anticipation. To settle them down, the announcer stated that the pilot of the wrecked airplane was all right and would make an appearance shortly.

In about thirty minutes the airshow manager escorted Britt to the announcer's stand and made the following introduction: "Ladies and gentlemen, I have here a very lucky man. This is Lieutenant Jimmy Britt, the Marine pilot that just bailed out of his airplane." After the cheering was over and the crowd finally quieted down, the announcer asked Jimmy if he had anything to say to the crowd. "Yes sir," said Jimmy, "I'm going out now and get drunk." And he did! From all that can be gathered, drinking got underway shortly after and ended in a big party at the McAllister Hotel.

Colonel Rowell (Fig. 6-5), who witnessed the accident, was worried over the adverse comments that he was certain would come from the Navy

Bureau of Aeronautics and the Chief of Naval Operations. VF-9M had been warned on several occasions about its "gusto" for staging dramatic performances; now, on its first show with the new Boeings, one had been destroyed.

In answer to a telegram sent by Rowell to headquarters, it was ordered that a board of investigation be convened immediately following the squadron's return to Quantico to determine the cause of the accident.

In a verbal statement to Sandy shortly after the mishap, Britt indicated he was bewildered as to what actually happened. Gunnery Sgt.

Fig. 6-5. Lt. Colonel Ross E. "Rusty" Rowell (courtesy U.S. Navy).

Hugh A. "Zero" Blanks, in charge of the ground crew, was instructed by Sandy to go over the crashed F4B-4 piece by piece and, if at all possible, try to determine if there had been a structural failure. Further, Sandy gave direction to crew chiefs that the remaining airplanes were to have a complete inspection before the next day's show—even if it meant working all night.

As expected, Britt's accident brought many thousand more spectators to the show the next day to see the Marines' perform their daring stunts. However, the shows on Saturday and Sunday was toned down and each performance was completed without mishap.

Monday morning VF-9M departed Miami at 0930 for home, staying overnight at Savannah after a 100-mile battle with rain and fog. They arrived at Brown Field shortly after noon the following day. Flying time for the return trip was 7 hours 35 minutes.

The following morning Rowell appointed Pugh, Cloud and Chappell to head the investigation of Britt's crash. On 11 January the following report was compiled from the available evidence and sent for Rowell's approval before being forwarded to the Bureau of Aeronautics.

> On 6 January 1933 a formation of six airplanes was flying a tactical formation at the Municipal Airport, Miami, Florida. Upon diving out of a Lufberry circle, the fifth airplane in column rolled to the right from an altitude of approximately twelve hundred feet and went into a right spin from which it did not recover. The pilot loosened his belt and was thrown clear of the plane at less than 300 feet.
>
> It is the opinion of the Board that the plane hit a slip-stream from which it was knocked into an outside spin. The airplane appeared to have sufficient speed as it spun about twice in a diagonal direction before it started spinning vertically.
>
> Upon an examination of the airplane, it was noted that the aileron control rod leading to the right aileron was broken off about six inches from where it was connected to the base of the stick. The stick itself was broken off at the middle. All other control connections were intact but badly smashed. A possible cause: broken right aileron tube connection.
>
> It is recommended that any serviceable parts of the airplane and engine be salvaged and that both be stricken from the Navy list.
>
> (signed)
Clarence J. Chappell
(Senior Board Member)

The report was signed by Rowell on 14 January and forwarded to the Navy Department as requested. A letter was received shortly after stating that the Bureau had removed the airplane and engine from its records. Both Rowell and Sandy felt relieved, as this was a good indication the matter was dropped.

The Marines' commitment in Nicaragua ended in January and eased the pilot shortage considerably. Headquarters followed with a dispatch

Fig. 6-6. Pilots of VF-9M in May 1933. L/R: Staff Sgt. Gordon Heritage; Gunnery Sgt. John Carter; 2nd Lt. Frank Schwable; 1st Lt. Sandy Sanderson; 2nd Lt. Perry Parmelee; 1st Lt. Pierson Conradt; 1st Lt. Elmer Saltzman; 1st Lt. Edward Pugh; 1st Lt. Tom Walker; 2nd Lt. Frank Wirsig; 1st Lt. Jimmy Britt and 1st Lt. Al Kreiser (courtesy BGen. F.H. Wirsig).

directing VF-9M to fill its pilot needs as required. Sandy immediately asked for the four pilots he used for the Miami show: Britt, Cloud, Saltzman and Walker, plus Al Kreiser, Perry Parmelee, Frank Schwable and Frank Wirsig. All were top-notch pilots and, except for Parmelee and Saltzman, were former squadron members. Four outstanding enlisted pilots already in the squadron were sergeants: Johnny Carter, Gordon Heritage, Fred Smith and Cracker Williams. Counting Pugh and Sandy, VF-9M now had 14 pilots (Fig. 6-6).

During the next few weeks Sandy and Wirsig, who became squadron operations officer, worked the men without let-up. Gunnery exercises were scheduled for 4 April and VF-9M hoped to make a good showing with its new airplanes. However, weather shortened their training period to slightly more than two weeks.

Custom Airplanes

Meanwhile, a few modifications were made to the F4B-4's. Recalling those days, Brigadier General Edward L. Pugh, USMC, (ret) said, "I was engineering officer at the time and I flew the first F4B-4 in the Marine Corps, serial number 9010, on 23 September 1932. After we had them for awhile, I made a few minor alterations. Inasmuch as we did not expect to be using them aboard aircraft carriers, we removed the arresting hook and covered the hole with a small metal plate to keep the mud and stones from splashing up into the fuselage (Fig. 6-7). This also lightened the plane and helped to improve its performance. We also removed the solid-rubber tire from the tail wheel and replaced it with a pneumatic one. We did this because, when landing on turf and mud fields, the solid-rubber tire dug into the ground like a tail skid and ruined the wheel bearings prematurely."

Another modification was to the engine exhaust stacks, as they often came loose. Frank Schwable just missed death one morning during formation practice when the bayonet stack from the number one cylinder of his F4B-4 flew off and split the top of his helmet open as it sailed by without so much as a scratch to himself. After this narrow escape all airplanes were grounded until the exhaust stacks could be redesigned.

To enable the F4B-4's to fly upside down at airshows, the crew chiefs bored out a carburetor jet just slightly larger than the main one in the carburetor and inserted it in the fuel line ahead of the carburetor intake. This prevented flooding of the carburetors when flying upside down, assuring quick response from the engine so necessary in close-formation flying.

At 0800 hours on 4 April 1933, VF-9M departed for the annual gunnery exercises at Norfolk, Virginia. They were to billet at the Naval Air Station there and conduct their gunnery practice from the National Guard field at Virginia Beach. Each morning they were to fly to the Guard field, located just back of the town, and return to Norfolk in the afternoon.

To tow targets with the F4B-4's, Ed Pugh designed a rack that attached underneath the fuselage to the auxiliary fuel tank mountings. The tow line was attached to this rack by means of a detachable ring controlled from the cockpit. This allowed the pilot to release the target when desired.

To get the target sleeve airborne, it was laid out on the ground at the opposite end of the field and in the direction that the tow plane would be making its takeoff run. The tow line was connected to the airplane and run forward to the target. As the airplane passed the target on its takeoff run, the pilot pulled his airplane upward into a steep climb, yanking the target into the air behind him.

Only three planes at a time fired at the target sleeve and they used various approaches. After each three-plane section completed its gunnery runs, the tow plane flew over the field at low altitude and released the target sleeve for inspection by the score keepers.

The bullets fired from each of the three airplanes were painted a different color for identification—usually red, green and yellow. They left their colors on the target if it had been hit, thus allowing the score keepers to tally the exact score of each pilot. The tow plane then took off with another target for the next section of three planes. The process was repeated until all pilots in the squadron had fired at the target. This practice went on for several days until time to fire for the official record.

The official gunnery exercises were conducted by the Navy at several locations. Each pilot was given a total of 120 rounds of ammunition. Individual scores were kept during the matches by the Navy score teams and, when added up at the conclusion, gave each squadron its total score. When the scores of all fighter squadrons in the Navy and Marine Corps were totaled, the one with the highest score was awarded the gunnery

Fig. 6-7. To reduce weight, arresting hooks were removed from all VF-9M F4B-4's. Metal cover was bolted on to cover hole in bottom of fuselage (courtesy BGen. E.L. Pugh).

trophy for the year and prize money. Similar contests were held for observation and bombing squadrons. Naturally, there was fierce competition among many of the squadrons. At the conclusion of the official scoring, VF-9M had placed only fifth. Sandy was very disappointed but vowed that next year things would be different. Actually, the squadron had done fairly well, considering that several of its pilots were new and not fully indoctrinated in flying the new F4B-4's.

The Thirst Quenchers

Several of the squadron's more enterprising enlisted men had a secret place (they thought) where they made homebrew. It was in a dugout deep in the woods west of Brown Field. Known as the "Foxhole," it produced most of the brew consumed by the enlisted personnel at Quantico and a good share consumed by the officers, too. The men had dug partially into the side of a small hill and covered the excavation with camouflaged boards to avoid detection. Besides brew, various kinds of wine and brandy were also fermented to accommodate various tastes.

Occasionally, impromptu bombing demonstrations were held for visiting dignitaries on the west side of Brown Field. These were known to strike terror among the drinking flock because the resulting vibrations frequently damaged crocks and kegs of the precious liquids in the dug-out. Except for this, bombing was planned far enough in advance for dug-out personnel to take precautionary measures.

One night a humorous incident occurred during a night-flying practice mission. The VO Squadron had departed in the afternoon on a tactical navigation problem to Norfolk and was not scheduled to return until sometime after dark. Private Glen J. "Jack" Carter—*Braumeister* extraordinaire—and his buddy Corporal Edward J. "Filthy" McMahon had been in the foxhole most of the afternoon busily engaged in bottling some of the "bubbly" for a party later in the evening. Finishing their chores after dark, the men loaded two mattress covers with bottles of assorted liquids to take back for the evening's festivities. Not wanting to take the long way around, they decided to walk across the center of the field. After all, everything looked quiet and no one would suspect a thing. As the two men reached mid field, the VO Squadron appeared overhead out of nowhere, and someone switched on the field's big landing light, turning night into day.

The heavy load the two men were carrying was too much to run with. In their surprise, they momentarily froze, not knowing what to do. As the first section of the squadron came over the fence at the south end of the field to land, both men suddenly realized what was going to happen pretty damn soon if they didn't get a fast move on. To keep from being run down by airplanes, they had no choice but to drop their precious cargo and run for their lives. It has been said that the crash of broken bottles could be heard above the roar of the airplane's engines. Luckily all planes missed the broken glass, and an accident was avoided. The field security officer was called on the carpet in Rowell's office and ordered to find the guilty persons. Naturally, no one knew who the culprits were. After the airplanes landed, someone quickly retrieved the bedding from the center of the field, assuring the safety of the two men.

By morning the story has spread over most of Quantico, and Rowell had to laugh to himself. However, it was his duty to issue a warning that such an episode must never occur again.

Several days later, when the wind was blowing from the right direction, the aroma from the spilled spirits could still be detected.

Carter and McMahon always seemed to be in some kind of trouble. When Carter was assigned to Aviation Service Company, he ran the engine test stands in the rear of the engine-overhaul building. He and "Filthy" rigged up a small still in the attic of the engine control room to increase their booze production. Sometimes it gave off some interesting odors, but this didn't bother the two Marines, who didn't worry about anyone finding out. They hardly ever had visitors due to the noise from the running engines. Recalling a surprise visit to this area, Master Sergeant Glenn Carter said, "One time Major Francis T. 'Cocky' Evans and my boss, Lieutenant Franklin G. Cowie, decided to pull a surprise inspection on all support facilities at Brown Field. As they came in to inspect the control room, the damn whiskey still picked this exact time to spring a leak. As the two officers stood there talking, several drops of the liquid dripped from overhead and landed on the floor at their feet. I started talking as fast as I could about my job and the engine test in progress to keep their attention. I didn't know if they noticed the dripping, but there was no way they could avoid the smell. Major Evans just cleared his throat, gave a wry smile and continued on with the inspection. Soon as they left on the remainder of the inspection tour, we worked like hell and moved everything out of the building. We knew damn well that Lieutenant Cowie would be back. Sure enough he returned, but by then there was no trace of alcohol.

"There was another character in our fun group. His name was 'Stiope' Gooding. Everyone called us the 'Gold-dust Twins.' If there was any trouble in the Marines anywhere on the East Coast, in Panama, or Nicaragua, we were either in the middle of it, or were blamed for it, or our buddies speculated that we started it and then took to the hills. Why, one night we even took over a whole town in Nicaragua when we got drunk. Guess maybe I'd better skip the details and let that one pass as I'm sure there may be someone still looking for us."

Chapter 7

An 18-Plane Squadron

On 1 July 1933 Fighting Squadron Ten (VF-10M), based at North Island Naval Air Station, in San Diego, was redesignated Bombing Squadron Four. It had 12 new Boeing F4B-4's, and Major Geiger ordered that they be reassigned to VF-9M pending agreement from Rear Admiral Ernest J. "Jesus"King, the new tough Chief of the Bureau of Aeronautics. Admiral King became the Bureau's chief following the tragic death of Admiral Moffett in the crash of the giant Navy Airship, *USS Akron*, on April 4 off the coast of New Jersey.

Geiger somehow convinced the admiral that transfer of the planes was in the best interests of the Marines, and Service Order No. 1488, dated 24 June 1933, directed that F4B-4 aircraft Serial Numbers 9016, 9017, and 9035 through 9038 and 9420 through 9245 be detached from VF-10M on 1 July and transferred by air to Squadron VF-9M at Quantico. The last paragraph of the order stated: "Further orders will be issued regarding the ferrying of the airplanes to Quantico." It was signed by Lieutenant Commander H.B. Sallada.

This was a real break for VF-9M. It would make it possible to have an 18-plane squadron with nine airplanes as spares!

Sandy, afraid that the Navy might change its mind and order the airplane kept in its aircraft pool as spares, lost no time in finding a way to get them to Quantico. The Marine group commander at North Island agreed to furnish pilots to fly six of the airplanes to Quantico, but told Sandy that he would have to send pilots for the remaining six.

Looking for a way to get there, Sandy learned that two airplanes at Quantico, a Vought O2U-1 and the squadron's old Curtiss RC-1 Kingbird, were to be transferred to North Island. He couldn't have a better set-up than this. He and Ed Pugh departed on 5 July flying the O2U-1, with Frank Wirsig, Al Kreiser, Jimmy Britt and T.J. Walker following in the Kingbird. All arrived at San Diego Naval Air Station on 8 July.

Impatient to get started, the 12-plane formation of F4B-4's left the station on the morning of 11 July for Quantico. Except for a half day lost at

Fig. 7-1. Helldivers of VO-7M practicing saturation bombing on Brown Field (courtesy BGen. B.C. Batterton).

McAlester, Oklahoma, because of bad weather, the trip home was uneventful. Flying time was 20 hours and 10 minutes.

Sandy Sanderson, Airplane Rustler

Sandy, in his anxiety to get the new planes to Quantico, flew them away before the required paper work was completed and signed. Thus, when the transfer papers came across the desk of Capt. John H. Hoover, the commanding officer of North Island, he had several questions to ask. It was his impression that the planes were to be placed in the Navy pool as spares for the Navy Squadrons. When informed that the aircraft had already departed for Quantico, he was furious. A letter was immediately written over his signature to the Bureau of Aeronautics, pointing out that the airplanes in question had not been properly checked out through his command.

Admiral King, responding in a letter of 27 July, stated in part: "It is advised that the Bureau does not consider it necessary to apply the provisions of reference (d) checking of men and aircraft through the station) to Marine Corps aircraft when such aircraft are being transferred within the Marine Corps. The responsibility rests in the Commanding Officer Marines, West Coast Expeditionary Force. If conditions exist at San Diego which, in the opinion of the Commanding Officer, makes it desirable for Marine airplanes and pilots to be checked through the air station, the Bureau will, upon receipt of such recommendations, consider including the Marine Corps planes under the provisions of reference (d)."

The letter from Admiral King closed the matter. Sometime later, when told of the commotion he had caused, Sandy remarked: "Well, you know *me*. I'm *always* at the center of trouble. Besides, it's good to stir up the brass once in a while. It gives them something to do."

Upon Sandy's return to Brown Field, he read a letter from the Bureau of Aeronautics, signed by Admiral King and forwarded by Major Geiger. It authorized VF-9M to become a full 18-plane squadron with six aircraft as spares. Another letter attached and written by Geiger authorized an increase in pilot strength to 22 men to man the new planes. To say that Sandy was overwhelmed was putting it mildly. Of the 28 F4B-4's allotted to the Marines, VF-9M had received them *all*, making it the largest squadron ever in the Corps until WWII.

To celebrate the occasion, Sandy arranged a small party at the Officer's Club. Raising his glass in a toast, he said, "This squadron has come a long way since Colonel Turner first gave it to me in 1925. It's had some rough times, but I predict that within a short time it will be the best damn squadron in the history of the Marine Corps!" There wasn't a man who didn't drink to *that*.

Practice Makes Perfect

The month of August, 1933 was probably the busiest of the squadron's existance. In addition to its stepped-up training schedule in preparation for the upcoming Chicago Air Show over Labor Day weekend, several battle and landing-force problems were executed much to the satisfaction of the Commandant of the Marine Corps (Figs. 7-1, 7-2). *Naval Aviation News* of 1 September 1933 described them in part as follows:

> *A landing force problem was held on Tuesday on the beach just north of the Quantico dock. Colonel Rowell, with General Brecken-ridge as passenger, led the six-plane, low-altitude attack on a target just off the beach, each plane dropping five miniature bombs in trail. Immediately following the two-seaters came twelve F4B-4's led by Lieutenant Sanderson in a high-altitude attack on the same target. The*

Fig. 7-2. Lt. Ed Pugh scores a "hit" on small pyramid target during dive bombing practice at Brown Field (courtesy Marine Corps).

attack was made in column, each plane dropping a bomb on each of four dives. During the high altitude attack four smoke planes led by Lieutenant Chappell made nine smoke runs down the beach at intervals of one-half minute. The troops in the boats landed in the smoke and were on the beach before they could be seen. Both squadrons returned to the scene of action at zero hour and simulated machine-gun attacks. The demonstrations was repeated on Friday with the Marine Reserve Brigade making the landing. Altogether these were the best demonstrations that have been put on thus far.

Another item in the *News* described a simulated attack by Quantico-based squadrons on ground troops the following week.

The Reserve Brigade, on its return to Washington, requested aerial attacks on Tuesday and Wednesday while hiking up the Maryland shore. Lieutenant Chappell laid a smoke screen to cover a simulated bombing and strafing attack by VF-9M. On Wednesday the smoke screen was repeated, and a six-plane formation from VO-7M launched a low-altitude bombing attack on the Reservists, using one-pound bags of flour for the bombs. The crew chiefs in the rear cockpits demonstrated real skill in tossing the bombs. It was reported that one bomb scored a direct hit on the head of a Reserve, but no damage was done other than slight discoloration. It was also reported that half of the enemy would have been casualties, assuming the effective radius of a bomb to be 50 feet.

During the three weeks preceeding the Chicago show, Frank Wirsig, VF-9M's busy operations and training officer, scheduled and completed no less than 37 squadron training flights, most of which were more than two hours of duration. Flying of this type coupled with tactical flying can put less durable men under considerable strain. Much credit must be given to the mechanics and crew chiefs for their untiring efforts to assure that the airplanes were ready for each day's flight schedule.

On 21 August the Navy Bureau of Aeronautics, examining a routine aircraft allotment report, noticed that VF-9M was in possession of 27 Boeing F4B-4's. That was three more than authorized. The Bureau, looking for several airplanes to replace those lost in a flood at Anacostia, brought the irregularity to the attention of Admiral King. On 23 August a letter was received by Col. Geiger, specifying that all F4B-4's in Squadron VF-9M in excess of the number authorized be turned over to the Bureau and requesting that they be ready for flyaway on 28 August.

Outsmarting the Navy

Geiger, knowing of a little-used way to outfox the Navy and save one of the Boeings, hastly telephoned Rowell at Quantico and suggested that he quickly assign one of the planes to Utility Squadron Six-M (VJ-6M) for engineering purposes. It worked and only two Boeings were lost in the transaction. When informed of what had taken place, Admiral King remarked, "I like a man that can think for himself."

The Marines' attendance at the upcoming Chicago show was causing considerable excitement. An article in the Quantico newspaper on 18 August 1933, said:

> *Brown Field is going to do Chicago and the Exposition 'Up Brown' from the first to the fourth of September when Lieutenant Colonel Ross E. Rowell, Commanding Officer of Brown Field, personally leads the largest flight of planes ever flown away from Quantico for exposition and demonstration purposes. General Balbo, the "Wop Hopper," as one radio announcer called him, who is visiting this country with a squadron of Italian planes, didn't cause any commotion in Chicago, but the excitement in the Windy City at the height of the Al Capone reign will be far overshadowed by the show that Colonel Rowell will put on with his squadron of Helldivers and 12 of the latest thing in fighting aircraft commanded by First Lieutenant Lawson H.M. (His Majesty) Sanderson.*
>
> *For the first time the general public will be exposed to a real smoke screen demonstration lead by First Lieutenant C.J. Chappell, Commanding Officer of VO Squadron Seven-M, with Master Sergeant Harry L. "Doc" Blackwell flying the assisting plane. Come on out to the field and see the daily practice flights for the Chicago show and you will have an idea of just what the fair-goers will have coming when the 'Devil Dog Dare Devils' take charge of the situation. Lieutenant Tom Ennis, Publicity Director of the flight, says: 'Chicago ain't seen nothing yet until it watches our smoke."*

His statement proved to be true.

1933 International Air Races

At 0800 hours on 1 September 1933 VF-9M left Brown Field for the International Air Races held in conjunction with the Century of Progress (World's Fair) at Chicago, Illinois. Orders called for one fuel stop at Dayton's Wright Field, with emergency fields designated at Cumberland, Maryland; Wheeling, West Virginia; and Fort Wayne, Indiana. Observation Squadron VO-7M, commanded by Colonel Rowell, and sporting its new red, white and blue markings, had departed 15-minutes earlier with seven Curtiss 02C-1 Helldivers (Fig. 7-3). They were to follow the same route except that to avoid congestion, would make their fuel stop at Columbus, Ohio.

The Ford RR-5 Trimoter transport of Utility Squadron VJ-6M, flown by Captain Harold C. Major, also departed at 0745 with the ground crew and all equipment necessary to sustain the two squadrons at Chicago. It was to proceed independently and wait for VF-9M at Dayton to assist in refueling its planes.

As pre-arranged, the two squadrons rendezvoused over Gary, Indiana, at 1530 and proceeded around lake Michigan to the Fairgrounds. At the

Fig. 7-3. Curtiss "Helldiver" of VO-7M showing non-regulation red, white and blue markings (courtesy National Archives).

World's Fair the expected arrival of the Marines had been announced several times during the afternoon and everyone was thrilled as the two squadrons circled at low altitude over the hugh exposition before landing at Chicago's Curtiss-Reynolds airport.

For the next three days the Marines had the audience standing with their screaming power dives, Squirrel Cage, dive bombing and a new maneuver: the squadron line reversement.

The squadron line reversement was similar to a line of troops marching single file towards another file of troops. Just before the leaders of each file meet face-to-face, both files—to avoid a collision—do an about-face and march in the opposite direction, still in perfect formation. And so with VF-9M. Each division flew out several miles in opposite directions, formed a single line (trail formation), and started their return to the field at the same altitude and in line with each other. The two six-plane lines now approached each other on a collision course. Just as it appeared that the two lead planes were about to collide, all planes of both files looped upward and rolled upright at the top of their loops. This brought them out, still in single file but heading in the opposite direction back to their starting point. It was a very dangerous maneuver and it required that all airplanes in each line to pull up at precisely the same time or they would run into each other—exactly as troops would if they failed to execute an about-face at the same time. It was performed at low altitude and was exciting to watch from the ground.

As a fitting climax to their Chicago performance, the two squadrons gave the large crowd an aerial display of the use of smoke in military maneuvers. While they were getting into position, the announcer explained: "Ladies and gentlemen, for the first time ever you are about to witness a beautiful demonstration of how Marines lay and use smoke as as aid to troop landings." As he continued, out of nowhere two planes from the VO Squadron, flown by Buddy Chappell and Doc Blackwell, came across the field at less than 50 feet altitude, leaving behind a hugh smoke screen that hugged the ground, blocking from view anything on the other side. As they passed from view, from overhead came the screeching Helldivers (Fig. 7-4) of the VO Squadron, lead by Rusty Rowell, in a simulated dive-bombing attact. When the last bomber completed its dive, six of Sandy's F4B-4's suddenly burst through the smoke screen, simulating a strafing run with machine guns to clear the beach for troops supposedly coming ashore behind the heavy layer of smoke. Overhead, the remaining six airplanes of VF-9M were weaving in and out, simulating air cover for the whole operation.

Just before the demonstration came to a close, there was a sudden shift in wind direction, and smoke began blowing into the grandstands. No one had anticipated the effect of the chemicals contained in the smoke. Within a short time many spectators noticed color changes in their clothing, especially the women. Rumor had it that some of the ladies "unmentionables" sort of disintegrated a short time afterward. To this date it is not known how the Marines got out of that one.

The Marines waved farewell to Chicago at 0900 on Tuesday morning. Their treatment had been nothing less than royal during their stay, and radio and press coverage was excellent. Retracing their route, Sandy led

Fig. 7-4. Smoke generator between landing gear of Helldiver used for maneuvers and public demonstrations. At the Chicago show, it produced somewhat startling results (courtesy W.T. Larkins).

his squadron over Brown Field at 1630 where family, friends, and the Marine Band were waiting to greet them.

The following weeks carried a busy schedule. Additional pilots were added to the roster, and training schedules were stepped up by Wirsig to accommodate the new arrivals. Successive shows and demonstrations were carried out the remainder of September. On the 19th, at the Coast Guard Air Station, Cape May, New Jersey; an air show on the 21st for the staff officers of the 7th Regiment at Quantico; and on 29 September, attacks were simulated on ground targets in support of troop landings near Quantico for the benefit of the Marine Corps Schools. September was indeed a busy month.

A Prestigious Appearance

On 30 September Rowell informed Sandy that his squadron was to be one of several feature attractions as the National Charity Air Pageant in New York on 7-8 October. The pageant, staged to raise money for the poor, was similar to the one held two years previously. Sanctioned by the National Aeronautic Association, it promised to be the largest ever, with all of "who's who" in aviation attending.

Geiger, informed that many of the nation's influential congressmen and senators were attending the two-day affair, *plus* numerous leading citizens and dignitaries, telephoned Rowell to order a "maximum effort" for the show. No way was Geiger going to let this opportunity to show off his Marines pass.

In view of this, Sandy was determined to debut at this show with an 18-plane squadron. Weekend leaves were cancelled and a seven-day working schedule invoked. Brown Field suddenly became alive day and night. Crew chiefs often worked far into the night to have airplanes ready for the next day's flight schedule. On Friday, the day before the show, Sandy ordered all work to cease at noontime so that everyone could relax and rest.

At 0810 on 7 October 1933, VF-9M took off from Brown Field with 19 F4B-4's for Roosevelt Field, Long Island, New York. Departing ahead of VF-9M at 0745 was VO-7M with 13 Helldivers (Fig. 7-5) followed by two Ford transport planes carrying mechanics, staff officers and equipment. Last to take off were several small aircraft carrying newsmen and dignitaries from Washington. The two squadrons joined over Staten Island and arrived over Roosevelt Field at 1015 where they landed for public display before the airshow in the afternoon.

The turn-out for this giant airshow was much greater than anyone had anticipated. Not only was the airport crowded to capacity, but all roads for several miles around were blocked with traffic trying to get close enough to see the show.

At exactly 1515 in the afternoon the air show announcer turned the microphone over to Tom Ennis, public relations officer from Quantico, to give a running account of the Marines' portion of the show.

Fig. 7-5. VO-7M working on its formation flying prior to going to the New York's Charity Air Pageant in October 1933 (courtesy U.S. Navy).

"Ladies and gentlemen, you are about to witness a flying demonstration of two crack squadrons of the United States Marine Corps from Quantico, Virginia. Under the command of Lieutenant Colonel Ross E. Rowell, they will perform tactical maneuver plus others that will keep you on the very edge of your seat, I promise you."

The VO squadron made its takeoff first in the two six-plane divisions, followed by Sandy, leading his entire squadron of 18 planes in a close-formation take-off. This thrilled Sandy almost as much as it did the huge crowd. It was the first time the squadron had been at a field large enough to try this, and it came off perfectly.

From this moment on, the audience seemed to be completely engrossed in the Marines' hair-raising maneuvers. The two squadrons worked beautifully together. Each gave demonstrations (both singly and together) of close-formation flying and dive bombing. Dive bombing always thrilled the audience, as the planes dived straight down—engines wide open—and let their bombs explode on the target. Several more maneuvers were performed, including a giant dogfight and an attack on the Helldivers staged by the fighter planes. This brought the two squadrons to their final maneuver, which was described by the announcer:

"Now ladies and gentlemen and honored guests. You are for the first time about to witness one of the most exciting, death-defying displays of flying ever performed before the public. Called a Squirrel Cage, it was made famous by none other than Lieutenant Sandy Sanderson, commanding officer of Fighting Squadron Nine, that has been so ably performing for you here today. He will be assisted by the observation squadron." As the crowd sat silently staring upward, Sandy leveled off at 8,000 feet and gave the hand signal for the squadron to form an echelon to the right.

While this was taking place, Rusty Rowell with the Helldivers had formed two tight six-plane circles, one at 2,500 feet and the other at 4,000 feet - one above the other - but going in opposite directions.

Observing that the Helldivers were in position, Sandy gave the "tally ho" signal to start the Squirrel Cage. Diving down to the left to pick up speed, he eased his plane up and over into the first loop. He was followed by the other planes - one by one - at three-second intervals until the entire squadron was going around in loops. Incidentally, in the previous two weeks, Sandy found that in order to accommodate 18 airplanes in a squirrel cage, it was necessary to make each loop slightly more offset; in other words, when all 18 airplanes were going around, it looked as if they were following the coils of a giant spring laying on its side. Sandy continued the Squirrel Cage until he was above the circling Helldivers. Then, as he came down the backside of his last loop, he continued straight down, executing several vertical rolls as he dived. Each plane in the squadron followed single file until all were in a vertical column of diving, rolling and screeching airplanes, each going through the center of the two circles of Helldivers below at almost 300 miles per hour. As each F4B-4 cleared through the last circle of Helldivers, it pulled out of its dive so as to pass in front of the hugh crowd at approximately 50 feet altitude (Fig. 7-6). The noise from the wide-open engines was so intense that most people had to cover their ears. After landing, the two squadrons were cheered for several minutes and according to "oldtimers" who were there, the two squadrons outdid themselves.

Their performance at the New York show gave Marine Aviation the extra shot in the arm it needed. Admiral King was delighted by their exposure and quickly commended Geiger and Rowell for the fine show. In weeks ahead the Congress and Senate suddenly became more receptive to the needs of Marine Aviation; accordingly, the Admiral revised the Navy's budget by increasing the Marines' portion. If approved, it was Geiger's intention to replace the aging Helldivers with the new Great Lakes BG-1 dive bomber presently under test by the Navy.

Sandy was learning many new things about commanding an 18-plane exhibition squadron. Problems consistently appeared that had to be solved immediately. There were just too many close calls. This was not *ordinary* formation flying they were engaged in; it was a business that could get you killed in one-hell-of-a-hurry, and he was aware that one little mistake was all it would take.

Sandy knew that one of the secrets was timing. When 18 airplanes fly wing-to-tail and wingtip-to-wingtip, everyone must *absolutely* understand each maneuver and at all times be exactly where he is supposed to be and,

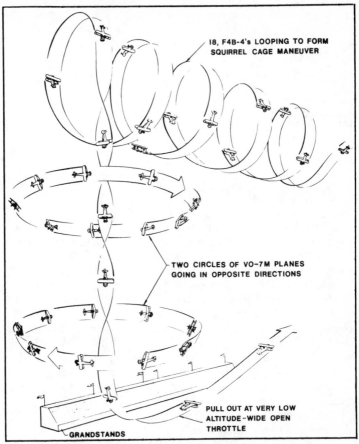

Fig. 7-6. VF-9M's famous "Squirrel Cage" performed with Squadron VO-7M. This maneuver was unequaled and was the "Coup de Maitre" of their show (Illustration by Tom George).

at the precise time. He must be able to identify every switch, lever and valve in the cockpit by feel, never for a moment taking his eyes from his wingman to look inside for anything. This means that pilot and airplane must be molded into one, never for a second letting the airplane fly the pilot. Each day, before and after flying, a briefing was held to discuss any problem. Sandy was a perfectionist; he often remarked to his pilots, "When you men leave this squadron, other flying will be easy." Commenting on this Brigadier General Frank Dailey, USMC (ret), said, "You know, after I left the squadron I often remembered Sandy's words, which proved to be true. He was probably the best pilot ever produced by the Marine Corps, and I'm sure he used to get impatient trying to teach us to fly as well as he could."

Chapter 8

A Boeing To Spare

As the squadron became more proficient in its airwork, Sandy established new goals. He disliked the sight of an 18-plane exhibition squadron wandering disorganized all over an airport like a bunch of greenhorns. When taking off and landing, he demanded that everyone must, as in airwork, be where he was supposed to be at all times. This occasionally posed a problem at Brown Field, which was very short and narrow with a creek on the north side and a hill on the south side. It was the smallest fully operational military airfield in service. As many former Marines will attest, just being able to fly from this cramped little field under all conditions was a feat in itself. Without runways, it often became so muddy that only the most skillful pilots could manage a take off or landing without nosing up or ground looping. As for formation take-offs and landings, if the squadron could manage this on Brown Field, it would look beautiful anywhere else. However, an occasional accident can happen just because someone—just for a second—violates a rule.

A case in point: On the afternoon of 6 November, Second Lieutenant Frank Schwable almost lost his life while he was on the ground, waiting to take-off.

On this day, the Operations Section of VF-9M had scheduled an 18-plane formation training flight. Sandy, impressed with the first-class flying of Lt. Schwable in the most difficult position in the squadron, better known as "Tailend Charlie," recommended to the operations officer that Schwable be assigned as section leader of the second section of the first division for training. This was his first assignment as such. Assigned to lead the fourth section, second division for the first time was 2nd Lt. Edward C. Dyer.

Crossed Signals

After starting engines Sandy gave the command by radio: Taxi single file along the hangar line to the south end of Brown Field for take-off into the North.

Quickly forming his three-plane section, Sandy taxied into takeoff position approximately 100 yards from the south border of the field. He then asked Schwable, in F4B-4 9038 if he was ready with his section, as the two sections were to take off together as a six-plane division.

Having only a radio receiver in his plane, Schwable gave a signal by hand that he understood what was said, but did not give the customary signal required of a section leader. This was to move the ailerons of his airplane up and down that he was ready for takeoff. Unknown to Sandy, because of a starting difficulty back at the ramp, Schwable's two wingmen had not yet joined him.

Sandy then said "Standby for takeoff," and gave a warning of crosswind from the left. When he again looked rearward and failed to receive the required aileron signal, he attributed the oversight to Schwable being somewhat nervous about leading a three-plane section for the first time. Sandy's view was blocked by his own wingmen so that he was unable to see if Schwable's wingmen were in position.

Completing his cockpit check, Sandy again spoke into the mike: "Standby for takeoff." Schwable, realizing that his hand signals were not getting across because he was positioned directly behind his commanding officer, gave the aileron signal out of desperation, even though he was still waiting for his two wingmen, who were now at the end of the squadron line and unable to get into position with Schwable.

Sandy immediately departed with his section, leaving Schwable waiting, thus setting the stage for what was about to happen. According to the field operational rules, Schwable should have departed with the first section. His wingmen could have joined him in flight.

Further, 1st Lt. Al Kreiser, who was leading the second division, had also planned on a division takeoff, but failed to take position with his section ahead of Dyer's because of a starting difficulty *he* had at the warmup apron. Thus, Dyer advanced and took position with his section about 40 yards directly in rear of Schwable, with Sgt. Neal G. "Cracker" Williams in the number three (right wing) position. Number two position (left wing) was a blank file in this section.

Having heard Sandy give the take-off command followed by the roar of engines up ahead, Dyer inferred that Schwable had departed with the first section as planned. Dyer looked both left and right, but made the mistake of not turning his airplane to see if anyone was in front of him. It's impossible to see straight ahead from the cockpit of an F4B-4 when it's on the ground without turning. Further, he should have checked with his wingman, who could see Schwable had not departed but, for reasons unknown, he did not.

Dyer then gave the ready signal—a movement of the ailerons—and opened his throttle for takeoff. His wingman having only a radio receiver was unable to warn him. Almost immediately he struck Schwable's F4B-4. Schwable, hearing the sudden roar of Dyer's plane approaching from behind, quickly opened the throttle of his plane and at the same time ducked down and forward in the cockpit. This action undoubtedly saved his life as the propeller of Dyer's F4B-4 chewed the rear fuselage on Schwable's plane from the tail section up to the cockpit (Fig. 8-1). Luckily Schwable escaped uninjured. Needless to say, after this accident much discussion was in order about the squadron field operations order number 44, which specifies that *"No section other than the first one shall be formed for take-off until the preceding section has been formed."*

The wrecking of Lt. Schwable's F4B-4, Serial Number 9034 (side number 20), was later to cause much controversy and embarrassment to the Quantico Marines.

A three-man trouble board composed of Maj. Francis T. Evans, Capt. Harold C. Major, and 1st Lt. Glenn M. Britt was convened to investigate the accident. Their findings charged 40% of the accident to supervisory personnel, 30% to Schwable for not taking off with the first section, even though his wingmen were not in position, and 30% to Dyer for forming his section before the preceding section had been formed, thus violating Marine Operations Order No. 44.

However, near the bottom of the accident report there is a line that reads "Recommendation on disposition of aircraft." On this line the Trouble Board typed: "It is recommended that this airplane (Serial Number 9038) be surveyed and stricken from the list of Naval aircraft."

It was this statement that set in motion the chain of events leading to the assignment of a new serial number for this aircraft.

The accident report was filed with the Navy Bureau of Aeronautics on 17 November. A reply from the Bureau on the disposition of the airplane was not received at Brown Field until two and one-half months later; 31 January 1934, to be exact. The letter stated that the subject aircraft had been stricken from the official list of Naval aircraft and that it was to be scrapped after all serviceable parts were salvaged.

In the meantime, Master Sgt. Earl Zalanka, in charge of the Assembly and Repair shop, was not one to let a challenge go by. After several weeks passed without word on the airplane's fate, he decided to see what he could do with the damaged aft section of the fuselage. The sergeant was an expert metalsmith, carpenter, electrician and all-around handyman. He had learned his trade well during the Marines' early days of flying, when airplane parts had to be fashioned from anything at hand.

In less than four months, Sgt. Zalanka, working in his spare time, accomplished the impossible by completely rebuilding the fuselage from the cockpit rearward. The sergeant then requisitioned a new vertical fin and rudder from storage and, with two of his helpers, reassembled the entire airplane, using the balance of its original parts.

Feeling very proud, Zalanka told Lt. Pugh, VF-9M's engineering officer, of what he had accomplished and informed him the airplane was ready for test flying. Pugh was first amazed, then pleased, but his feelings turned to apprehension as he suddenly remembered that serial number

Fig. 8-1. Frank Schwable's number "20" (serial no. 9038) left, after it was rammed from the rear by Ed Dyer's number "8" (serial 9238) during takeoff accident at Brown Field 6 November 1933 (courtesy BGen.F.H.Schwable).

9038 was *no longer legally in the Navy*. He suggested to the sergeant that he say nothing until he talked with Sanderson about it.

After a conference with Sandy, it was decided that the boss, Rusty Rowell, the group commander at Quantico, be informed at once. The two officers took off for his office, but for reasons unknown they were unable to see him. They were unaware at this time that the Colonel had already been informed of the project several hours before.

The Fighter That Wasn't

Immediately after Rowell received word that an illegal F4B-4 was on the station, he hastily summoned 1st Lt. Franklin G. Cowie, the chief engineering officer of Brown Field, to his office for an explanation. Cowie, knowing the airplane had been officially stricken by the Navy, disclaimed any knowledge of the project.

The following morning Lt. Pugh and Sgt. Zalanka were called on the carpet by Rowell to explain why the airplane had been repaired without authorization. Pugh thought the sergeant had accomplished the impossible and told the colonel so. Apparently that was the *wrong* thing to say, or Ed's timing was off.

Recalling that meeting of many years ago, Sgt. Zalanka (now retired) said, "We sure did catch hell. Rowell paced back and forth, using all the well-known Marine phrases plus some new ones. After he vented his anger be broke out in a grin and said: 'Sergeant, you did a damn good job. We'll find a way to outfox the Navy and put that airplane back in service.'"

Quantico, not being authorized to do major airframe overhauls or manufacture aircraft parts, as did the bases at San Diego, Norfolk and the Naval Aircraft Factory, was in strict violation of Naval regulations for having rebuilt a fuselage, especially an all-metal one such as the F4B-4. Rowell quickly ordered that it not be flown and that it be kept under wraps until a course of action could be decided upon.

The next day Rowell explained the situation by telephone to Major Geiger, Officer-in-Charge of Marine Aviation at Headquarters Marine Corps, Washington, D.C. Geiger was amused and agreed to help. As Marine Aviator No. 5, he had been in a few tough scrapes himself through the years and enjoyed bucking the system. He advised Rowell to write a letter to the Navy Bureau of Aeronautics and state that the trouble board had erred in its recommendation that F4B-4, serial number 9038, be stricken. Further, that the airplane had been rebuilt from factory new spare parts and that the use of serial number 9038 be continued. Of course, this was against regulations, inasmuch as the airplane was already stricken from the Navy list of aircraft.

This was done and a hot letter was shot back immediately from the Bureau and signed by none other than the Chief himself—Admiral Ernest J. "Jesus" King. His letter to Rowell stated that under no circumstances was this permissable and pointed out in *no* uncertain terms that this was a direct violation of Naval regulations and further stated that the airplane should be dismantled as ordered. After a cooling-off period, several more letters were exchanged between Quantico and the Bureau without the matter being settled.

Finally, through the joint efforts of Major Geiger and the involvement of others, a letter was written by the Bureau to Rowell on 9 June 1934, relenting its stand. It gave approval for the airplane to be flown in regular service and went on to explain that, even though the airplane was essentially the same as before, it had officially been stricken from the list of Navy aircraft. Therefore, the use of its original serial number 9038 was disapproved. In conclusion, it stated that the airplane had been added to the list of Naval aircraft as a new one and was hereby assigned a new serial number of 9719. The letter was signed by Commander Patrick N.L. Bellinger, by direction of Admiral King.

To win out over the Navy, especially Admiral King, was cause for rejoicing by the Quantico Marines. Several years later, when Colonel Rowell moved to Washington to become the new Director of Marine Aviation, he learned from a former aide of Admiral King what the Admiral had said when he ordered the letter to be written: "For God's sake, *let* those crazy Marines fly that damn airplane if they want to! I don't want to see or hear any more about it, *ever!*"

Assigning a new serial number to the airplane later proved to be an unwise decision by the Bureau because of the excessive amount of correspondence between various government agencies and air commands to convince people that the serial number 9719, so far out of sequence for Boeing F4B-4's, was indeed correct. On 25 June it was test-flown by Pugh, and returned to active service with VF-9M, carrying its original side number 20. Its new serial number was not added to the vertical fin.

Back To Routine

Throughout the month of November, night flying was conducted along with several sessions of machine gun and dive bombing practice. On 9 November, VF-9M and VO-7M worked out a rendezvous and attack problem on the railroad junction at Unionville, Virginia. The people of the community and surrounding territory enjoyed the maneuvers immensely. The following paragraph is from a letter received from Mr. R.W. Martin of Unionville.

"I am writing to assure you of my sincere appreciation and thanks for your kindness in having the planes of the U.S. Marine Corps visit our community on Thursday last. It was really a treat to us country folk, and so many have expressed their approval and appreciation of the opportunity of witnessing the U.S. Marine Corps planes in action."

On Friday, 10 November, 60 British Royal Marines were guests of Quantico. After they inspected all airplanes on the ground, VF-9M took to the air for a special flying demonstration, much to their enjoyment.

On Tuesday morning, 21 November, word was received from Naval Operations to prepare both tactical squadrons and hold them in readiness to search for Lieutenant Commander T. G. Settle and his stratosphere balloon, which had taken off the day before from Akron to break the world altitude record. All planes were hastily fueled and assigned search sectors. Shortly afterwards, word was received to get under way. It is believed that a record was established when, in exactly five minutes, both squadrons were airborne. Lieutenant T. J. Walker of VF-9M sighted the balloon in a wooded sector shortly after crossing the Delaware River into New Jersey. He continued to circle until it was located by a ground search party.

VF-9M's schedule was still busy. At this time, tryouts for pilots wanting to join the squadron were conducted, but few had the qualifications Sandy was looking for. Brigadier General Pugh, USMC (ret), said "We really put the newcomers to the test. Hence, VF-9M was considered *the* squadron, for we surely did separate the goats from the sheep. The saying then was that if a pilot couldn't take it, he would be sent to the VO squadron which, by our standards, was a disgrace. This seems somewhat amusing to me now, but then it really was the survival of the fittest. You just couldn't get into our squadron unless you were exceptional."

For the Marine Corps, the most notable event of the 1930's was the establishment of the Fleet Marine Force on 8 December 1933. This placed the Marine Corps within the fleet organization as "an integral part thereof, subject to the orders for tactical employment of the Commander-in-Chief, U.S. Fleet." This was wonderful news to Marine Aviation. It took them out of the Expeditionary Forces and committed them to an over-riding wartime mission. For practical purposes it placed Marine Aviation on the same footing as Naval Aviation. This gave the Marines something they could sink their teeth into and they seized their new assignment with gusto.

On Saturday, 16 December, all Quantico squadrons participated in a tactical demonstration over Washington in connection with the commemoration exercises of the first flight made at Kitty Hawk, North Carolina, by the Wright Brothers. Utility Squadron Six (VJ-6M), not to be left out, hastily made up a six-plane squadron of its own that—although admirable and slightly comical—brought many favorable comments. It consisted of a Bellanca RA-3 leading the Vee formation, with two Leoning OL-9's on each side. Two Ford Trimotor transports were on each side of the Loenings, with their Pitcairn XOP-1 autogyro closing the gap. And it worked! Despite differences in cruising speeds and some slipping and skidding by the big Fords, it was a very presentable formation.

Secret Missions

During the week before the 1933 Christmas holidays, Sandy led his squadron on a low-level cruise over the Virginia hills, looking for smoke rising up through the trees. This usually signified a whisky still. When smoke was sighted, he dispatched a three-plane section to peel off and go screaming down to investigate. After a few circles over the spot a signal was usually received from the ground. The planes responded by waggling their wings, and the man on the ground knew that later in the evening some Marine would be out for a load of "white lightning."

Actually this happened quite frequently among squadrons at Quantico. Brigadier General Frank Wirsig, USMC (ret), tells how it was done. "We marked the location of the smoke on our map, and that evening, with a charred oak keg, we payed a visit to that location. We always managed to swap our empty keg for a full one. On returning home, we put the keg in the bathtub and filled it with water. This swelled the keg. Lieutenants couldn't afford any leakage and, besides, it helped to age the contents. Wives were not too happy about this, but we all managed. Captains and majors put their kegs on the house radiators, as they could afford some leakage. I don't know *what* the colonels did, as we didn't have many in those days."

On 22 December all flight operations were secured for the holidays. A total of 5,648 flying hours was accumulated for the year. It was a record for those times and it required real dedication on the part of pilots, as a large portion of the flying was conducted in the winter months.

Miami—A Great Host

The first order of business for the new year of 1934 was participation in the annual All-American Maneuvers on 11, 12 and 13 January at Miami. Second only to the National Air Races at Cleveland, it drew tremendous crowds and only top performers were invited.

On 10 January, just as the morning began to dawn, Sandy ordered his squadron to taxi single file to the north end of Brown Field. Take-off was planned toward the south and would be by six-plane divisions. The weather was cold and because of the heavy clothing they were forced to wear, many pilots found it almost impossible to squeeze into the small cockpits of the F4B-4's. A small crowd of families and well-wishers gathered to say goodby and watch the take-off. At exactly 0815 Sandy gave the command and the first division started its take-off roll. Flying time to Miami was six hours and forty minutes. Refueling stops were made at Charleston, South Carolina and Jacksonville.

The city of Miami was an excellent host to aviation. It sponsored luncheons, parties and dinner-dances that were gala affairs. The Marines were looked on with favor and managed to get more than their share of the good life. Sandy's 15 years as an outstanding and colorful aviator automatically qualified him as a preferred guest at any party, and he tried to make them all.

On the first day of the show, Sandy immediately established VF-9M's reputation by leading the entire squadron of 18-planes in a close-formation take-off. It left no doubts that the audience was about to see a real performance. Major General A.W. Kreiser, USMC (ret), leader of the second division, said "Sandy always put on a good show. He was the greatest all-around pilot produced by the Marine Corps. Our routine after take-off usually consisted of several low passes across the field in a

Fig. 8-2. Three-plane section of VF-9M dive bombing at the 1934 Miami All-American Maneuvers (courtesy G.W. Romer).

demonstration of close formation flying. This gave us a chance to feel out the air for smoothness. The formations were very close and were worked out by Sandy and Rowell especially for air shows. This was usually followed with the squadron breaking into sections and climbing for altitude, whereby Sandy lined us up in either right or left echelon formation, depending on the circumstances. From this formation we could enter most any maneuver the squadron leader decided upon. We performed 18-plane loops, dive-bombing (Fig. 8-2), and our now-famous Squirrel Cage that ended with all planes flying by the grandstand at less than 50 feet off the ground, engines wide open."

The general also described the dive-bombing: "After take-off, the ground crew towed the target onto the field. It was a six-foot by ten-foot wood and canvas affair painted bright orange to make it visible. We used miniature bombs which, in addition to giving off smoke, produced a loud enough sound to make it realistic. Sandy would peel off from echelon formation and dive straight down, followed by plane number two, three and so on, in single file. To the audience it was a spectacular show to watch the planes come hurling down, engines roaring and wires screeching, each plane letting off its bombs, producing a cloud of smoke. We always hit and destroyed our target."

Departure for home was scheduled for the morning of 15 January. However, because of a farewell party lasting til early dawn, it was nearly noon before the order to "start engines" was given (Fig. 8-3). The

Fig. 8-3. One of VJ-6M's two Ford Trimotor Transports at the 1934 Miami Races. Indespensable, these planes were used to transport personnel and support equipment (courtesy Steve Hudek).

squadron arrived home at noon the following day after bad weather forced an over-night stay at Savannah.

One week after returning from Miami, the annual bombing practice got underway (Fig. 8-4). Sandy wanted his squadron to look good that year and openly stated that if bombing scores were not improved considerably from the previous year, some heads would roll. The ultimatum had been passed down to him by Rusty Rowell and presumably came from Geiger. Improve they did! They moved from the previous year's standing of fifth

Fig. 8-4. Number "19" with two 100 lb. bombs attached. Sgt. Berg of the photo lab is in the cockpit (courtesy Marine Corps).

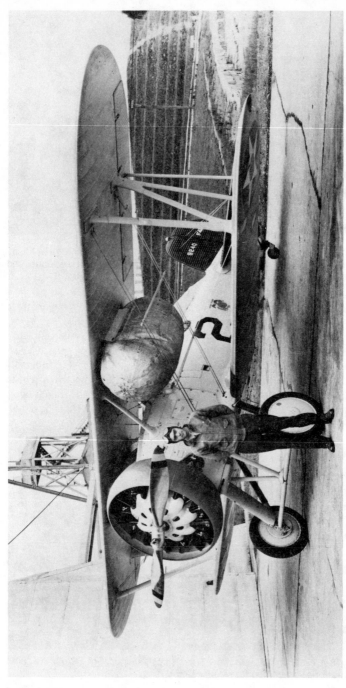

Fig. 8-5. F4B-4 with flotation bags extended for inspection (courtesy Marine Corps).

place to third place. It was not where Sandy had hoped they would end, but they *were* improving.

On Wednesday, 21 February, VF-9M departed for the Naval Air Station at Norfolk, where they would be based for the next six weeks while conducting the annual gunnery exercises. As before, during the day they operated from the National Guard field at Virginia Beach, and at the end of the day's firing they returned to Norfolk. As the days progressed it became apparent that VF-9M was racking up some excellent scores and might stand a good chance at winning the highly coveted gunnery trophy.

The Officer's Club at Norfolk was, as usual, filled with this type of conversation each evening and friendly bets were made among the Navy and Marine pilots. Sandy warned his pilots about revealing their scores and suggested that they not get too cocky because it wasn't over yet.

Days and weeks of constant gunnery practice can become boring, so to liven things up a bit pilots sometimes engaged in a little spirited horseplay such as low-level flying, flathatting, and chasing each other around the sky. Sandy knew what was going on but said nothing. He felt it was important that they have some fun. After all, their scores were the best ever recorded for the squadron.

However, a few days before they were to commence firing for record, the Norfolk base commander summoned Sandy to his office regarding several complaints received from citizens in the Virginia Beach area. The complaints were of low-flying airplanes buzzing ships, livestock, the beach area and generally scaring hell out of the countryside. Sandy tried to pass it off lightly. "You know how civilians are, they don't know one airplane from another," he said. The admiral then proceeded to read a paragraph from one of the letters. "The airplanes had red, white, and blue tails with large numbers on their sides and under the right lower wing. (Fig. 8-5). The pilots seemed to be bent on killing themselves. They flew between my house and barn and sideways between two trees in my pasture, causing my livestock to panic and tear down a large section of fence." The Admiral reminded Sandy that no other fighter squadron in Naval service carried those non-regulation markings.

Chapter 9

The Death of Cloud

Leaving the admiral's office, Sandy was slightly disturbed at being put in this position without any warning. However, the more he pondered the situation, the more humorous it became. He remembered doing the same thing only a few years back and knew he would do it again, except now that he was a commanding officer, *he* had to set a good example. So he decided to talk to the men—but only after gunnery was over because he didn't want to put a damper on their spirit at the wrong time. After all, while he had told the admiral he would put a stop to it, he hadn't said *when*.

Finally came the day of reckoning (Fig. 9-1, 9-2). VF-9M was to shoot for the official record. Navy referees and umpires were on hand to oversee procedures and document the scores. All went well the first two days and fantastic shooting was recorded by most of the pilots. On the morning of the third day, as the exercises were coming to a close, a tragic accident took the life of Lieutenant Cloud, the squadron executive officer. A superb aviator, he was one of the best liked men in the squadron and ranked among the best in Marine Aviation. His death left the entire squadron in a state of shock and bewilderment. A court of inquiry report described the accident as follows:

"On 12 April 1934 at about 1100 hours Lieutenant Cloud's section, composed of Lieutenants John Wehle and Edward A. Montgomery, was firing formation battle practice on a target sleeve being towed by Lieutenant Tom Ennis at 3,000 feet southward and about a mile off shore. The section was in right echelon at 4,000 feet, preparing to make its second pass at the sleeve below. As Lieutenant Cloud dove on the sleeve, he pressed in a little too close before he commenced firing, and as he pulled up, the left upper wing of his plane caught on the target sleeve, causing it and part of the tow line to wrap around the wing and aileron. The plane then zoomed upward and immediately went into a spin to the left. After about three turns it then went into a dive, with the target coming loose from the wing and lodging on the left stabilizer before it hit the water. The plane sank immediately. Lieutenant Cloud managed to jump

Fig. 9-1. Frank Schwable's number "6" (9236) at the National Guard Field, Virginia Beach, Virginia, during 1934 Gunnery exercises. Rack under fuselage is for towing target sleeves (courtesy J.R. Pritchard).

from his disabled plane and his chute was seen to open at about 800 feet. He landed safely and was seen to get out of his parachute harness. He disappeared in about four minutes before rescue could be made. It is believed the weight from the heavy cloths he was wearing because of the cold weather was responsible for his drowning."

Lieutenant Wehle described Cloud's last minutes in the water:

"Immediately after Cloud's plane hit the water I saw his chute open. He landed within 100 yards of where the plane sank. I circled and saw him land safely in the water and get out of his chute harness. He then floated on his back. I flew to two fishing boats about a mile away; however, they evidently did not see the accident and failed to understand my signals. I returned to Dave, and he was half out of his heavy flying suit and was still floating on his back. I got out of my chute and rebuckled my safety belt and was intending to land in the water alongside him to help keep him afloat. When I looked for him he was gone. I flew around for about 10 minutes but could find no trace of him. I then returned to the field and led Lieutenant Sanderson out to where the accident happened. An oil slick, a few small pieces of fabric and the sleeve floating on the water marked the approximate location. A Coast Guard boat and the two fishing boats that I had tried to signal were now headed toward the scene of the crash. Tom Ennis had alerted the Coast Guard by landing his F4B-4 on the beach right in front of their station at Dam Neck, just below Virginia Beach. I flew over then and guided them to the wreckage on the water and returned to the field at Virginia Beach and landed."

A very disturbing aspect of the accident was that Cloud parachuted safely from his airplane only to be drowned because of the heavy clothing he was wearing. This unwarranted death helped hasten the development of

111

Fig. 9-2. Refueling three VF-9M planes at Virginia Beach are Hugh Edwards (left) and John E. Curtis. Dave Cloud died during these exercises on 12 April 1934 (courtesy J.R. Pritchard).

a lightweight life vest later given the name "Mae West" by the aviators in World War II.

The Coast Guard conducted an air and sea search for several days but failed to locate the body.

Cloud's death was a jolt not only to the squadron but to everyone in Marine Aviation. Sandy used it to hammer home to his pilots once again the importance of remaining alert at all times and striving for perfection; that one moment of carelessness can quickly cost the life of even the best of pilots.

Out of respect, Sandy immediately called off the gunnery exercises. He met with Navy officials the following morning and they agreed that sufficient firing had been completed to satisfy their requirements.

Joint Maneuvers

After a few days rest, the squadron turned its attention to the joint Navy-Marine maneuvers in the Caribbean on 9 through 12 May. In addition to the study of naval tactics, all pilots became busily engaged in the study of special search procedures and air support, techniques which many of the pilots had learned under actual battle practice in Nicaragua. The six spare F4B-4's (Fig. 9-3) were rotated through the squadron, thus allowing time for the regular ones (Fig. 9-4) to be overhauled.

Fig. 9-3. White-tailed number "22" rotated through squadron as spare. Pilot, Staff Sgt. Gordon W Heritage, NAP (courtesy National Archives).

Orders for the fleet maneuvers came down on 20 April. Their base of operations was San Juan, Puerto Rico, and the squadron's departure was scheduled for 30 April.

Pilots reported to the operations office at 0530 on the morning of departure for final briefing (Fig. 9-5). All were anxious to get started. The weather for the last of April was not at its best in Quantico; however, takeoff time of 0630 still looked good. Considerable rain and fog was reported enroute between Savannah and Jacksonville. Because of their slow speed, the two Ford Trimotors transports carrying the mechanics were to proceed independently. Their takeoff was scheduled for 0600. Lt. William D. Saunders, pilot of one transport, departed on schedule; Capt. Harold C. Major, pilot of the second transport, was unable to leave until 1030 because of a faulty magneto on one engine.

Promptly at 0630, VF-9M departed Brown Field with 18 F4B-4's. The round-trip flight to Puerto Rico was more than 5,000 miles. It was the largest mass over-water flight ever staged by the Marines, and reporters and cameramen were at the field to record the event. Colonel Rowell, the task force commander, flew the spare F4B-4 and 2nd Lt. Perry O. "Pop" Parmelee left with the squadron's utility plane, a Loening OL-9 Amphibian.

A few miles out from Quantico, Sandy ordered the squadron to spread out. A long flight in close formation is very tiring, and this allowed the pilots to relax somewhat. The day's destination was Miami, with refueling stops at Fort Bragg and Jacksonville.

As the squadron cruised along, Sandy's thoughts were about VF-9M, and the wonderful privilege it was to be associated with such a fine group of men. Just a few years earlier, he had had no idea he would one day command the largest—and to his way of thinking, also the best—fighter squadron in Marine Corps history. Each of the men was specially chosen for his flying ability and personal traits. Sure, there were a few "hellraisers" among the group, but he wouldn't want it any other way. In fact, he was no saint himself! He knew each man could always be counted on to give his utmost when necessary. Just before leaving Brown Field, a reporter had asked Sandy to name his best pilots. He had replied, "Each and every one in this squadron is the best, and you be damn sure and write it that way!"

While refueling at Fort Bragg, Frank Wirsig reported weather between Savannah and Jacksonville did not show any improvement and that further south, towards Miami, it was fast deteriorating. As they proceeded southward, the ceiling and visibility began approaching instrument conditions and Sandy decided to land at Savannah to check the latest weather reports. The Weather Bureau reported ceilings varying between 100 and 300 feet and visibility less than a mile.

Sandy decided to continue on, however. He thought their chances of getting through would be improved if each division was allowed to proceed independently; if weather deteriorated enroute to the point that is became

Fig. 9-4. VF-9M working on formation routines near Quantico. Red, white and blue tails can easily be seen. Sanderson's number "0" is in the second line, this end (courtesy BGen. F.H. Wirsig).

115

Fig. 9-5. Capt. Harold C. Major, Group Operations Officer, briefing VF-9M pilots for their trip to the 1934 Navy-Marine Maneuvers in the Caribbean (courtesy BGen. E.L. Pugh).

unsafe for divisions to remain intact, sections could-at their discretion-break away and proceed on their own. Rowell agreed. After refueling the three divisions made their take-off at three-minute intervals to minimize the possibility of a collision.

Everyone made it to Jacksonville except Al Kreiser's section, the transport, and the utility plane. For the next two hours there were no reports of the planes and it was feared that they might have gone down in the ocean. A burden was lifted from Sandy's shoulders when, shortly after, he received a telephone call from Kreiser that he and his section plus the transport and the utility plane had just arrived safely at their destination—the Opa-Locka Naval Air Station at Miami. They had followed the shore line by flying just a few feet above the beaches until the weather cleared approximately 100 miles north of Miami. Moments after Kreiser's call, a radio message was received from Harold Major in the second transport that was forced to leave Brown Field late. Major said that he was now in the clear north of Miami and expected to land in 30 minutes. Everyone was now accounted for and both Sandy and Rowell vowed to exercise more caution and judgment in the future. Severe weather in the Jacksonville area delayed their arrival in Miami for two days.

New Friends: USS Macon

As will be remembered, VF-9M was very popular in the Miami area. Several days prior to its arrival, newspapers picked up the story that it was

Fig. 9-6. *USS Macon* moored at Opa-Locka. *Macon* took part in the 1934 Navy-Marine maneuvers in the Caribbean (courtesy BGen.F.H. Wirsig).

expected on 2 May and the city of Miami extended an "open house" to all its members. Sandy thought this was extremely generous in view of the fact that the giant Navy airship, *USS Macon* (Fig. 9-6), which was to take part in the war games, had been moored at Opa-Locka since 22 April. However, Miami never seemed to tire of entertaining the military. The Mayor indicated he was prepared to host one and all indefinitely. In the evening of 3 May a large dinner and dance was given in their honor at the McAllister Hotel where excellent food, wine, women and song were in great abundance.

All Marine flight personnel reported to the operations office at Opa-Locka the morning of 4 May for a final briefing on the overwater flight to Guantanamo Bay, Cuba (Fig. 9-7). Several were nursing hangovers. Rowell warned Sandy that the press was on hand and no matter how rough the pilots might feel, they had better make a good showing of take-off. It seems Rowell had done a little bragging the night before. There were hand shakes all around with new-found friends from the crew of the *Macon*, which was to depart Opa-Locka the folowing day to join the maneuvers and take part in exercise "M".

At 1000 hours VF-9M began its takeoff and a beautiful one it was. The squadron pulled in tight, then returned across the field at low altitude in a salute to the *Macon*. It then proceeded to downtown Miami, where thousands watched as it flew low over the city in salute to a wonderful host.

Leaving the city on a gentle climb, the squadron started for the overwater flight to Cuba. Because of the cold, Sandy leveled off at 8,000 feet and spread the squadron out. Following the Florida Keys to Marathon, he set course due south for the island of Cuba. The flight of Camaguey was uneventful and flying time was three hours and five minutes.

Fig. 9-7. VF-9M at Opa-Locka Naval Air Station preparing to depart for San Juan, on 4 May 1934. Airship *USS Macon* in background (courtesy BGen. E.L. Pugh).

Potable Adventure

Deteriorating weather conditions reported across Cuba prompted Rowell to cancel the flight to Guantanamo and remain overnight at Camaguey. The city, in the heart of the sugar section of Cuba, was considered an excellent liberty town. While mechanics checked the planes and attended to minor squawks, the pilots pitched in to help with refueling the planes so they could get into town early for a good time. All of a sudden most had forgotten about their hangovers of the night before. Brigadier General Frank Schwable, USMC (ret), remembered the occasion.

"There were practically no facilities at the Camaguey airfield except 50-gallon drums of gas, so we helped to refuel the planes with small hand pumps. That turned out to be real work in the hot sun. Finishing the task, we went to town for the night. After cleaning up a bit, Ed Dyer and I went to the closest bar and asked the waitress for the coolest drink in the place. She suggested a Daiquiri. We had never heard of a Daiquiri but we said to serve them up. As it was hot and we were tired, I guess we never tasted anything so cool, delightful and refreshing as those drinks were. I quickly ordered a second one along with Dyer and when the waitress brought the second one, we ordered the third-and so on-so we wouldn't have to wait. By the time the third quick one had hit bottom, the first one was hitting me between the eyes. The second one made me lean considerably to port and the rest just pushed me over. I don't know how I got home that night—except I sure had friends in that squadron. I can testify to the excellence of the drinks at Camaguey but will never know what its food was like because I don't think I ever had any."

Surprisingly, everyone was accounted for the next morning although, for some reason, many could barely stand the roar of the aircraft engines as they were started. Nearly all of the local townspeople turned out to say goodbye—especially the girls!

The squadron's destination for the day was Port-au-Prince, Haiti, with a refueling stop at Guantanamo Bay. In exactly one hour and forty-five minutes, Sandy circled Hicacal Beach, the landing field at Guantanamo (Fig. 9-8). Conditions there were not much better than at Camaguey and required fueling the planes with hand pumps. Departing two hours later, course was set for Port-au-Prince.

Marines had been stationed in Haiti for fifteen years. Most aviation personnel enjoyed their tour of duty there, even though living conditions at times left a lot to be desired. Several pilots then in VF-9M had spent a few wonderful years there earlier in their careers and were looking forward to the visit. Observation Squadron Nine (VO-9M), then stationed at Port-au-Prince, was also looking forward to VF-9M's visit and had made provisions to "roll out the carpet" on the arrival of the Marines' most famous squadron. Actually Rowell and his task force from Quantico were not prepared for the enthusiastic welcome they received. An official

Fig. 9-8. Landing area at Hicacal Beach, Guantanamo Bay, Cuba. VF-9M planes refueled here with hand pumps (courtesy National Archives).

Fig. 9-9. Pilots of VF-9M on arrival at Port-Au-Prince, Haiti, on 4 May 1934. Welcoming committee in white suits are (L/R): Mr. Normal Armour, American Minister to Haiti; President Lescauz of Haiti; General Little, Commandant of Marines in Haiti (courtesy BGen. F.G. Dailey).

welcoming committee included President Lescauz of Haiti, Mr. Norman Armour, the American Minister to Haiti and General Little, commandant of the Marines stationed there (Fig. 9-9).

On the morning of the third day everyone came to the conclusion that he had had enough. It will never be known how all survived the parties and festivities. Many were not fully recovered from the Miami and Camaquey visits when they arrived. For sure, it would have exhausted the stamina of anyone less physically qualified.

The day's flight had San Juan, Puerto Rico, as its final destination. Leaving Port-au-Prince amidst cheers at 0900, Sandy made a tight formation flight over the field in farewell until their return in about one week. The 425-mile flight was to be made in two segments, with lunch and refueling planned for Santo Domingo.

At 1535 Sandy brought the squadron over the city of San Juan in a beautiful parade formation, then landed at the Pan American Airfield, which would be home base during the war games.

Blue Fleet at War

After reporting to the commanding general that his task force was aboard, Rowell gave strict orders that parties and drinking must cease and that everyone must report bright-eyed the following morning for briefing in their first battle exercise.

In the war games, the enemy, called the Gray Fleet, had seized Puerto Rico and the Virgin Islands. The Blue Fleet had the task of destroying the Gray Fleet and retaking the islands. On 10 May, VF-9M's assignment was to support a landing by a large force of Marines on the island of Culebra. The island was considered a strategic one in the retaking of Puerto Rico and had to be seized at all costs. The Gray forces were well entrenched and would have to be taken by surprise. VF-9M's mission: neutralize enemy ground targets, employing dive bombing and machine-gun fire. The squadron was a master at this and after four separate attacks the war games referee ruled that the Marines had successfuly seized the island.

On 11 May the exercises officially ended, and Sandy prepared to depart for home the following day. However, the people of San Juan were not going to let VF-9M leave without performing its great airshow. Everyone on the island was invited to attend by the Governor.

In the morning of 13 May the 22 airplanes departed San Juan for Port-au-Prince (Fig. 9-10)—direct, without a planned stop at Santo Domingo. Because of heavy rain squalls some detouring enroute was necessary; however, the flight was made in three hours and ten minutes.

Again Observation Squadron Nine rolled out the carpet for Sandy and his squadron. It appeared that the island rum makers had been working overtime to replenish the stock depleted during VF-9M's visit the previous week.

On the morning of 15 May Colonel Rowell informed everyone that the day's destination was Miami, with only one stop in between. Moans and groans could be heard from several pilots who had aquired diarrhea and weren't sure they could last the 425-mile trip to Camaguey, their only stop. At the conclusion of the briefing session many of the men immediately headed for the base sick bay for medicine to cause binding. It was indeed difficult for Rowell and Sandy to hold straight faces.

As for the Marines stationed at Port-au-Prince, stories are told that it was *months* before they recovered from VF-9M's two stopovers there!

Fig. 9-10. Bowen Field, Port-Au-Prince, Haiti. VF-9M preparing to leave for return flight home on 15 May 1934 (courtesy BGen. E.L. Pugh).

Flight time to Camaguey was three hours, and a most welcome stop it was. Many pilots were at the limit of their restraint and the local privy and surrounding woods were occupied in record time. Refueling the planes in the hot sun helped sweat out the booze and in less than two hours they were underway for the 420-mile flight to Miami. They arrived over the Opa-Locka Air Station after a flight of two hours and fifty minutes.

The *Macon* had preceeded them and was preparing to depart the following morning for California. Her crew and the Marines again renewed friendships; however, Rowell ordered that excessive drinking and celebrating in Miami be kept to a minimum because he was planning to leave the following morning.

At exactly 0707 hours on 16 May the *Macon* cast away its mooring lines and commenced its departure for Moffett Field, California. All VF-9M members were on hand to bid her farewell. Sandy wished he could use the giant airship in his shows. He could think of many stunts using the airship that would surely dazzle the public.

Shortly after 0830, VF-9M got underway for Jacksonville. Rowell, the two transports and the utility plane had departed ten minutes earlier for the same destination. The flight up the east coast was uneventful except for magneto trouble with Ed Pugh's F4B-4. By the time repairs could be made, the expected bad weather forced all to remain in Jacksonville overnight.

The following morning, the weather was still "stinko" and Rowell delayed their departure another day. At this point he didn't want anything to happen. The next day (18 May), all planes took off for Fort Bragg, their last stop before home.

Knowing that a group would probably be waiting to welcome them, Rowell ordered that a formation be assembled just prior to their arrival. At 1630 Rowell's F4B-4 passed over Brown Field at 1,000 feet, flanked on each side by the two Ford transports, with the old Loening OL-9 flying the slot position. Just moments behind came Sandy, leading his squadron over the field at 800 feet in one of the tightest formations ever (Fig. 9-11).

On the ground, everyone was waving. Most of Quantico's population turned out for their arrival. As the airplanes taxied up to the line and shut down their engines, wives, sweethearts, friends, the press, and newsreel cameramen all tried to get past the line of military police. After an official welcome by the commanding general, everyone was allowed to mingle. It was indeed a great homecoming.

On Monday morning when all were assembled at Operations awaiting orders for the day, Sandy read a letter to them that brought happiness and congratulations all around. It was from the Bureau of Aeronautics and stated that VF-9M had attained the top gunnery score for fighter squadrons for the 1933-1934 year. Sandy was extremely proud of his unruly bunch—as was the entire Marine Corps. However, each man expressed sorrow that Dave Cloud was unable to take part in the trophy presentation.

Fig. 9-11. Squadron has just been given the command "right echelon" by Sanderson in number 11. They had 90 seconds to comply (courtesy BGen. F.G. Dailey).

His contribution had been greatly responsible for the squadron attaining the honor.

On 14 June all participants in the mass flight to San Juan were honored in an official letter from the Commandant of the Marine Corps to the Commanding General at Quantico, citing all for their participation in the war games. Paragraph two, three and four of the citation reads as follows:

2. Leaving Brown Field, Quantico, Virginia, on 30 April 1934, twenty-two aircraft made a formation flight to San Juan, Puerto Rico, participated in the Fleet Maneuvers, and returned without casualty to their home base on 18 May, 1934. The flight covered a distance of 5,700 miles, of which nearly 1,000 miles was over sea, across three foreign countries, and was carried out in the face of tropical storms of the rainy season. The task force not only reached its advanced airdrome in Puerto Rico on schedule, but participated in four missions supporting the landing of the Fleet Marine Force on the island of Culebra on 10 May, and again on 11 May took part in a major air problem with the Fleet some 50 miles at sea south of Puerto Rico.

3. This aerial operation was a manifestation of high efficiency and devotion to duty on the part of each of the officers and enlisted men and is a source of gratification to the Commandant, who takes pride in extending a well merited commendation to them.

4. A copy of this letter will be attached to the record of each Marine Officer and to the service record of each enlisted man concerned.

(Signed) John H. Russell

Chapter 10

The Rogers Era Begins

A few days after returning from the maneuvers, everyone within the squadron had heard the latest rumor: Sandy was soon to be relieved as skipper. To every man in the squadron this was a very important crisis. All agreed that it was Sandy, more than anyone, who had molded VF-9M into the Marines' top fighter squadron; no one until then had ever given it a thought that someday he would be transferred. Some rumors even had it that the squadron was to be disbanded.

On 15 June Sandy finally called a meeting of the entire squadron. He couldn't remain silent any longer. The unrest was beginning to affect their flying. "I've called you men here," he said, "to squelch the many untrue rumors that are floating around, especially one. You men known damn well the Marine Corps wouldn't disband the best squadron in its history. Only one of the rumors is true. I will be relieved of command at the end of this month. After a 30-day leave I'll be attending school. As to who will replace me, I'm not at liberty to say as yet. A final decision has not been made. However, I'm sure an excellent selection will be made. You men will know as soon as I do. Now, let's knock it off and get back to work."

Speculation was running high after a few days as to who would take command; or, rather, who could possibly be good enough to take Sandy's place. One thing was for sure: all agreed he would have to be a man of exceptional qualities; one who not only could keep a highly-spirited group of men under control, but one whom the entire squadron would respect at all times. All the men in VF-9M were experts in their profession—the cream of the crop. Their enthusiasm and spirit should never be broken—only dampened from time to time, when necessary, to keep them in line.

To illustrate the point, Brigadier General Frank Dailey likes to tell this story on Sandy.

"There was an urgent need for an airplane to be delivered to the Naval Air Station at North Island, on the west coast. At this time an individual cross-country flight across the United States was still quite rare. Sandy assigned one of our pilots to deliver the plane, which he did successfully. However, his flight out and return took about two weeks. On his return he was feeling good, having accomplished his mission, and was congratulated by all his fellow pilots in the squadron. He went into Sandy's office expecting a pat on the back for a job well done. Sandy, sitting at his desk, looked up slowly and said: 'What in the hell did you do? *Taxi* that airplane all the way there?' "

Tex Takes Over

On 5 July 1934 Captain Ford O. Rogers (Fig. 10-1) took over the command of VF-9M. Headquarters had done well in its selection of Captain Rogers, and Lt. Col. Geiger, Director of Marine Aviation, personally recommended Rogers for this important command.

Rogers, known by everyone as "Tex" because of his birth in Waco, Texas, was also known as a hot shot fighter pilot throughout the Marine Corps and at that time was one of only four World War I Marine aviators on active duty. He and Sandy were old friends, having entered many races together around the country in the 1920's. In fact he and Sandy used to put on a very funny comedy flying routine with two World War I German airplanes. The planes were Fokker D-7's and were named "Hans" and "Fritz." Wearing German uniforms, they were a tremendous hit at airshows of their day. Sandy was indeed happy that Tex was chosen as his replacement.

Captain Rogers' flying career started when he was sent to Miami Naval Air Station in February, 1918, after placing ninth out of a class of 63 men who successfully passed the examination for a commission in the Marines. After completing his training at Miami, where he soloed a "Jenny" in two and half hours flying time, he was sent to the Pensacola Naval Air Station to finish his training, qualifying as a Naval Aviator on 4 April, 1918.

From Pensacola, Rogers was assigned as a pilot in Squadron B, commanded by Lt. William M. McIlvain, and sailed for France on 30 April, 1918, on board the *USS DeKalb*. In France, Tex, along with several others, was loaned to the Royal Air Force, Fifth Bombing Group, Squadron 218, and flew DeHavilland DH-4's and DH-9's in bombing raids against the German submarine bases in Ostend, Zeebruge and Ghent.

After the war, Tex Rogers had many interesting assignments all the way from air racing to helping the controversial General Billy Mitchell bomb the German Battleship *Ostfriesland* in tests off the Virginia Capes on 21 July 1921. In 1924 he was sent to the Anacostia Naval Air Station, Washington, D.C., as a test pilot for all Navy land planes. From 1926 to 1929 he was assigned to Headquarters Marine Corps as a staff officer. After a tour of duty in Haiti as squadron commander, Tex was assigned to the Naval Aircraft Factory at Philadelphia as Chief Engineering Test Pilot, and it was from this assignment that he came to take command of VF-9M.

Fig. 10-1. New "Skipper" of VF-9M, Capt. Ford O. "Tex" Rogers, July 1934 (courtesy L.I. Beatty).

According to Rogers, his three-year command of VF-9M was the most rewarding of his entire 30 years in Marine Aviation.

The first thing that Rogers did as the new skipper was to purposely fly every position within the squadron so that he could better understand the many problems pilots had to cope with in an 18-plane stunt team. Further, he moved his pilots around so that they learned to fly every position within the squadron as well as their own. This was one of the secrets that made VF-9M so outstanding in its future years. He knew that if they were to stay the best, there was only one way to do it, and during the next few weeks he put the men through some of the toughest training to date, averaging two and sometimes three 18-plane formations a day. Brown Field (Fig. 10-2) became a beehive of activity. Master Sergeant Morris K. "Sap" Kurtz, the squadron line chief, seemed to be everywhere, making sure that he had 18-airplanes always on the line and ready to go.

It didn't take long until all of the officers and men in the squadron knew that Tex, like Sandy, was a real pro. Not only was he an expert aviator, he set about reorganizing the squadron and boosted morale even further by giving everyone an assigned responsibility and putting his trust in them to do their very best without having to constantly check on them. Commenting on this, Brigadier General Frank Wirsig, USMC (ret) said:

"VF-9M was the best squadron I have ever been associated with and I've seen some damn good ones. Tex was one of the finest squadron

Fig. 10-2. Brown Field in 1934. New airfield can be seen under construction in upper left center on opposite side of railroad tracks (courtesy Marine Corps).

commanders I have ever known. He wasn't one to tell you something you already knew. He put his trust in everyone to do his best and they did."

On 8 August Sandy returned to Brown Field from a 30-day leave and was greeted warmly by everyone. Until his departure in a few days, he was attached to VF-9M. Tex invited him to fly with the squadron but Sandy refused, saying it would deprive one of the regular pilots of his training. The first morning, Sandy stood by until the squadron took off on a training flight, then walked to operations to await its return. However, Master Sergeant Kurtz, seeing the look on Sandy's face, ordered the mechanics to roll Sandy's Number "0" out of the hangar where it had been waiting his return. Sergeant Tom Griffis, who had been Sandy's crew chief, started the engine. Sandy, with a big grin on his face, grabbed his helmet and goggles and hopped in. To the delight of all Brown Field and Quantico, Sandy performed an outstanding one-man airshow that was talked about for some time.

A farewell party was given for Sandy, and what a party it was. Singing and dancing went on until the wee hours of the morning. If hangovers and headaches are any measuring stick, it was a *howling* success. All joined in wishing him well at his new assignment, where he would be attending the Army Air Corps Tactical School at Maxwell Field, Montgomery, Alabama. He would be missed.

1934 National Air Races

The first official airshow for Tex Rogers after assuming command was the world's classic event, the National Air Races at Cleveland, 31 August

128

through 3 September, 1934 (Fig. 10-3). That year, the show was to commemorate twenty-five years of air racing and promised to be the biggest ever, with all available seats and standing room sold out. As usual, the world's best racing planes and pilots would be competing. And the Army, Navy and Marines would be expected to show-off their newest airplanes and their flying prowess.

Tex faced tough competition. Representing the Army Air Corps was the famed 27th Pursuit Squadron from Selfridge Field, Michigan, flying its brand new Boeing P-26A monoplane fighters. The Navy's contribution was none other than Fighting Squadron Six (VF-6B), known as Felix-the-Cat Squadron (because of its insignia) and commanded by the very able Lieutenant Commander Ralph A. Ofstie (Fig. 10-4). Based aboard the aircraft carrier *USS Saratoga*, Fighting Six was also equipped with Boeing F4B-4 airplanes and considered one of the Navy's finest. However, the feeling of all in VF-9M was "We'll give 'em hell. We can outfly 'em."

Permission was granted for nine Helldivers of VO-7M (Fig. 10-5), commanded by 1st Lt. William L. "Skeeter" McKittrick, to assist VF-9M at the show. Four large transport planes from Utility Squadron VJ-6M, commanded by First Lieutenant William D. Saunders, carried all support-

Fig. 10-3. Preparing to depart for the 1934 Cleveland Air Races are (L/R): Capt. Ford O. Rogers, Commanding VF-9M; Lt. Col. Ross E. Rowell, Brown Field Group Commander; 1st Lt. William L. McKittrick, commanding VO-7M (courtesy U.S. Navy).

Fig. 10-4. The Navy's famed Fighting Squadron Six (VF-6), better known as "Felix-the-Cat" Squadron, showed up at the Cleveland Show to challenge VF-9M. L/R: LCdr. R.A. Ofstie, Commanding Officer and Lt. Ketchem, Executive Officer (courtesy U.S. Navy).

ing equipment and performing yeoman work as required. The task force would be under the command of Lt. Col. Rowell.

Thursday morning, 30 August, was takeoff time for Cleveland. Arriving at Brown Field at 0630, Tex found it buzzing with activity. Sap Kurtz, his line chief, had all the airplanes ready and lined up for inspection. At 0730 Rowell held a briefing session in the big hangar for pilots of the three participating squadrons. Take-off time was set at 0815 for VJ-6M, 0820 for VO-7M and 0830 for VF-9M.

Rowell, flying VF-9M's spare F4B-4, began his take-off at exactly 0815, followed by the other squadrons. A sizable crowd had gathered to see the squadrons off and the press was on hand for pictures and interviews. Once airborne, the squadrons joined up for a pass-in-parade formation for the photographers (Fig. 10-6).

The route to Cleveland was by way of Cumberland (Maryland) and Pittsburgh. Just west of Cumberland the VO and VF squadrons passed the transports and the three squadron leaders acknowledged by radio that all was well.

Twenty minutes past Pittsburgh, Tex heard Lt. Schwable, leader of the fourth section, say that his right wing man, Jack McQuade, was in trouble and dropping behind. Just a minute before, McQuade had changed his fuel-selector valve from the auxiliary fuel tank to the main tank but the fuel pressure hadn't come up. At the first sputter of his engine, McQuade began working the wobble pump to regain the lost fuel pressure but to no avail. A few seconds of this convinced him he was about to make a hurried forced landing. His altitude was now less than 1500 feet and he knew that his F4B-4 wouldn't glide too well with a dead engine.

He was still over somewhat hilly country and the only safe landing area he could glide to was a long, narrow field running east and west, just south of a small town that turned out to be Kent, Ohio. Running out of altitude fast, he had to make his approach from the west. That end of the field was bordered by high-tension wires running along Franklin Road. Not having sufficient altitude to go over the wires, McQuade had no choice but to go *under* them. On the opposite side of Franklin Road was a small cornfield. Making his approach over the tall corn, McQuade didn't see a small telephone pole, just slightly higher than the corn, until it was too late. He hit the pole with his left landing gear just before going under the wires. This threw his airplane sideways just as it touched ground, wiping out the landing gear completely. The airplane then skidded on its belly for approximately 50 feet before turning upside down. Quickly unbuckling his safety belt and removing himself from the wreckage, he waved to John Wehle and Al Kreiser, who were circling overhead, that he was all right.

In no time at all a crowd gathered at the site of the wreckage. Inquiring as to his whereabouts, McQuade was told that he had landed on the John Whitefield Farm on Franklin Road, Kent, Ohio. The mayor of Kent, Mr. W.I. Harvey, and the safety director, Mr. Francis Kerwin, arrived at the site and welcomed McQuade to the city. Patrolman James Moors was assigned to guard the wreckage, and McQuade was taken to town where he was treated for a cut on the nose and a few bruises by Doctor S.A. Brown.

In the meantime the rest of the squadron had landed at Cleveland, where Tex immediately contacted the State Police and gave them the

Fig. 10-5. Helldivers of VO-7M in their red, white and blue show markings joined with VF-9M at the 1934 Cleveland Air Races (courtesy Marine Corps.)

location of the downed airplane, requesting a report as soon as possible. One of the pilots, trying to keep Tex from worrying, remarked, "Don't you worry about ol' Jocko. He can take care of himself. Why, if I know him, by this time he is being toasted by all the city officials and having a grand time." And he *was*, too! Several hours later, when a car finally arrived to take him to Cleveland, he was enjoying himself so much he didn't want to leave.

The next crisis began shortly after their arrival at Cleveland. It was discovered that hotel reservations were lacking for the mechanics and crew chiefs. A canvas of the city's hotels resulted in the same answer—sorry, no vacancy. A call for help by one of the local radio stations produced results. An offer by a resident hotel for women only was too good to turn down. Recalling the incident, John Curtiss, a former crew chief, said:

"We were loaded into a bus and gave the driver the address. When we pulled up in front of the Devon Hall he couldn't believe his eyes. The hotel was strictly for women only, and to leave a bus load of Marines there was beyond his imagination. It was beyond *ours*, too! The fourth floor of the hotel was cleared for us and the self-serve elevator supposely was 'gimmicked' so that it would work only for that floor. This was done to keep us away from the girls. However, knowing Marines, that didn't last long. Also, we were allowed to take any meals in their dining room if we so desired. Some of the gals took part in the poker games going on each night in the parlors and did pretty well, too. At night, when we returned to the hotel by taxi, the driver would always ask if you wanted him to wait. When told we were living there, you should have seen the astonished look on his face. This has given me many a chuckle over the years."

Opening day of the giant air show saw a tremendous turnout. Thousands payed for standing room only; many more thousands were turned away for the Sunday and Labor Day shows.

The Army and Navy shows, with their flawless demonstration of tactical formations, were first rate. An Army trio calling themselves "The Men on the Flying Trapeze," led by Captain Claire Chennault, (later of Flying Tiger fame) put on a daring show of aerobatics. However, for a large aerobatic squadron, none could surpass VF-9M's performance.

Each day the huge audience gave the Marine flyers their undivided attention. Billed as the Marine Corps' crack squadron, the show included such specialities as the Squirrel Cage, Snake Dance, Squadron Line Reversement, Daisy Chain and many other crowd-chilling maneuvers. The announcer would then remark: "Now, ladies and gentlemen, if you will look to your right you will see the Marines' famous "Helldivers" approaching. Under the command of Lieutenant William L. McKittrick, it is the squadron that fought the bandits for so long in Nicaragua. Officially known as Observation Squadron Seven, they will now join with Fighting Squadron Nine to demonstrate tactical maneuvers."

The two squadrons' demonstration of the Marines' use of bombs and smoke as an aid to establishing a beachhead for invasion troops was always

Fig. 10-6. Tex Rogers leading his 18-plane formation to the 1934 Cleveland Air Races on 20 August. Squadron is composed of three six-plane divisions (courtesy Marine Corps).

a crowd pleaser. However, remembering their past experience and embarrassment in Chicago when the wind changed, the chemical make-up of the liquid for the smoke screen had been altered to prevent harm to the ladies' dresses and underwear in case it blew into the grandstands.

Dive bombing by both squadrons climaxed the 35-minute show each day and, as always, left a profound effect on the audience. For the last two days Tex added an extra thrill for the audience by leading his entire 18-plane squadron straight down in close formation, letting off all bombs at the same time. This brought the audience to its feet, and at the conclusion of the demonstration the air show announcer remarked, "There's just no way of outdoing the Marines."

Again, as in the past, no one was able to top VF-9M's performance. The official publication for the National Air Races said the squadron's four-day appearance: "They have glorified the National Air Races with their presence."

The squadron's return home on Tuesday morning was un-eventful. Believe it or not, all were glad it was over. It meant rest and sleep. Each night of their stay at Cleveland, many parties had been in progress, mostly given by large aviation companies and their suppliers. Probably one of the more rugged affairs was the ball given for the Marines on Saturday night by the Leatherneck Club, the local Marine Reserve Unit. Several former squadron members have said that the air races were rugged affairs for the aviators; only the *real* tough ones could hold up under flying all day and drinking all night.

After a two-day rest Tex called a meeting of his pilots on Friday morning. The result was a stepped-up training schedule that continued for the next three months.

VF-9M-Superstars

Things were happening at a fast pace for VF-9M. Invitations to perform were coming from all parts of the United States, Canada, and Mexico. According to Marine Headquarters, it was the most popular squadron in military service. Even as things stood, its schedule for the upcoming year of 1935 was overloaded and Tex could see trouble in store if his pilots didn't pay more attention to detail. Sure, the show looked good to huge civilian audiences, but he noticed several rough edges that had to be smoothed out.

In the meeting, Tex laid all the facts on the table. He outlined what lay ahead and what he expected of his men. Never one to lecture his pilots, he called for suggestions. It was not his way to scold or give anyone hell. He wanted pilots who felt they were not giving their all and maybe not doing some things exactly right to make suggestions for improving themselves. He believed this technique worked far better than a hell-and-damnation lecture, making all the suggestions himself. Even though Tex didn't give the impression of being a perfectionest, he was. However, he used his own methods of obtaining perfection from others. Looking back on those days, Major General "Sandy" Sanderson commented:

"Tex Rogers was a great squadron commander. He did a great job with VF-9M. He was much better than I was. He knew how to get the most out of his men and make them think it was their idea. As I remember, he didn't care much for regulations; he just wanted to get the job done. He was an easy-going Texan and everybody liked him. However, anyone who got the idea he was a softie was sure in for a helluva surprise."

Tex held the same kind of meeting with his crew chiefs and mechanics and their contribution was even more important. Many of their suggestions on maintenance and care of the F4B-4's were passed along to the Fleet squadrons by the Bureau of Aeronautics that eventually resulted in several modifications on this type airplane.

As the weeks went by a notable change in all squadron activities could be detected. Every day possible, all pilots were airborne. Some worked on three-plane section tactics, others on six-plane division maneuvers, including gunnery and bombing. At week's end, Tex would drill all in 18-plane squadron formations.

Only three public appearances were made during this period: The observance of Navy Day on 27 October; a demonstration for the Adjutant and Inspector General of the Marine Corps on 21 November; and a flyover at Washington on 17 December in honor of the Wright brothers' flight.

The squadron's fast pace continued until Friday, 21 December, when Tex ordered everyone home for the holidays. They were not to report back until 4 January 1935. The two-week vacation was surely welcomed by the enlisted men, who had worked extremely hard during the previous three months. It's not an easy task to keep 18 or more airplanes flying every day. A few days earlier, Rusty Rowell had suggested to Tex—it was *almost* an order—that maybe he should ease up on the squadron. Remarked Tex, "Hell, *I'm* not doing it. They're doing it on their *own*. I just happen to agree with all of the suggestions they put forth. They want to be the best squadron in service and I'll be damned if I'm going to stand in their way. As their commander I just sort of point the way and they do the rest. 'Course, maybe I do give 'em a little jab now and then or maybe a suggestion here and there, but I always manage to make 'em think it was *their* idea. Don't worry, I know my boys and I'll take good care of them."

By 0800 on 4 January 1935 all pilots had signed in at operations and were waiting for Tex to appear. As he entered, all stood at attention. After a warm greeting and the usual exchange of friendly conversation, Operations Officer Frank Wirsig called for order.

The first topic for discussion was the All-American Air Races at Miami, scheduled for 11 through 13 January. With little time left, Tex informed them that as of that moment, two full formation flights would be flown daily in preparation for the show.

The next item on the agenda was the busy schedule planned for the year. According to Rusty Rowell, Headquarters had committed the squadron to 20 airshows and were considering several additional requests. Further, the annual bombing and gunnery exercises were scheduled for 6

February and would run approximately six weeks. On top of that, a course in instrument and night flying was to begin soon and could last for several months. Not counting unforeseen problems that often arise—weather, maintenance, sickness,—it would be a *very* tough schedule to complete.

Back to Miami—The Hard Way

Operations Order No. OP-VF-1935-1 called for VF-9M to depart Brown Field with 19 Boeing F4B-4's on 8 January for the Miami Air Races. Observation Squadron VO-7M, consisting of 12 Curtiss O2C-1 Helldivers commanded by "Skeeter" McKittrick, would accompany VF-9M. Capt. Harold Major, flying the big Curtiss R4C-1 Condor, would be carrying several dignitaries from Washington, including Brig. Gen. George Richards, the Paymaster of the Marine Corps. First Lt. Raymond C. Scollin was to fly the crew chiefs in the Ford RR-5 transport. As usual, the task force was under the command of Lt. Col. Rusty Rowell.

A large weather front over the east coast and extending as far west as Texas detained their departure. The next day the weather was no better. The cloud ceiling and visibility were near zero, with no letup in slight for several days.

On the morning of 10 January there was a slight improvement. Tex knew if they didn't get underway shortly, it would be impossible to arrive in Miami for opening day. By 1000 hours it was go now or never; Rusty Rowell agreed. Within 30 minutes the two squadrons were airborne, followed by the supporting aircraft. The first scheduled stop was Pope Field at Fort Bragg.

Several times enroute Tex was tempted to turn back. It was so cold he didn't know if they could hold out until they reached Pope Field. Snow squalls cut visibility to near zero, making it very difficult to follow the iron compass (railroad tracks), the only reliable means of navigation they could count on.

Just past Richmond, Virginia, the snow turned to freezing rain. The faces and goggles of the pilots became coated with ice. On several of the F4B-4's the large radio mast became coated with ice, thus producing a vibration so intense that pilots began thinking about a possible forced landing. Luckily, not enough ice accumulated on the airplanes to force them down.

A few miles out of Pope Field, visibility improved enough so that the pilots could spot the field on the horizon. All became jubilant, knowing that in a few minutes they would be able to thaw out with a few shots of booze at the Fort Bragg Officer's Club. However, the flight was not over yet, as several pilots found out when the squadron began its break-up to land. Several found they couldn't reduce power because the throttles had frozen at cruising speed. Tex instructed them to fly away from the field, turn around and make a long straight-in approach and —when they were sure they could glide to the field—to turn both the master switch and the fuel selector valve to the off position and land with a dead engine. All made it without mishap.

McKittrick and his 12 Helldivers were having the same problems. The crew chiefs in the rear seats of the planes looked like frozen statues. A few good stiff ones from a bottle took care of *that*. Needless to say, flying in winter in open-cockpit airplanes could be a "chilling" affair and required that each pilot possess that certain something not found in the average person.

Word was received that the two transports had made it to Jacksonville and would continue on to Miami the following morning.

The Fort Bragg weather bureau informed Tex that he, too, could possibly make it to Jacksonville; however, he thought his men had been through enough and decided to call it a day. The forecast was for improving weather conditions in the morning and he figured that if he could get away early enough, he could still make it to Miami in time for the show.

The forecast was accurate; the weather showed considerable improvement, with some rain forecast north of Jacksonville. Thanking the Army for its hospitality, the two squadrons were airborne by 0800.

The weather wasn't too bad; it was getting warmer as they pushed southward. About an hour out of Jacksonville the sky began to blacken and the rain that the weather bureau had promised began to appear. Tex spread the squadron out as the rain increased. Then all hell broke loose. Recalling the incident, Brigadier General Ed Pugh said:

"There was a solid wall of water just as if someone had turned a large fire hose on the airplanes. It was almost impossible to believe my engine was still running. Water was coming in from everywhere and the bottom of the fuselage was filling up faster than it could run out. In just a few minutes I was soaked, but at least the rain was warm. I had flown in rain many times in my life, but this was the worst. It's a wonder some of the planes didn't run into each other. When we flew out of it, the squadron was scattered all over, but everyone came through all right. When we landed at Jacksonville, we found the rain had removed the paint from the leading edges of the tail surfaces."

At Jacksonville, Tex made a telephone call to the commanding officer of the Opa-Locka Naval Air Station to inform him that the two squadrons would arrive by 1430 and to let the Miami airport manager know that they would be there in time to perform. Miami's airport was only one mile south and adjacent to the Opa-Locka Naval Air Station.

Approximately 10 miles north of Opa-Locka, Tex was informed by radio that the Marines' portion of the airshow would be scheduled any time they were ready. This gave plenty of time for the two squadrons to slip into Opa-Locka to fuel and arm all planes with demonstration bombs.

McKittrick's Helldivers were fueled and armed first, with all hands pitching in to repeat the procedure on the F4B-4's. Both squadrons were serviced in record time and were airborne by 1515. Tex took his squadron several miles to the west, where he climbed to 10,000 feet, then turned south to await instructions. McKittrick flew his squadron north to wait.

Rowell, who had arrived in the Curtiss Condor transport in advance of the two squadrons, had informed the air-race manager that the Marines would be ready to perform anytime after 1530 hours. This was passed on to the airshow announcer. "Ladies and gentlemen," said the announcer, "I have just been informed that the next portion of today's show will be two squadrons of the United States Marines from Quantico, Virginia. Detained because of bad weather, the two squadrons have been flying all day just to thrill us here in Miami with their breath-taking maneuvers. Making up the

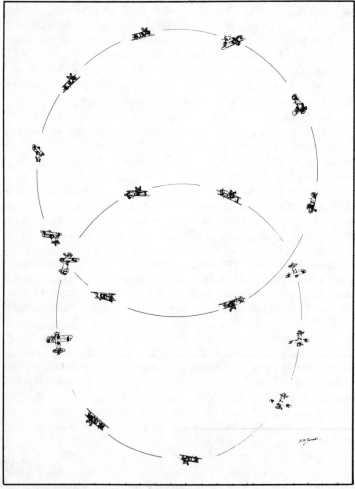

Fig. 10-7. Intersecting loops performed with nine planes in each circle (illustration by B.W. Campbell).

Marine's performance will be none other than the famous Fighting Squadron Nine, commanded by Captain Ford Rogers. Assisting Fighting Nine will be the Helldivers, commanded by Lieutenant William McKittrick. The entire Marine contingent is under the command of Lieutenant Colonel Ross E. Rowell, commanding officer of the Marine Air Station at Quantico."

As the announcer continued with his glowing praise, Rowell waiting in the transport plane picked up the mike and said: "Tex, you and Mac are on. Make it look good."

Tex, now several miles south, immediately gave his squadron the command to dive and peeled off to the left, followed by the other planes in succession until all 18 were hurling down at 275 miles per hour in a vertical column of roaring engines and screeching wires! McKittrick's Helldivers, diving from the north, were timing their decent so as to meet VF-9M over the airport and pass, close as possible, over the top of each fighter. From the stands, it would look as though many of the planes were going to collide as they approached head on.

The announcer was saying "We can expect the Marines to arrive most any minute now," when he suddenly stopped and looked up towards the south. He then turned to the north! As the roar increased, the entire audience got to its feet and looked into the sky to see what was producing such a mighty roar. The announcer suddenly blurted out: "My God, the Marines have already arrived and *what* an arrival!" Tex started his dive pullout at the south end of the field, then rolled his plane on its left side as he passed across in front of the audience at less than 100 feet altitude. As each member of his squadron followed, the Helldivers were coming across the field from the north at wide open throttle, heading right for the fighter squadron—just missing each plane by a few feet as they passed. (Fig. 10-7). Most spectators held their ears because of the tremendous noise produced by the wide-open engines.

The Marines then continued their 25-minute show with the Squirrel Cage, Snake Dance, bomb dropping, and a simulated support of a beachhead landing by attacking through a smoke screen. At the conclusion of their performance, the two squadrons landed on the Miami airport, where the huge audience gave them a standing ovation.

Miami, as always, was an outstanding host and there were many parties in their honor, including a dinner-dance hosted by the mayor at the Biltmore Country Club.

All good things must end. The Marines left for home on 15 January and arrived at Brown Field the next day after staying overnight again at Pope Field, Fort Bragg.

Chapter 11

A Hole in the Overcast

For some time, the Navy Bureau of Aeronautics had been working on an improvement for its .50-caliber aircraft machine guns. By altering the guns slightly, a new experimental long-range ammunition could be fired. After more than a year of testing, the new ammunition looked very promising and was now considered ready for squadron testing.

The chief ordnance officer within the Bureau asked Admiral King if he had any preference as to which squadron the task should be assigned. "I certainly do," replied the Admiral. "It should be assigned to VF-9M at Quantico. I'm sure they can prove its worth. Clear it with Roy Geiger and Rusty Rowell."

On 18 January, Rogers was summoned to Rowell's office to discuss the project. Also attending was Al Kreiser, the squadron ordnance officer and Ed Pugh, the engineering officer. They agreed that there would be no problem. A slight change within the airplanes for storing the ammunition belts was all that was required and this could be accomplished in time for the upcoming gunnery exercises. By 1 February, all airplanes were modified, bore-sighted, harmonized to each pilot's preference, and test-fired.

Shortly after 0800 on 6 February, VF-9M left Brown Field (Fig. 11-1) for gunnery and bombing exercises at the Marine's new air facility at Parris Island, South Carolina. They were scheduled to continue for approximately six weeks, and most wives were not too happy because it was nearly 600 miles from Quantico, too great a distance to commute home on weekends. However, Tex, who was an old softie where women were concerned, promised them that if the squadron returned to Parris Island again in the fall, something would be worked out so they could go along. The wives would not forget this.

Weather conditions on the first leg of the flight to Parris Island were very similar to those on the recently completed Miami flight. Snow and freezing rain were encountered until they were well past Richmond and forced Frank Schwable, who had volunteered to ferry the squadron's old

Fig. 11-1. Pilots had to cope with muddy conditions at Brown Field for many years, causing many ground accidents (courtesy Marine Corps).

Loening Amphibian, to make a forced landing in a farmer's field near South Hill, Virginia. He was wined and dined by two wonderful old ladies and was unable to continue his trip until the following morning.

The exercises officially began on 11 February, and for weeks everyone was extremely busy and caught up in the excitement of the "great aerial contest."

Flying operations were conducted each day, except Sunday, from 0800 till noon. Bombing was conducted on targets erected in the mouth of the Broad River; aerial gunnery was fired on towed targets several miles offshore over the Atlantic Ocean.

Afternoons were used by all personnel in preparation for the next day's operations. Guns, ammunition, bombs, and bomb racks were checked by the armorers. Mechanics serviced the airplanes and checked them from engine to tailwheel until crew chiefs were satisfied. Pilots filled out evaluation reports, tabulated gunnery and bombing scores and, when finished, attended informal "bull sessions" to improve their scores and flying technique.

Commenting on a few problems of a crew chief, John Curtiss said, "At this time the Boeings were beginning to show excessive cam wear in the machine gun synchronizers and occasionally a bullet would go through one of the propeller blades. It was no fault of the armorer crew, however. If a new prop wasn't readily available, we would take a ball-peen hammer and pound out the raised area where the bullet went through, then dress it up with a file. The hole gave a nice whistling sound to the props and you could always tell when your plane was coming back to the line. The propellers took quite a beating in those days. There were no paved runways and it didn't take long for them to get nicked up. A good double-cut file was a handy tool for a crew chief to keep props dressed down and smooth. To combat salt-air corrosion we wiped down the blades with used engine oil. The carbon in the old oil served as a mild abrasive and helped to give them that polished look."

Teamwork Pays Off

Rogers encouraged everyone to make suggestions and contribute any ideas about gunnery, bombing, or flying, no matter how impractical they might seem. It was team work such as this that led VF-9M to develop several maneuvers and methods of approaching a target that were later used with success in World War II. "We were constantly seeking maneuvers and new methods of approach which could be used in time of war," remarked Brigadier General Pugh. "We continued with this idea in all of our exercises. The Navy had established certain rules and approaches to be followed in gunnery competition for fighter squadrons, but it was obvious to us that only a few of these could be used in combat. We in VF-9M felt that we should be realistic in our gunnery practice, so we did just that. It was VF-9M that developed what we considered the proper approach for a fighter plane to attach an enemy. We termed it the 'roundhouse' approach. It was first used by my division, which was comprised of pilots Frank Wirsig, Ed Montgomery, Frank Schwable, Glen Herndon, 'Cracker' Williams and myself. This approach was used throughout World War II very successfully."

On Wednesday, 13 March, VF-9M finished the competetive exercises. As one crew chief, Sergeant Alexander A. "Red" Case, remembers, "There was a *hell* of a lot of money that changed hands before the day was over. Probably the heaviest betting was among the plane crews. Each one bet on his pilot to win, with a grand jackpot to go to the plane crew whose pilot accumulated the highest score at the end of the exercised."

The squadron arrived home on 15 March where wives, friends and reporters were waiting to welcome them.

The next day Rowell received a favorable report on the experimental long-range ammunition. In fact, VF-9M had used it while firing for the record that would be used to determine its official standing within Naval Aviation. Other than the comment that "it shook hell out of the planes from nose to tail," most pilots liked the new ammunition. They agreed that in most instances they could commence firing further from the target and break off sooner, eliminating the necessity for pressing in too close, which had been partially responsible for the death of Dave Cloud.

On 26 March Tex learned that his squadron had barely missed obtaining the highest scores in bombing and gunnery. It was a letdown after being the winner the previous year. He met with his pilots the following morning and told them that each of them was going to increase his score by 15 percent—if they had to fly day and night to do it. VF-9M was going to be the top squadron in everything "come hell or high water." With that, Tex walked out. Almost a full minute passed before anyone said a word. It was the first time most of them had seen Tex riled.

New Lessons, New Problems

The next two months were very busy ones. In fact, the month of May 1935 became known by all hands as "The month that was." Operations Officer Wirsig could be seen going all directions at the same time. In addition to training flights for several reserve pilots who had joined the squadron, a new instrument-flying course was underway for all regular pilots. Designed by Capt. Karl S. Day, the course was composed of 35 hours of classroom instruction and a minimum of 25 hours of instrument-flying instruction. Four pilots from VF-9M were assigned to each class, along with pilots from other squadrons. During the month, heavy rains descended on Brown Field, creating hazardous operations for several days at a time. It was during one of these wet spells that the Bureau of Aeronautics sent an urgent request to Rusty Rowell, asking that pilots from VF-9M be assigned to fly several BG-1 dive bombers to squadrons on the west coast. That did it! Tex complained loudly to Rowell about the use of his pilots to ferry airplanes when the squadron was faced with such a heavy work load. Rowell agreed, but due to the pressing need for the new planes, all squadrons had to participate in their delivery. Of the ten pilots requested, VF-9M was to furnish only four. Because of the weather at this time of year, those asssigned the task were not too happy, either. The flight almost started in disaster but ended in a rather humorous way.

The delivery flight left Brown Field on 3 May for the west coast—or so it was thought. The five plane formation was under the command of Skeeter McKittrick, who, despite the deplorable weather, had decided to go. The four pilots from VF-9M were Frank Schwable and Tom Ennis, flying in one of the planes, and Ed Montgomery and Jack McQuade flying together in another. The further south they flew, the more the weather deteriorated. This required the formation to pull in very tight, as McKittrick's airplane had the only radio range receiver on board. The others had to follow him. The ceiling came down to the tree tops, and what happened next is described by Brigadier General Schwable.

"We were trying to stay underneath the clouds, as the airplanes were not equipped for instrument flying, nor were we. When the clouds came down and met the ground and trees, that was too much for us. There was just no place to go and the formation exploded in five different directions. As Tom Ennis and I were in the last plane to the right, we made a steep climbing turn to the right and climbed through several thousand feet of solid overcast, finally breaking out on top in the clear blue sky. We both relaxed for a minute after that sweating climb, not knowing just where in that soup the other planes were and worrying about the illegal instrument flying we just did, as little or none of it was done in those days.

"After flying for some time, we found a hole in the overcast large enough to spiral down through, otherwise we probably would have had to jump, which was a horrible thought. After descending through the hole in the clouds, we found the ceiling underneath still very low and visibility almost zero. Not knowing where we were, we turned north and vaguely recognized what looked to us like the shores of the lower Potomac River. We followed the shore line, going up and then back down each cove, as visibility was so bad we couldn't see across any of them. We finally came upon Brown Field and, after making a hurried landing and wiping the sweat from our brows, we both thanked God that we were down out of that mess.

"Moments after landing we were called to operations. There was Rusty Rowell, the boss, who looked at us as if we were just about the lowest, most stupid and lousiest pilots that ever came under his command. Our weak explanations didn't seem to phase him, so we got the hell out of there soon as possible, again praising the Lord for our safe landing.

"After lunch, we returned to operations and learned that McKittrick made it to Fort Bragg, our destination. About an hour later word came that another plane was down near Danville, Virginia, on its nose in a farmer's field. No word from the other two. Rowell was beginning to look worried—*quite* worried in fact—and even managed a smile at Tom Ennis and me a couple of times.

"Almost an hour later, a vague report came in that the fourth plane was down somewhere, with its two pilots okay. As time went on, Rowell became more and more worried and as his worries increased, Tom and I seemed to gain stature in his eyes. Quite late, when Rowell became really worried, word was received that Jack McQuade and Ed Montgomery had landed in *Wyoming*! You can imagine the consternation *that* caused the boss. Wyoming was pretty far off in those days. It happens that the telegram forgot to say, Wyoming, *Delaware*!

"By the time we got word from McQuade, I believe Rowell thought Tom Ennis and myself were the two best flyers, with the soundest judgment and greatest skills, that had ever been assigned to his command because we got our airplane home safely and early and caused no one any worry or concern."

In spite of a few obstacles of burdensome proportions, six airshows were still performed as scheduled. On 2 May an airshow was staged at Chancellorsville for the thousands gathered to witness the reenactment of the great Civil War battle fought there. On 11 May, there was a bombing demonstration in the morning for the Navy Brass and a troop landing exercise for Marine Ground Staff officers in the afternoon; on 18 May, an airshow and bombing demonstration for the United States Congress and friends; on the 24th, a special show by all of Brown Field for the Argentine Military staff; and on the 25th, a wonderful show and all around get-together for the Washington Press Club. On this occasion, Rowell reminded the entire air station to look its best, as the news media in the past had been very favorable in its coverage of Marine Aviation.

On 30 May an important change took place in the top command of Marine Aviation. At the conclusion of an inspection of all facilities at

Fig. 11-2. Lt. Col. Roy S. "Jiggs" Geiger, Marine Aviator Number Five, took over as Group Commander of Aircraft One, Quantico, Virginia, on 1 June 1935. Geiger, like Turner, was a real promoter of Marine Aviation (courtesy Marine Corps).

Fig. 11-3. Douglas R2D-1 Transport of Utility Squadron VJ-6M at the Toronto Air Pageant (courtesy BGen. F.H. Wirsig).

Brown Field, orders were read officially transfering command of Aircraft One, Fleet Marine Force, Quantico, Virginia, to Lt. Col. Roy S. Geiger (Fig. 11-2). On this date he and Rowell were exchanging jobs. Geiger was pleased to be returning to Quantico. He missed flying to the shows with the squadrons. Rowell's appointment as the new Director of Marine Aviation brought a sigh of relief to some who were afraid an officer less sympathetic to aviation would get the appointment to the all-important post in Washington. Rowell was an all-out promoter of Marine Aviation and would, without doubt, see that the objectives set by Turner and Geiger were continued.

King's Jubilee in Toronto

The next show was scheduled for Toronto, Canada, on 15 June. Officially called the Toronto Air Pageant, it was to be the highlight of a week-long King's Jubilee celebration. The day before their departure they had a good practice session when an open house and airshow was staged at Brown Field for the Shriner's annual convention in Washington. This put unusual pressure on the enlisted men to make things ready for takeoff the following morning, but all station personnel pitched in to help.

Promptly at 0730 on 14 July, 19 F4B-4's and two transports (Fig. 11-3), under the command of Col. Geiger began their departure for Toronto. An enroute stop at Buffalo, New York, brought out a large crowd as their arrival had been announced on radio.

At 1100 the 21 airplanes left Buffalo for their final destination. As scheduled, the task force passed in review over downtown Toronto at noon as thousands looked skyward and waved (Fig. 11-4). Geiger then lead the planes to a landing at the Toronto Flying Club Field for public viewing.

What a welcome the Canadians gave the Marines! They were taken to the Royal York Hotel, the largest and finest in Canada, where they were housed in its best rooms. That evening Colonel Gieger and Captain Rogers were guest of a local broadcasting station. Each gave a short talk followed by a question-and-answer session.

A former crew chief, John E. Curtiss, had this to say about the city's hospitality:

"When we checked into our rooms, each man had a litre of cold 'City Club' beer. After dinner we had a wonderful evening on the town. I especially remember the Toronto policeman, who were something special to put up with us. One policeman, when we had to leave a pub at closing time, showed us an alley entrance so that we could re-enter and continue on into the wee-small hours in the morning. The next morning we knew *that* was a mistake."

The following day VF-9M performed before one of its most enthusiastic crowds. Faced with this and such generous hospitality the night before, Tex flew the longest continuous airshow ever performed by a squadron before the public. It included every known maneuver they had trained for—and a few they hadn't. It continued for more than an hour.

That evening all were invited by the Royal Canadian Air Force to a lavish banquet and dance at the Royal York. According to Tex, he had never attended a more elaborate affair.

Fig. 11-4. VF-9M flying over Toronto, Canada, on their arrival 14 July 1935. They were the main attraction at the Air Pageant (courtesy BGen. E.L. Pugh).

Fig. 11-5. Staff Sgt. Theodore A. "Pete" Petras, one of VF-9M's outstanding enlisted pilots (courtesy Col. T.A. Petras).

In view of the night before, it was indeed fortunate that the 21 airplanes finally got under way early the next afternoon. They arrived at Brown Field at 1730 hours.

On 20 July the Mayor of Toronto, the Honorable James Simpson, sent a letter to Major General Russell, Commandant of the Marine Corps, in connection with VF-9M's participation in the Toronto Air Pageant:

> *Dear General Russell:*
>
> *May I, on behalf of the citizens of Toronto, express to you, as Commandant of the United States Marine Corps, our thanks for permitting a detachment from your Corps to visit Toronto on the occasion of the Toronto Flying Club's sixth Annual Air Pageant.*
>
> *Many thousands of citizens viewed the breath-taking exhibition of aeronautics in which your splendid aviators played such a great part. The thrilling display of the Marines was of major importance and contributed very greatly to the success of the Pageant. The spontaneous outbursts of applause which greeted them was an indication of their popularity with the spectators. They conducted themselves magnificently both in the air and on the ground and thoroughly maintained the prestige of your service.*
>
> *Such friendly visits between the services of our respective countries do much to cement the goodwill and high regard which happily exists between us.*
>
> *Again, on behalf of the Toronto Flying Club and the citizens of Toronto, I express our appreciation for this goodwill visit.*
>
> *Yours Sincerely,*
> */s/ James Simpson*

Four new pilots (Fig. 11-5) joined the squadron in July and were progressing very well under the watchful eye of Frank Wirsig. Further, three second lieutenants from the reserves had joined and were doing an outstanding job. One of the reservists, Daniel W. Torrey, later became commanding officer of the squadron after the start of World War II.

At this time however, Lt. Ed Pugh, a six-year veteran of VF-9M, received orders transferring him to the west coast. Pugh, an outstanding fellow and pilot, was a great loss to the squadron. First Lieutenant Glen G. Herndon, who was Pugh's assistant, was named by Tex to become the engineering officer.

1935 National Air Races

The National Air Races were scheduled for 30 August through 2 September and VF-9M had accepted its standing invitation. A super show was planned in company with Observation Squadron VO-7M, who had received 16 new Vought 03U-6 airplanes to replace the colorful but aging Helldivers.

Little Brown Field was a busy place the last two weeks of August (Fig. 11-6). Wirsig had stepped up squadron operations from one to two full 18-plane formations daily. Capt. Byron F. Johnson, who took over command of VO-7M on 11 July from McKittrick, was in the air every day

Fig. 11-6. Loading practice bombs on F4B-4 number "21" (9241) at Brown Field in 1935. This is currently the only F4B-4 in existance. It is presently displayed in the NASM, Washington, D.C. (courtesy Marine Corps).

with a 12-plane formation familiarizing themselves with their new Vought Scout Bombers.

At 0730 on 29 August, VF-9M began its take-off roll on Brown Field with 18 F4B-4's for the world's greatest airshow (Fig. 11-7). Following closely behind with 13 Vought 03U-6's was VO-7M commanded by Captain Byron Johnson (Fig. 11-8). Numerous support aircraft had flown out earlier, including two large transports with VF-9M's crew chiefs and all necessary equipment and supplies. Col. Geiger, flying the spare F4B-4 for VF-9M, was in command of the entire task force.

The route was by way of Pittsburgh, where it was decided to make a stop because of weather. Departing after a brief lay-over, the two squadrons arrived at Cleveland before noon, where they flew in close formation over the city before landing at municipal airport.

Mr. W.S. Wilson and Mr. W.H. Martin, who were the appointed liaison officers for the Marines, were waiting to greet the two squadrons. They had been working for months securing first class hotel accommodations and transportation and making all other arrangements to insure that the Marines' stay was a pleasant one.

As usual, Cleveland opened its doors wide for the visiting Marines. Parties, banquets, dances, and all kinds of festivities were held each night over the entire city. However, after a few nights of this, it became boring, so a few broke away for a little bar hopping. Frank Wirsig recalls a humorous anecdote on a fellow pilot who was proceeding to get drunk and, for obvious reasons, must go unnamed.

"Several of us were out on the town and about 1 o'clock in the morning one of the pilots met a girl in a bar. A little while later he was heard to offer her five dollars to spend the night in his hotel room. That was a *lot* of money in those days so, after a short discussion, she agreed. He asked her to wait for him at the end of the bar while he went to get a bottle and a cab. Returning in a few minutes, he walked up to a girl at the end of the bar. Taking her by the arm, he said, 'Let's go, honey. I've got the booze and a cab.' Both disappeared through the door, heading for his hotel. The next night we returned to the same bar. Shortly after we sat down and ordered a drink, a girl came up to our fellow pilot with fire in her eyes and said: 'A hell of a damn Marine *you* are, you lousy bastard! I waited for you at the end of the bar for over an hour last night and you never came back. You S.O.B., you owe me the five dollars anyway for waiting so long! *He had taken the wrong girl*, one who had been waiting at the opposite end of the bar. With a puzzled look on his face, he took out his wallet, gave her the five dollars and said, 'Take it, honey. You wasn't any good anyway.'"

Opening day of the mammoth airshow was marred by low clouds, rain and haze. Many of the scheduled events were cancelled, including the Marine's show, so back to town for *another* night of fun!

Saturday dawned with greatly improved weather. Both squadrons took to the air at 1430 to dazzle the air-race fans with the Marines' brand of flying. The next three days they kept the audience gasping as Rogers and

Fig. 11-7. Formation on way to 1935 Cleveland Air Races. This formation was typical for cross country flying (courtesy Marine Corps).

Fig. 11-8. Joining VF-9M at the 1935 Cleveland Show was Squadron VO-7M, commanded by Capt. Byron F. Johnson, with its new Vought O3U-6 scout bombers (courtesy BGen. B.C. Batterton).

Johnson led their squadrons through beautiful maneuvers designed to impress audiences (Fig. 11-9). The *Cleveland Plain Dealer* summed up the Marine's three-day performance by saying: "The Marines gave a thrilling performance as usual, which bears out its slogan: 'The Marines have landed and the situation is well in hand.'"

Adverse weather conditions again moved over the Ohio Valley and the Cleveland area, grounding the Marines for two more days. Finally, on Thursday morning, 5 September, with hangovers and bloodshot eyes, the Corps' finest got under way for home. Approximately two hours' flying time from Cleveland, the task force caught up with the weather front that had plagued them for the previous two days. Geiger ordered all planes to turn back and land at Pittsburgh. The Pittsburgh Weather Bureau informed Geiger that the front streached from New York southward through Virginia and that Quantico would not improve for at least 24 hours. It was decided to stay overnight in Pittsburgh. Several members of VF-9M groaned and the consensus was that they didn't know if they could stand another night away from home. Tails were dragging and, worst of all, they were broke.

Recalling the stopover, ex-crew chief John Curtiss said, "We had a good time at Pittsburgh even if we were low on money. That evening after dinner several of us decided to pool our money for a bottle to take back to our hotel room. We stopped in a liquor store but were informed that they could not sell liquor by the bottle to anyone in uniform. We were shown a copy of the state law posted on the wall and, after reading it several time, we discovered that all other branches of service—soldiers, sailors, Coast Guard and National Guard—were spelled out but, there was no *specific* mention made of the *Marines*. This sort of perturbed the man but, after a little arguing, we got our bottle."

All planes touched down at Brown Field by noon the following morning (Fig. 11-10). Tex was preparing to leave for home when he was given a message to stop by Geiger's office. As he walked through the door, Geiger extended his hand and said, "Congratulation, Major Rogers. You have officially been promoted to the rank of Major as of 1 September." Tex had known for sometime that he was up for promotion, but was happy to hear it officially. Geiger also suggested to Tex that, as a major, he should try to improve his military appearance. Tex was known for his lack of military dress and disdain for most military regulations. Rusty Rowell had often shown disapproval of Tex's dress, especially when he appeared at staff meetings with his shirt open and necktie pulled down. He always promised to do better, but somehow never seemed to.

Retired Brigadier General B.C. Batterton said, "Tex was somewhat on the non-regulation side. He often wore any color socks or sweaters with his uniform that he wanted to. 'Course, this sometimes caused dismay

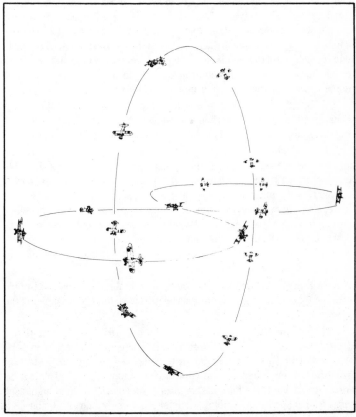

Fig. 11-9. VF-9M performed "loops through figure eight" with 18 F4B-4's (illustration by B.W. Campbell).

among superiors and the spit-and polish set, but Tex didn't seem to mind. He knew his job and knew it well. There wasn't anything the men wouldn't do for Tex. He had the loyalty of the squadron to the highest degree. He would stick his neck out all the way for anyone in his squadron, down to the lowest private, and fight to the last ditch for any promotions that he thought his outfit deserved. As a result of his action, you can see that he had the respect and trust of the squadron from top to bottom."

Reward for the Troops

On 14 September, Tex received an official letter from the Chief of Naval Operations that produced a big smile on his face and rejoicing by all in the squadron. It will be remembered that Tex was disappointed when they did not win the top spot while test-firing the new 50-caliber machine gun ammunition at Parris Island; however, this letter greatly reduced the pain. Paragraph One stated: "VF Squadron 9M is considered to have contributed to the advancement of the art of aircraft gunnery during the gunnery year 1934-1935. This decision is based upon the general excellence of the scores attained and of the new procedures established for combat." The crew enjoyed the last paragraph of the letter, which read: "In due recognition of the excellent work of the crew, the Commanding Officer of VF Squadron 9M is therefore authorized to pay prize money of five dollars each to the twenty-three members of the crew."

A letter of this sort from the Chief of Naval Operations was considered an honor. Remarked Roy Geiger, "It recognized the outstanding contribution that VF-9M made to Naval Aviation."

During September and October aerial gunnery flights were increased and the developed film from the camera guns showed a considerable increase in marksmanship. The pilots showed more aggressiveness during dogfights with other squadron members. The number of "kills" was increasing daily and rivalries began to develop among pilots and divisions within the squadron. Arguments sometimes broke out after gunnery practice as to "who killed who" and lasted until the film was developed and shown. It appeared that Tex was going to get his 15-percent increase in gunnery scores and possibly more.

As if the men didn't have anything to do in the day time, the Bureau ordered that night tactical operations be increased for the remainder of the year.

Night flying always brought many spectators to the field. The F4B-4's did not have landing lights but used magnesium flares. Metal shields were attached to the bottom side of the lower wings near the tips for protection from the burning flares. As the pilot made his approach for a landing, he would ignite one of the flares. This made a spectacular sight at night as it left a trail of sparks and smoke. Many of the flares would still be burning after landing. Brown Field being so small, the pilots had to keep taxiing around until the flares burned out to dispell any danger of setting the lower

Fig. 11-10. F4B-4's lined up on Brown Field for inspection. Section markings on engine cowls were used briefly to satisfy the Navy Brass (courtesy Marine Corps).

wings on fire. It looked like a huge Fouth of July display and contributed greatly to the after-dinner entertainment of the residents of Quantico.

On 15 October Colonel Geiger received a communication from the Chief of Naval Operations stating that VF-9M and one other squadron he might designate would again take part in the Navy war games in the Caribbean, scheduled to commence in early January. In view of this, Geiger notified Tex that the annual gunnery exercises planned for January and February were to moved up into November and December. Tex assured Geiger that his squadron would be ready anytime after the Washington Navy Day show on 27 October. Considering the gunnery scores obtained in the past few weeks with camera guns, he knew his pilots were ready.

The gunnery schedule and the Navy war games required that the men be away from home for approximately three months. Wives began to needle their husbands to take them along to Parris Island. Reminded that he had promised this earlier in the year, Tex, though somewhat doubtful, agreed that families who wanted could join their husbands there. This prompted eight of his pilots to ask permission to drive their families to Parris Island in their personnal cars. Tex agreed; he told them to go ahead and that he would find other pilots to fly their airplanes for them.

Chapter 12

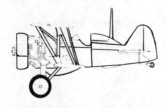

The Flying Country Club

At 1000 hours on 6 November, VF-9M made ready to depart Brown Field for Parris Island. Tex ordered there would be no formal take-off because of the eight inexperienced men he had obtained to replace his pilots. Not too much publicity had been created and he was confident they could leave unnoticed. After all, he reasoned, it wasn't necessary to look sharp just to leave Brown Field. What he *didn't* know was that he was setting the stage to receive from Geiger a wrath he would remember for some time.

Unbeknownst to Tex, several important members of the House Appropriations Committee for Naval Affairs were calling on the Commandant at Quantico. Because of their departure, VF-9M was unable to perform an airshow for these important visitors. However, Geiger invited them over to Brown Field to witness the squadron's takeoff. He assured them it would be beautiful to watch the Marine's finest roar down the small field in six-plane division formation. He further boasted that no other squadron did this on a daily basis from a field only 2400 feet long and less than 1000 feet wide.

Geiger and guests arrived just as most of the squadron airplanes were rolling to the north end of the field for take-off into the south. Tex pulled over to the northwest edge of the field and gave the signal to follow at will. As he roared down the field, his two wingmen were in fairly close; however, those that followed were in any and all positions and directions as they rolled down the field.

Geiger watched with disbelief. He just could not believe this was "the show squadron of Marine Aviation," his pride and joy, bouncing down the field like a bunch of student pilots. He was sure there would be a collision before all could get off the ground. To say that he was speechless was surely an understatement. After making an excuse to his visitors, Geiger quickly summoned his aide to find out—"what in hell is going on around here," and to send a telegram to Fort Bragg, the squadron's first stop enroute.

Tex in Trouble

By the time Tex arrived at the Fort Bragg airfield, his squadron was looking pretty good. The new men were fast learners. While the planes were being refueled, Tex went to operations to file an arrival report to Brown Field. As he entered the office, the duty sergeant handed him a telegram from Quantico.

> To: Major F.O. Rogers, Ex-Commanding Officer VF Squadron 9M.
>
> I'll get you for this if it's the last thing I do.
>
> (signed) Geiger.

Tex knew he was in trouble. He *especially* didn't like the wording "*Ex*-Commanding Officer." However he said nothing to his men. The flight continued to Parris Island, arriving there at 1630.

After a formal welcome by the Commanding General of Parris Island, he was handed another telegram from Quantico by the general's aide.

> To: Major F.O. Rogers: Commanding Officer of VF Squadron 9M.
>
> Demand an explanation by telephone immediately! It damn well better be good.
>
> (signed) Geiger.

After giving Geiger plenty of time to cool down, Tex called and explained exactly what had happened and the reason for the sloppy take-off. Geiger replied, "You have put me in a *very* embarrassing position and it had better *never* happen again."

Several days later, Geiger sent a formal apology to the congressmen with an explanation as outlined by Tex. They thought it very humorous, expressed concern that Major Rogers might be reprimanded and suggested that he be commended for the importance he attached to the families of his men.

"Boy, did I get out of *that* one," remarked Major General Rogers. "I had met most of the congressmen on that committee at one time or another when I was a staff officer at Marine Corps Headquarters in Washington, back in 1929. Two weeks later, Geiger came down to Parris Island to see how we were doing, and after seeing our gunnery scores, he was in a big way and laughed about what happened. It was never mentioned again."

Everyone in the squadron was elated about the scores. Tex knew they were on their way to receiving the top gunnery award. Pilots like Glen Herndon, Frank Schwable, Pete Petras and Cracker Williams just couldn't miss.

On Thursday, 5 December, the squadron left sunny Parris Island (Fig. 12-1) for home. Rusty Rowell flew down from Washington to greet

Fig. 12-1. Page Field, Parris Island, South Carolina. All Quantico Squadrons conducted gunnery exercises here after 1934. Dirigible mooring circle can be seen in upper center (courtesy Marine Corps).

the returning flyers and to inform them their gunnery scores were, so far, the highest of any squadron.

On 20 December, VF-9M closed down flying operations for the year and there was no doubt that a new squadron record had been established. A total of 8,640 flying hours were accumulated for the year, making it the busiest fighter squadron in Marine history. Asked to comment on this, Major General "Tex" Rogers said:

"In 1935 my squadron accomplished one of the biggest work loads in history. As I remember, we set a record by performing at more than 20 airshows in the United States and Canada. This alone was an onerous chore. Only retired senior aviators from those days can appreciate the long hours that the squadron spent flying in all kinds of weather and in open-cockpit airplanes which had no navigation equipment to speak of. In most instances we spent days enroute to and from our destination. We did this in addition to carrying out our military duties. Believe me, it could get damn cold up there.

"As far as I'm concerned, I had the best men in aviation. They were a rugged group—the cream of the crop. My operations officer, Frank Wirsig, was the best instructor that I have ever seen in my life. He sure put the finishing touch to all the pilots like no one else could. When Frank said a man was ready to fly any position within the squadron, why, he sure as hell *was*. Frank was an expert and he was patient, which was more than I could have been. We were indeed fortunate to have him."

Only Athletes Need Apply

Due to VF-9M's success and popularity, many pilots within the Marines were constantly trying to get assigned to it. It was considered the ultimate in one's career, and a major stepping stone to future assignments and promotions. Very few, however, had the qualifications demanded by Tex or were able to pass the severe tests that were required. Those that made the grade considered themselves very fortunate, and to those on the outside looking in, they were the elite of Marine Aviation. Tex had one qualification that he considered of prime importance. Each man, in addition to being an excellent pilot, had to possess a better-than-average background in a competitive sport. Tex, himself an outstanding athlete and polo player, knew that anyone with a background in sports such as football, baseball, or basketball had the extra stamina, the better sense of timing and the greater love of teamwork so necessary to this type of flying. It has been said that during the years that he was commanding officer, no greater array of athletes was ever banded together in one squadron.

"All my pilots were experts in some kind of competitive sport," remarked General Rogers. "One man in particular was Staff Sergeant Theodore A. 'Pete' Petras. He was one of the finest natural athletes that I have ever known. He was fantastic. He was a one-man tackle team, an excellent baseball and polo player, a top wrestler and just about anything else you can name. And he always stood at the top in all squadron activities. And with it all, he had such a wonderful personality that in later years, Admiral Byrd and three former Commandants of the Marine Corps selected him as their personal pilot. Incidently, he won his wings while still a private!"

In the meantime, the world's only 18-plane stunt team was beginning to acquire another kind of reputation. Within the military services it was said that they did not care about rules and regulations, did not practice good military conduct and more or less did as it pleased. Many spit-and-polish Navy and Marine Commanders were irked at VF-9M's seemingly non-regulation status, and at times they openly made sarcastic remarks using names such as; "Roger's Flying Circus," and the "Civilian Air Force." At a high-level staff meeting, when the subject of aviation came up, one ground general refered to VF-9M as "Rogers' Rogues." Many other names were coined for the squadron but one name—"The Flying Country Club"—was enjoyed by the whole squadron and many of the oldtimers still refer to it by that name.

To a certain extent, many of the allegations were true. In all fairness it must be remembered that VF-9M was constantly on the move and dealing with the public. It would have been impossible to accomplish and contain such intensive activity within strict military regulations. On many occasions it became necessary to bend regulations somewhat, to meet the squadron needs or circumstances at the time. As history bears out, fame has always had its critics and VF-9M was no exception.

Caribbean War Games

On 6 January 1936, squadron personnel were back on the job and making preparations to take part in the Naval War Games then getting underway in the Caribbean. As the squadron would be absent for approximately 40 days, all previous commitments for airshows were cancelled for the next two months. The men were looking forward to the trip, with its warm weather and good times, so, Col. Geiger planned to leave at the earliest possible date so there would be time to rest and relax along the way and after arrival.

On 10 January the task force of 37 airplanes got under way at 0900 on the first leg of the Trip. First to take off was VF-9M, with 19 Boeing F4B-4's, followed by the newly formed Bombing Squadron Six (VB-6M), with 12 Great Lakes BG-1 Dire Bombers commanded by Capt. William J. Wallace. Last to depart was Utility Squadron Six, (VJ-6M) commanded by Capt. Schilt, with three large transports and two small airplanes to support the task force. Geiger was flying the spare dive bomber for VB-6M.

After lunching and refueling at Fort Bragg, the task force arrived at Jacksonville, where it remained an extra day because of weather.

On 12 January , all arrived in Miami, which once again played host to the "best damn squadron in the world." They had such a good time it was two days before Geiger could get all his Marines together to continue the trip.

Departing Opa-Locka Naval Air Station at 0930 on 14 January, the task force headed out over the Caribbean for Cuba.

"After leaving Miami, we stopped at Moron, Cuba, for fuel and a nice big drink of water to put out the fire after our escapades in Miami," recalls Brigadier General Frank Schwable. "Shortly after takeoff for Guantanamo, we settled down to a nice wide, open cruising formation to admire the beautiful, clear, peaceful day that nature had given the Caribbean. The monotony of flying straight and level all but put us to sleep. I was flying tail-end Charlie and could see the whole squadron ahead. Suddenly, without warning or apparent cause, one plane in the squadron began to go through all kinds of maneuvers—rolls, split S's and violent yaws. This continued for what seemed a long time; however, I guess it was only a few minutes. Then all quieted down and settled back to normal. Looking ahead, I determined the pilot of the plane was Frank Wirsig. Not wanting to ask questions by radio, no one said a word.

"After our arrival at Guantanamo we got the explanation. Frank was cruising along about half asleep, enjoying the beautiful scenery, same as the rest of us, when he happened to look down in the cockpit and saw a pair of eyes staring back at him from between the rudder pedals. Well you can't have passengers in a single-seater airplane, so this one had to go. First Frank had tried to stomp on that—whatever it was—with one foot, naturally starting the airplane into a violent yaw as, in the excitement, his other foot was still pushing on the opposite rudder pedal. Then a shift of feet, and the whole process would repeat itself; then a slow roll to try and drop it out, etc. As I said before, the answer was simple. Someone had put a frog in Frank's airplane as a joke. But who knows *what* might have joined you in a strange Cuban field?"

On the 15th, the task force left Guantanamo for San Juan, Puerto Rico, with stops enroute in Port-au-Prince, Haiti, and Santo Domingo, Dominican Republic. The flight was uneventful and total flight time was 5 hours and 45 minutes.

The Marines received a rousing welcome at San Juan, where they were greeted by the governor. After brief ceremonies, everyone was invited to a night on the town. It was dangerous to drink water in the islands. Most of the pilots supported this idea and did their best to subsist on beer and rum.

Life on a Golf Course

Leaving the task force at San Juan, VF-9M got underway to Charlotte Amalie, on the island of St. Thomas. There was no airport on St. Thomas; only an official landing area at the Charlotte Amalie golf course, where a new airport was under construction (Fig. 12-2). Arriving over the area at noon, Tex instructed his pilots to land single file on the north-south

Fig. 12-2. Golf Course at Charlotte Amalie, St. Thomas, V.I., that squadrons used during the 1936 Navy-Marine Maneuvers. Planes landed uphill; took off downhill (courtesy BGen. B.C. Batterton).

Fig. 12-3. Squadron VO-7M on golf course (Camp Bourne) during 1936 maneuvers (courtesy U.S. Navy).

fairway, the only landing area open. This fairway was not level, so all takeoffs, formation or otherwise, were made to the south towards the bay, which was downhill; all landings were made uphill to the north, towards the mountains. For the next 30 days, all VF-9M's operations were conducted from this golf course. The small landing and takeoff area didn't bother the Marines. Flying from Brown Field was almost as difficult and often more dangerous because of the mud.

Observation Squadron Nine (VO-9M) also operating from the golf course with its nine planes, had a radio command station set up to receive messages during the war games (Fig. 12-3). VF-9M's orders were to stand by until further notice.

At their arrival, all Marine aircraft were now deployed as directed. A message was sent by the Brigade Commander aboard the battleship *Uss Arkansas* to the Commanding General, Fleet Marine Force, on board the battleship *USS Wyoming*: "All airplanes of Aircraft One have arrived after a very successful and expeditial flight and are ready for service in good shape."

For three days things were quiet. The airplanes were washed down and made ready to go on a moment's notice; the nights were used to keep the island's bars and rum distilleries in business.

On 20 January the squadron came alive. An unconfirmed report was received that the enemy was within striking distance of the Virgin Islands. Tex dispatched two of his divisions as separate scouting forces and the third was sent to the island of Culebra to act as aerial scouts and help to defend it in case of an attack. The Red Fleet was not sighted. Several landing and aerial exercises were conducted by the Navy to smooth out any rough edges during the remaining days of the war games.

Bombing Squadron VB-6M flew over from San Juan on 27 January, to join VF-9M in dedicating a new landing field at Christiansted, on the island of St. Croix (Fig. 12-4). All Marines were given a feast along with a complete tour of the island. The ceremonies were closes with an aerial review and a show by Tex and his squadron.

In the next two weeks, 336 squadron hours were flown in defense of the islands and support of troop landings (Figs. 12-5, 12-6). Attempts were made by the Red Fleet to put troops ashore on several islands but all were repulsed. Most of the enemy ships were deemed "sunk" by Navy and Marine battle observers. The battles seemed almost real, as this was the first time that live bombs of any size were used. The enemy had to withdraw to lick its wounds and a truce was called while the war planners went back to the drawing board.

Fig. 12-4. Squadrons VF-9M and VB-6M dedicated new landing field at Christiansted, on the island of St. Croix, V.I. on 27 January 1936 (courtesy Marine Corps).

Fig. 12-5. Landing Field on island of Culebra. During 1936 maneuvers, several VF-9M planes operated as aerial scouts from this field (courtesy U.S. Navy).

During the truce, a large celebration was held on 8 February to thank to the people of San Juan for being such wonderful hosts to the Navy and Marines. At the governor's request, Tex brought his squadron from St. Thomas to put on its "famous show" as it had the year before.

As expected, VF-9M completely captivated its audience at San Juan. During the "finale," the Squirrel Cage, Tex looked up from the bottom of a loop just in time to see plane No. 6 flip out of position at the top of a slow loop, then spin downward, completing a two-turn spin and narrowly missing another airplane before recovering. As will be remembered, Sanderson barely cheated death when he and Brice collided after a similar event at the Cleveland Air Races in 1931. Tex was boiling mad and quickly gave the command to end the show. The pilot in question was 1st Lt. R. B. Burchard. He was one of the reserve Marines who had flown with VF-9M many times under Sanderson and was a highly competent pilot.

Later landing, Tex quickly walked over to find out what happened. Burchard, looking sheepish, admitted that he had—among other things—a case of whisky stowed in the headrest compartment back of the cockpit. The extra weight was just enough to move the CG (center of gravity) to the rear, causing his airplane to easily stall and spin. He apologized and assured Tex that it would never happen again. Tex remarked, "I know *damn well* it won't."

In the early morning of 13 February VF-9M made its last tactical flight in the war games and was officially released from any further duty at noon. A radio message from Geiger in the early afternoon ordered that preparations be made to leave for home the following day. Though some of the men were beginning to show signs of homesickness, most agreed they had enjoyed the past month in the islands, with its beautiful weather (Fig. 12-7). In the words of one former squadron member, Brig. Gen. Edward A. Montgomery, "We really had it rough during our stay on St. Thomas. While the airport was under construction, we used one of the fairways of the St. Thomas golf course as our landing strip and used the club house as our operations shack and living quarters. Probably the only thing that kept life from becoming unbearable was a beautiful 50-gallon piece of 'antique furniture'—sometimes known as a rum barrel—which was mysteriously kept filled by a St. Thomas friend of the squadron. There was no conflict of interest here, but of course his establishment in downtown Charlotte Amalie enjoyed the patronage of the drinking brethren amongst us. As you can see, maneuvers in the Caribbean were pretty rugged affairs in those days, especially for us aviators."

Several of the men wanted one last fling in town before leaving for home. Jocko McQuade, up to his usual tricks, was the center of attraction at one bar and tried to provoke a fight with everyone he met. A few of the

Fig. 12-6. Squadron VO-7M flying over the *USS Arkansas* during the 1936 Caribbean Maneuvers. Culebra Island can be seen in the background (courtesy Marine Corps).

Fig. 12-7. Lt. Dan Torrey's #14 flipped over during landing on golf course at St. Thomas, 21 January 1936 (courtesy BGen. D.W. Torrey).

enlisted men, who were feeling no pain themselves, loaded him on a truck and drove him back to the field amidst some very salty language and his shouts: "I can whip anybody in the whole damn Marine Corps and maybe the whole world!"

This was just too good for a few of the men to pass up. Several began taunting McQuade with, "Bet you can't lick Pete Petras." "Hell, I can take him with one arm tied behind my back," shouted McQuade. After bets were made all around, the whole gang went to the tent where Petras was sleeping. Sticking his head in, McQuade said, "Get the hell out of that bed, Pete. I'm going to give you something you'll always remember." After trying unsuccessfully to calm down McQuade, Petras, still half asleep, finally got out of bed and said, "Well, if I can't talk you out of this, what will it be—wrestling, fists, or a duel with guns?"

"Don't be funny," said McQuade. "You're supposed to be a good wrestler, I'll show you a thing or two." Before McQuade knew what was happening, Petras picked him up and threw him over his shoulder, McQuade making a big thud when he hit the ground. Petras then calmly got back into bed.

McQuade, shaking his head a few times, pulled himself up and said, "Dammit Pete, you were just lucky that time. You caught me off balance. You can't do it again. Now get out of that bed and *fight like a man!*" Seeing there was just no way to calm McQuade, Petras got out of bed again and repeated the performance two more times. Suddenly, the enlisted men scattered faster than customers in a bawdy house police raid as Master Sergeant Morris Kurtz appeared. Taking McQuade by the arm, he politely but firmly escorted him to his bunk, where several of his buddies took over. Needless to say, the next day McQuade received a stern lecture, headache and all, about fighting. This was an absolute no-no with Tex. It was learned later that Sergeant Kurtz, who ruled his men with an iron hand, took care of McQuade's agitaters.

Corporal Brucci Races the Wyoming

At 0900 on 14 February, VF-9M took off from the golf course airstrip on St. Thomas to join the Bombing Squadron at San Juan an remain there overnight. The task force was to leave for Port-au-Prince by way of Santo Domingo the following day, and personnel not leaving St. Thomas with the squadron were to return to Quantico aboard the battleship *Wyoming,* anchored off the island of Culebra. However, to get to the *Wyoming* it was necessary to board the Coast Guard cutter *Woodcock* at 0700 hours. All were on board at the scheduled sailing time except Corporal Eugene J. Bracci. The ship's skipper was persuaded to wait until 0730 for him. Recalling the incident, Capt. Richard E. Gilmore, a former crew chief, said:

"The *Woodcock* cast off at exactly 0730. After we got underway and were about 500 yards from the dock, we looked back and there was Corporal Bracci waving his arms; however, we had to keep going to make the *Wyoming* on schedule.

"The Marines on board the *Wyoming* were commanded by a very tough officer and all hands, including the ship's crew, were lined up for inspection. We in VF-9M made it too late to participate in the inspection, so we were ordered to sit aft by a barbette until it was over. While waiting for the captain and the colonel to appear, everyone was standing at ease. Soon we noticed a small dot bobbing in the waves a couple of miles astern. As we watched, we could see it was coming our way. Soon it was close enough for us to recognize Corporal Bracci. He was sitting in an 8-foot rowboat with the blackest Negro you ever saw doing the rowing.

"Bracci was sitting in the stern of the boat with his arms folded, his overseas cap on the back of his head, the knot of his field scarf under one side of his collar, and he was grinning from ear to ear. As he bounded up the gangplank, the Officer of the Deck hurried over and demanded, 'Who are you, where did you come from and state your presence here?'

Bracci just said, politely, 'Request permission to come aboard, sir.'

Before the OOD could answer, Bracci saluted, knocking his cap off, but retrieved it quickly with his left hand behind him. He gave the officer a big grin, and quickly walked over and sat down with us. While this was taking place, the colonel and the ship's captain had walked out on the deck and viewed Bracci's unusual arrival. Both had considerable trouble keeping a straight face. All the Marines and ship's crew were about ready to burst with laughter but were afraid of receiving a reprimand. The junior officers began shouting 'attention' to settle the men down. When the colonel ordered Bracci to go below and prepare a statement, we knew he was in trouble."

After inspection, Bracci was called to the captain's quarters, where he and the colonel were waiting. When asked if he had prepared a statement, Bracci replied, "Yes, *sir!*" and handed the colonel a folded piece of paper. Bracci was ordered to stand at ease. Both officers read the statement but managed to contain themselves.

After a conversation in low tones the colonel spoke. "We will take your statement under advisement. You are excused." After Bracci disappeared through the door, both officers laughed aloud. After a minute or so the captain said, "He's a Marine. What do you recommend?"

"To hell with it," replied the colonel. The captain agreed, ripped the statement up and tossed it in the waste basket.

Incidently, the statement read:

Dear Sir:

I attended a rum-swizzle party because it was our last night here. The taxi driver and I stopped on the way back and took a little nap. That is the reason I missed the tug. Then, not having any more money, I bummed a ride in the rumble seat of an old car to the St. Thomas airfield and from there a pilot flew me to Culebra in the rear seat of an airplane. At Culebra, Sergeant Jake Bealer loaned me a horse and I rode it to the dock and a native rowed me out here in a boat. Thats all I've got to say.

/s/E.J. Bracci

The task force of 37 airplanes began their departure from San Juan at 0930 on 15 February for Port-au-Prince where they remained there overnight.

The following morning they commenced their flyaway at 1000. Climbing to 6,000 feet, Tex ordered his formation to loosen up; he knew several were not feeling too well from their night out on the town. It was decided to stay overnight at Moron, Cuba and proceed to Miami the following day. Flying time was 3 hours 54 minutes.

The Miami news on the 17th reported the arrival time of the task force, and a sizeable crowd was on hand at Opa-Locka to greet the fliers. Because of the festivities planned for them, Geiger agreed to stay an extra day. Of course, Miami had always commanded at least a one-day layover in the past.

The Colonel was proud of his boys in Miami. All managed to stay out of too much trouble, and on the morning of departure, all showed up at the air station on time, several chauffeured by new—found young ladies. Warned of an impending storm in northern Florida, he decided the task force could make it to Jacksonville and began take-off at 0930 hours.

As predicted, severe thunderstorms terminated the day's flying and all landed at Jacksonville for the night.

The task force left Jacksonville at 0800 the following morning. Bucking strong headwinds, they landed at Ft. Bragg at 1100 for lunch and fuel. After a forty-day absence from home, Geiger knew there would be a sizable crowd awaiting their arrival, so before departing Ft. Bragg, he outlined the formation he wanted for their fly-over of Brown Field. Approximately 10 minutes south of Quantico the three squadron assembled as ordered.

At Brown Field a welcome committee of approximately 1,000 people awaited their arrival. Among those present were Major General Charles F. Lyman, Commanding General of Quantico, Colonel Rowell, several

Fig. 12-8. Maj. Gen. Charles H. Lyman, Commanding Officer at Quantico, (left) greeting Col. Geiger on his return from maneuvers 20 February 1936 (courtesy BGen. F.H. Wirsig).

congressmen, radio and newspaper reporters. The rest was made up of families of the men, friends and persons interested in Marine Corps activities.

At 1500 the five-plane formation of Utility Squadron VJ-6M flew over Brown Field in a perfect "Vee" formation, with the old Ford Trimoter in the lead flanked by the two Douglas R2D-1 transports with a Vought SU-1 and a Grumman JF-2 on the left and right side respectively.

Less than one minute behind came Bombing Squadron Six in a 12-plane diamond formation, followed by VF-9M in three six-plane divisions. All were pulled in tight parade formation. While the three squadrons were landing, the Marine Band played the *Marine Hymn*. When all engines were shut down, General Lyman conducted the brief welcoming ceremonies (Fig. 12-8). As he spoke his last word, the field guards no longer tried to restrain the crowd and the flyers were engulfed by families and friends. It was good to be home after 40 days (Fig. 12-9).

Heavy rains decended on Brown Field during March and April, hampering flying operations for days at a time. However, the time wasn't wasted. It was a good time to catch up on ground work. Complete overhaul of airplanes and engines of the F4B-4's was accomplished. Tex encouraged all who wanted to take a vacation to do so during this period. The annual bombing exercises were scheduled to start as soon as field conditions permitted and he wanted every pilot to be rested and sharp.

This time was also used by the homebrew-and-booze experts to distill a new supply of the bubbly liquid for the drinking brethren. This was also an important squadron function. Sergeant John Curtiss describes a real windfall that came his way during this time.

"I sent one of the privates working for me to get some paint thinner. He returned with a 10-gallon can of grain alcohol. Well, this was just to good to be true. I re-distilled it, put in some of my secret additives to make it taste like rum and sold the stuff for $1.50 a pint. I made over $100 on the deal. That was real money then."

On 10 March, the Commandant of the Marine Corps, Major General John H. Russell, sent a letter to Colonel Geiger, commending his squadrons for their performance during the war games. Paragraphs three and four of the letter read as follows:

Fighting Squadron Nine-M is to be congratulated for its exceptional performance during the war games just completed. In addition to its excellent air support and search missions, it is commended for its outstanding tactical support of troop landings and extraordinary skillful flying while neutralizing targets, using both machine guns and bomb.

"This aerial operation was a manifestation of high efficiency and devotion to duty on the part of each officer and enlisted man. Therefore I, as Commandant, take great pleasure in extending a well-merited commendation to each of them. A copy of this letter will be attached to the service record of all personnel concerned."

Fig. 12-9. Capt. Vernon E. "Simon Legree" Megee, Executive Officer of VF-9M (courtesy Gen. V.E. Megee).

New Status

On 1 April Marine Aviation gained further recognition within the Navy Department. The previous Marine Corps Aviation Section under the Commandant was elevated to Division status and the title Officer-in-Charge of Marine Aviation became the Director of Marine Aviation. Colonel Ross E. Rowell, who held the old title, moved into the new position, serving in a dual capacity of advisor to the Commandant on aviation matters and head of the Marine Corps organization in the Navy Bureau of Aeronautics. This was another step in the right direction. Just 11 years previously, Marine Aviation had not appeared anywhere in the aviation organization of the Navy.

All were looking forward to the annual bombing practice that got underway on 14 April at Brown Field. Floating targets for the 100-pound, water-filled bombs were erected and achored 1,000 yards off-shore in the Potomac River. Referees and repair crew waited nearby in motor launches to tabulate scores and, if necessary repair the targets for the next planes. Several hundred people lined the river banks each day to watch the big water splashes and to bet on their favorite pilots.

The dive-bombing segment was conducted on the southwest edge of Brown Field with small, three pound bombs containing a shotgun type in the nose. On the ground was a 50-foot diameter circular target containing several smaller circles and a five-foot solid center. It was simular to a handgun target except, of course, for its size. The referee and scorekeeper ran out after each dive-bombing run and inserted colored pegs with the corresponding airplane numbers on them into the small holes produced by the bombs. As one scorekeeper remarked: "Sometimes it could get a little hazardous out there if the planes followed each other too close. I could hear the next plane making its dive before I was out of the target area."

On 22 May, an official letter to Tex Rogers from the Chief of Naval Operations was cause for a great deal of pleasure.

NAVY DEPARTMENT
Washington, D. C.

20 May 1936

From: Chief of Naval Operations
To: Commanding Officer VF-9M
Subj: Gunnery and Bombing Standings 1935-1936
1. Fighting Squadron Nine-M is to be congratulated for standing Number One in the Naval service in both gunnery and bombing for the 1935-1936 competition. The fact that no other squadron in Naval service received a merit equal to ninty-five percent of VF-9M's score is ample testimony of the excellence of personnel and its traning methods and of the fine team work and spirit of the entire squadron.
2. The Navy Department and the Marine Corps take great pride in having one of its organizations so highly honored and the Comman-dant, along with myself, extends heartiest congradulations.
/s/ D. F. Sellers

Tex immediately assembled the squadron and read the letter to them. However, news has a way of traveling. In less time than it takes to say "scuttlebutt," everyone knew what was in the letter before he read it. It was the first time the squadron had won both categories in the same year.

Enlisted men were especially happy as it meant prize money. After cheering and handshakes all around, Tex warned again that being the top squadron could have its drawbacks, too. "When you are on top the going really gets rough. There's no place else to go but down."

Tex was extremely proud of every man in the squadron. Men such as Frank Wirsig, Glenn Herndon, Jack McQuade, Frank Schwable and Dan Torrey had been with the squadron for several years and were its mainstay; also, enlisted pilots Irv Masters, Charlie Campbell, Bobby Roberts and Cracker Williams just could not be replaced. These men had come into the squadron under Sanderson and knew its operation well. Said Brigadier General Batterton: "We had a wonderful group of enlisted men—both pilots and crew chiefs—in the squadron, who were the backbone of Marine Aviation. Without them there is no way we could have stood number one for so many years. I remember when I joined the squadron, Tex appointed me as engineering officer, but he also said that our Line Chief, Master Sergeant Morris Kurtz, was the boss and that all I had to do was to sign my name on any reports when Sergeant Kurtz asked me to. If I hadn't, I would have been in trouble. This Kurtz was a real Marine Sergeant; a leader, if I ever saw one. He was quiet-spoken, very respectful, but his word was law among the enlisted men in the squadron, because he could back up any order he gave with his fists if it ever became necessary."

Brigadier General Wirsig also had glowing praise for the enlisted men in the squadron. "There are many things that could and should be said about Master Sergeant Morris Kurtz and the wonderful men he had under

Fig. 12-10. Preparing for inspection of the squadrons at Brown Field in July 1936 (courtesy Marine Corps).

Fig. 12-11. The staff of Aircraft One, Fleet Marine Force, Quantico, Virginia, in July 1936. Left/right: Maj. H.A. Carr; Capt. William P. "Pat" Kelley; Lt. Col. Francis P. "Pat" Mulcahy; Capt. John C. "Toby" Munn; Lt. Col. Roy S. "Jiggs" Geiger, the Commanding Officer; Lt. J.G. Wright, USN, Medical Corps; Maj. Claude A. "Sheriff" Larkin; Capt. William L. "Mac" McKittrick; Capt. Stanley E. Ridderhof; Capt. Harold R. "Bob" Lee (courtesy Marine Corps).

him. Those men really knew what made an airplane run. When we asked for 18 planes or more on the line, which was practically everyday, there were always 18 or more ready—even if it meant working all night (Fig. 12-10). In the seven years that I was with the squadron we did not have a court martial or a man in the brig. I'm damn sure no other squadron can equal that record."

Fighting Squadron Nine had surely been doing its promotional job well. It was the undisputed show squadron of Naval and Marine Aviation. Through its efforts, all operational squadrons within the Corps were flying the newest aircraft available with more new ones on the way. No longer did the Navy pass down to the Marines its old and worn-out airplanes. Now, in most instances, Marine squadrons received delivery of new aircraft direct from the factory. Things had changed considerably during the previous five years. Colonels Rowell and Geiger (Fig. 12-11) could see the rewards of their efforts.

However, at this time there was pressure building within the Navy Bureau for the Marines to back off in the promotion of their aviation branch. Several were sure the Navy's position was being threatened by the

Marines. To the surprise of all concerned, Rear Admiral King, the Navy Bureau's tough chief, let it be known that he admired anyone who seized the initiative with gusto as the Marines had and suggested that anyone so inclined to think otherwise should tend to his own knitting. The matter was dropped. Of course, it can be said that the Admiral was a good politician. Any thought of putting the Marines down at this time could have produced far—reaching and unwanted consequences. Many congressmen and senators who chaired committees and voted on military appropriation bills personally knew most Marine Aviators. They had watched with awe numerous performances of VF-9M at both civil and military functions and knew the pride that the American people had in the United States Marines. And, too, it was they who often motored to Quantico when they wanted to impress visiting dignitaries, especially heads of State from foreign countries. If a tour of Washington and other places in the United States didn't impress them, a tour of Quantico and an airshow at Brown Field certainly did.

Actually the Marines' publicity campaign had helped the Navy equally well and Admiral King was very much aware of this. Congress recently had voted increased appropriations for several new aircraft carriers and new airplanes to staff them. So, for the time being, VF-9M could continue its promotion of Marine Aviation and anything else it wanted to do.

Fig. 12-12. Major damage to #22 when pilot Lt. Lyle H. Meyer was momentarily blinded by floodlight during night landing practice on 20 July 1936 (courtesy Marine Corps).

Fig. 12-13. Eight of many enlisted pilots that served with VF-9M over the years. Left/right: Sergeants Harold R. Jordan; Neal G. "Cracker" Williams; Irvin V. Masters; Robert E.A. "Bob" Lillie; John S. Carter; Harry L. "Doc" Blackwell; Gordon W. Heritage; Fred H. Smith. Highly respected, NAP's were the backbone of Marine Aviation and stood at the top in all squadron activities (courtesy Col. H.R. Jordan).

Requests continued to pour into Quantico and Marine Headquarters from throughout the U.S. for VF-9M to perform at shows. However, since the squadron's return from maneuvers it had been busily engaged in advance training designed to deep it the Number One squadron in Marine Aviation. Further, the Navy Bureau of Aeronautics, looking for specialists to evaluate the merits of two important research projects, assigned them to VF-9M. One of the projects was the testing of air-to-air bombing using specially timed live bombs. This proved very ineffective in actual practice and the project was cancelled.

The second project was an extensive weather-flying program in which they were to fly every day possible in all types of weather. This was an important project to the Navy and required the utmost in flying skill. The latest radio equipment was installed in several of the Boeings and hundreds of hours were logged in both day and night "over-the-top" instrument flying in the testing and prove—out of this new equipment (Fig. 12-12). On the basis of the squadron's findings several new basic navigation and instrument let-down procedures were established and later used by the military to advantage in World War II.

176

In addition to these projects, the squadron continued with its regular training in bombing and gunnery, and when time permitted, worked on refinements for its airshows. The very nature of its activities also set it aside as the number one training squadron in fighter tactics.

Because of a modest expansion of Marine Aviation underway at this time, there was a continuing flow of young cadets and reserve pilots assigned to the squadron for short periods of training. Even though this was an added burden on all, especially Frank Wirsig, it provided a valuable service to the squadron. Tex Rogers had an understanding with Headquarters that any of the young pilots demonstrating outstanding flying quality and meeting all other requirements, especially the ability to get along with other people, could join the squadron on a permanent basis if he so desired. This was one way to assure that replacement pilots were of the highest caliber, thus maintaining the squadron's reputation and degree of readiness at all times. (Fig. 12-13, 12-14).

On 1 July, Captain Jack McQuade, First Lieutenants Raymond Hopper, Edward Montgomery, Glenn Herndon, Frank Schwable and Sergeant Irvin Masters were transferred to other commands. These men

Fig. 12-14. Pilot roster of VF-9M on 1 August 1936. Left/right: 1st Lts. Edward B. Carney; Gordan H. Knott; Carl W. Nelson; Capts. Boeker C. Batterton; Frank G. Dailey; Maj. Ford O. Rogers, (C.O.); Captain Frank H. Wirsig; 1st Lts. Carson A. Roberts; Robert R. Porter and Daniel W. Torrey. Standing left/right: Sgt. Theodore A. Petras; 2nd Lt. Pelham B. Withers; 1st Lt. Lyle H. Meyer; Tech. Sgt. Lee E. Roberts; 1st Lt. William K. Pottinger; and Master Sgt. Charles C. Campbell (courtesy Marine Corps).

Fig. 12-15. Office of Aircraft One, Fleet Marine Force, at Brown Field (courtesy Marine Corps).

were outstanding pilots, and always stood at the top in all squadron activities and would be hard to replace. Their departure certainly was not of their own choosing. Tex did his best to block their transfer but was overruled by Headquarters (Fig. 12-15). Each felt sorrow at leaving "Rogers' Rogues."

Chapter 13

The Saratoga Caper

For some time, it had been the wish of Colonels Rowell and Geiger that all Marine Aviators be qualified for aircraft carrier operations. This wish was also shared by Rear Admiral Arthur B. Cook, the new Chief of the Bureau of Aeronautics, who replaced Rear Admiral King on 12 June, 1936. Many of the Marine Aviators on the West Coast were so qualified, and two small Marine Scouting Squadrons (VS-14M and VS-15M) were based aboard the carriers *Saratoga* and *Lexington* from 2 November 1931 until 14 November 1934. By 1936, approximately 60 of the Marine's 145 aviators were carrier qualified.

In October, it was learned that, starting in February, 1937, the Navy would hold the largest fleet maneuvers ever undertaken. They were to be held in the Pacific and VF-9M, along with several other Marine squadrons, was to fly in the West Coast and take part. Again Rowell and Geiger requested that while there, the East Coast Marine squadrons be allowed to qualify for carrier operations.

In November, Geiger was notified by the Bureau of Aeronautics and the Chief of Naval Operations that his request was approved with the stipulation that it be done after completion of the maneuvers and providing that an aircraft carrier could be made available without jeopardizing other operations of the fleet.

This was the opportunity that Rowell and Geiger had been waiting for. When Tex heard about it, he didn't have much to say. He liked water for drinking and bathing but disliked flying over it. There were mixed feelings among the squadron members, but as everyone busied themselves in their duties, it was soon forgotten (Fig. 13-1).

In December, Lt. Thurston B. Clark, U.S. Navy, arrived at Brown Field to discuss the rudiments and the various Navy requirements for qualifying aboard carriers, and to give all pilots an introductory lesson in signals and landings. All proved to be apt students, and Clark could forsee no problems. Of course, a more detailed syllabus was to be presented on the West Coast before actual carrier qualifications began.

Fig. 13-1. Cartoon depicting the seasoned "Old Pros" calmly awaiting favorable weather conditions while the newcomers impatiently practice "suitcase" drill (courtesy Corp. Hyman).

On 23 December, VF-9M closed down its squadron activities for the year. Its heavy schedule of military duties during the year had curtailed its civilian activities somewhat; however, 10 airshows were performed during the year and a total of 7,000 flying hours were compiled. It was another great year for VF-9M (Fig. 13-2).

On Monday, 4 January 1937, Brown Field began preparing four of its five squadrons for the West Coast Naval Maneuvers. It was to be the largest exercise ever undertaken by the Navy up to that time and was scheduled to continue for approximately 30 days. During these maneuvers, the four squadrons of Aircraft One were to be based at the North Island Naval Air Station, San Diego, California (Fig. 13-3). They were expected to be away from home for at least six weeks.

Col. Geiger, who was commanding the task force, called a final briefing with the four squadron commanders the day before departure. He went over the route in detail again, adding last minute details on refueling stops, overnight stops and other pertinent data. In closing he reminded each one of the excellent flying record that Aircraft One enjoyed and specifically emphasized the importance of exercising caution. It was imperative that the Marines demonstrate to the Navy that an entire aircraft group could be safely moved across the United States. Large task forces had been flown to the Caribbean previously, but not of this size. He further

Fig. 13-2. Tight formations were everyday occurrence with "Rogers' Rogues". Occasional bumping of wingtips and tails caused much consternation among Crew Chiefs (courtesy Marine Corps).

Fig. 13-3. U.S. Naval Air Station on North Island, San Diego, California (courtesy U.S. Navy).

181

warned of the dangers from adverse weather they could encounter at that time of year.

Go West, Young Men

On Friday 22 January, VF-9M with 19 Boeing F4B-4's departed Brown Field at 0800 on the first leg of its flight to California. Following approximately five minutes behind VF-9M was Observation Squadron VO-7M. Its 13 Vought 03U-6 Corsair airplanes were under the command of Maj. Byron F. Johnson. Due to last minute problems, the other two squadrons were unable to depart as scheduled. Geiger elected to delay his departure and wait for them. He ordered VF-9M and VO-7M to wait at Fort Bragg until they caught up .

The following morning, the Colonel landed at Fort Bragg in his command plane, followed by Bombing Squadron VB-6M, with 13 Great Lakes BG-1 dive bombers commanded by Maj. William J. Wallace. Landing last was Utility Squadron VJ-6M, commanded by Capt. Schilt. It consisted of seven aircraft of various types, including three large transports.

The four squadrons departed Fort Bragg for a scheduled fuel and lunch stop at Atlanta. Overnight stops were at Birmingham, Alabama; San Antonio, Texas; and El Paso, Texas. Additional refueling stops were at Shreveport, Marfa, and Tuscon. The 52-plane task force arrived at San Diego's North Island Naval Air Station in the late afternoon of 27 February, where a sizable crowd awaited their arrival. Total flying time from Brown Field was 23.5 hours.

In its monthly report, *Naval Aviation News* said of the Marine's flight: "Fifty-two planes of Aircraft One, Fleet Marine Force arrived at North Island as scheduled. During the flight, each squadron made a position report at thirty-minute intervals to the command plane of Aircraft One. This permitted the Commanding Officer to know the position of all planes at all times and thus preserved the unity of command while allowing the squadrons to proceed individually. There was no trouble experienced in communication between the appointed radio guard plane and the liaison planes in the various squadrons and sections."

"The services rendered by the various Army airfields at which stops enroute were made were of the most efficient order and did much to facilitate the trip. The cooperation and courtesy shown by Army personnel at each stop was appreciated by all members of Aircraft One."

The arrival of the four squadrons at North Island signaled a week-long round of cocktail parties and other social activities. On these occasions, there was a lot of talk about VF-9M's non-regulation markings and the fact that its pilots were not carrier qualified. To "Rogers' Rogues," landing on a carrier flight deck required no special talent, and they so informed those doing the talking.

Many of the social activities came to a halt on 8 February, when two fleet-bombing exercises were carried out. That night a two-hour search problem was flown to San Clemente Island to locate and bomb the enemy ships sent to put troops ashore. As all knew, Tex wasn't too happy about flying over water, especially at night, and he was the butt of much kidding by his squadron members.

Bombing exercises continued daily during the week and on the night of the 10th, VF-9M was ordered to fly another night mission. At the briefing, Tex was heard grumbling about flying over water at night and reminded all to use caution. The mission was to bomb enemy targets on San Clemente Island in support of landings by ground Marines. At 2100 hours, Tex led his squadron off North Island by sections and climbed to 14,000 feet on his way to the target. Several pilots complained about the cold at that altitude, but Tex wanted plenty of airspace between his squadron and the ocean just in case it became necessary for anyone to glide back to shore. As it turned out, he made a wise decision. Shortly after they reached 14,000 feet, an oil line severed on Dan Torrey's Boeing. Only because of the extra altitude was he able to avoid ditching his plane in the ocean. He was able to glide to a landing on North Island, possibly saving his life.

Arriving over San Clemente Island, Tex brought his squadron around in a wide circle until the supporting airplanes below dropped flares to light up the target area. All made several dive-bombing runs on the island until it was declared "secured" by the war games referee. The next day Tex learned that the Naval camp on the island had not been notified in advance of the bombing and that a few of "Rogers' Rogues" mistook their camp for the target area. Most of the following day was spent digging the Navy men out of the cactus, where they had fled when the bombing started. Luckily no one was hurt—with bombs, that is!

Carrier Training

On 17 February, the fleet-landing exercises were terminated and Colonel Geiger was informed by the Navy that the aircraft carrier *USS Saratoga* would be available on 3 March for any squadrons he wished to qualify. Lt. Sperry Clarke, the Chief Landing Signal Officer from the carrier *USS Lexington*, was assigned to be their LSO for the qualifications; ground school for the Marines would start on the 19th.

One of the toughest jobs in the Navy is that of the LSO. He is selected, among other things, for his ability to understand people—especially aviators—and to instill in each of them confidence in their flying ability. When standing on the stern of an aircraft carrier with his signal paddles, the LSO must not make *any* mistakes. As an airplane approaches—no matter what type of airplane it may be—he must know *immediately* if its speed is too fast or too slow or if its approach is too high or too low. He must transmit this information instantly with his signal paddles so that the approaching pilot can make the necessary corrections. At the last split second he must determine of it is safe to give a "cut"—the signal for the pilot to land aboard—or give a "waveoff"—the signal for the pilot to apply power and go around to try for another landing approach. Often the LSO works with several types of airplanes of various landing and approach speeds in the landing pattern at the same time. And many times he takes the wrath of the air officer, who may think he is giving too many wave-offs or go-arounds and therefore taking too long to get all the airplanes aboard the carrier. Lastly, the LSO must be a qualified Naval Aviator. It is easy to see why he is not envied and why he has the respect of all Naval Aviators.

Promptly, on 19 February 1937, Lt. Clarke, considered the finest LSO in the Navy, began ground school for VF-9M pilots. It began with several blackboard sessions followed by a few mornings of field practice at an outlying field near the Mexican border known as Ream Field. Here a carrier flight deck was outlined on the field. It was used by Navy pilots to keep in practice when absent from carrier operations for extended periods of time.

Clarke always tried to analyze the personalities and flying habits of all his students. Knowing of VF-9M's splendid record and popularity, he wanted especially to understand this high-spirited group. He wasn't long in discovering that they were unlike any students he could remember—but he couldn't pinpoint it exactly. He was amazed at their flying ability and especially their sense of timing and judgment. Their approach to the carrier outline was always at the proper speed and altitude and, when he gave the "cut" signal, they always touched down at precisely the right spot. At times their attitude seemed to him to be one of indignation; at other times it seemed as if they thought they could do anything with an airplane and therefore considered the practice sessions a complete waste of time.

Actually, Clarke was very close to being right. The squadron, from Tex on down, more or less resented the entire exercise and figured that carrier flying had no place in their type of operation; that until it did, it was a waste of time. Since their arrival on North Island they had been kidded and hazed either directly or indirectly by the aviators stationed there. On many occasions, they overheard talk at the Officer's Club or at other social gatherings about the merits of flying from carriers. One of the most-repeated criticisms was: "You're not considered a *real* Naval aviator until you can land and take off from aircraft carriers."

Naturally, anyone in VF-9M overhearing such remarks had a tendency to become annoyed. Several vowed that, before they left for home, the Navy and other loud talkers would be singing a different tune. Flying from carriers was child's play.

"You know, it was pointed out to me by several of my friends not to take the remarks seriously," recalled General Rogers. "This was the only way many of the aviators had of getting back at my squadron. There was considerable jealousy of our freedom to move around and of the high favor we enjoyed in political circles in Washington. Further, we held the top spot for fighter squadrons in both bombing and gunnery. I guess taunting us about carriers was the only way to bolster their egos."

Actually, this was true. VF-9M had for years continuously enjoyed top publicity from the news media, and many squadrons felt they could do the same things if afforded the same opportunity. In all probability they could have.

A Phobia Cured

One evening several VF-9M pilots were talking in the Officer's Club about Tex Rogers and his fear of flying over water. It was decided to have a little fun at the skipper's expense. Enlisting the aid of Tex's crew chief, Sgt. Russell D. "Salty" May, they fashioned a pair of eyeglasses by cutting a beer can lengthways and fastening each half to frames of eye glasses. They cemented trees, grass and other objects inside the beer-can halves so that anyone wearing them would think he was flying over land.

Word quickly spread through Aircraft One of the project and everyone cooperated in keeping it a secret. Tex knew that something was going on, but was unable to find out what it was. Colonel Geiger, when asked if he would like to make the presentation, instantly replied, "I will be *delighted*" and set the morning of 26 February for the formal ceremony.

The Chief of Staff circulated a notice that all personnel of Aircraft One were to assemble in front of Operations at 1000 on 26 February for a special briefing.

At the assembly, Tex took his place at the head of his squadron. When the Colonel and his staff arrived, Tex called his men to attention. During a short speech by Geiger about the squadron's excellent showing in the maneuvers, Tex noticed smiles on many faces and wondered what in hell was going on.

The men were again called to attention and at this point Colonel Geiger called Major Rogers to front and center.

As he stepped forward and saluted, Tex's only thought was "What the hell did I do now?" Colonel Geiger said, "As you men all know, we in the Marines have always taken great pride in helping our own and in giving aid and comfort where needed. This is in keeping with the highest traditions of the United States Marine Corps. Therefore, Major Rogers, it is my pleasure, on behalf of your squadron and the staff of Aircraft One, to hereby present the *Royal Order of Water Blinders*!" At this point, the glasses were presented on a red cloth to Rogers (Fig. 13-4). The Colonel continued, "It is hoped that their use will be of great comfort throughout your career as a Marine Aviator and will provide many hours of pleasurable overwater flying."

As Tex accepted the glasses, he could feel a warm glow within and felt somewhat emotional. Quickly regaining his composure, he replied, "Colonel Geiger, I humbly accept this great honor and I will always remember and cherish this moment as one of the highlights in my career. I promise to do the utmost to uphold the Royal Order bestowed on me and to wear the Water Blinders with dignity on any and all overwater flights."

With that the assembly was dismissed and all rushed over to shake Tex's hand and have a good laugh at his expense.

On 1 March, final preparations began for the squadron's carrier qualifications, scheduled to commence on 3 March. Crew chiefs added tail hooks to all airplanes and removed the tail wheels with pneumatic tires and replaced them with solid rubber tires. As an added precaution, all landing gear fittings that showed any signs of wear were replaced. On 2 March Line Chief Morris Kurtz personally inspected each airplane and reported to Tex Rogers that all was ready.

The morning of 3 March dawned with the usual patches of ground fog around North Island. This day was to be a memorable one for VF-9M and the Navy.

By 0745 all pilots had gathered in the Operations Office for final briefing by Frank Wirsig and Carson Roberts. Roberts had just taken over as operations officer, following Wirsig's appointment as the squadron executive officer. There seemed to be a certain amount of excitement among the men as they stood around in small groups talking. Roberts and Bob Lee were the only VF-9M pilots that had been aboard carriers, and their fellow pilots were asking questions. Just as the briefing was about to get underway, a roar of laughter suddenly broke out; Tex stepped into the room wearing his "water blinders." He did this purposely to relax his men, who had seemed to be rather uptight the past few days.

"I thought maybe I could start the day off right by giving my boys a good laugh," said General Rogers, recalling the incident. "You know I could feel it in my bones that they were up to something, but I didn't say too much to them as I wasn't very enthused about the operation myself. I suspected there were a few who, with a little encouragement, might show off a little for the Navy and I tried to warn them not to try anything funny. As it turned out, I didn't set a very good example myself."

Colonel Geiger arrived at the conclusion of the briefing to wish them luck and to read a message just received from the *Saratoga*, stating it had departed San Diego, was steaming on a northwest course between Point Loma and San Clemente Island, and would be ready to receive VF-9M aboard anytime after 0900. Tex informed Geiger he would be ready to depart by 0830 and to radio the *Saratoga* to expect their arrival at approximately 0920.

At 0830 all pilots filed out of operations and ran for their planes. Engines had been started by the crew chiefs and were warmed and ready to go. At 0840 Tex announced over the microphone that take-off would be by divisions. As his division broke ground, he began a wide climbing turn to the left to allow the remaining two divisions to quickly join up with his. As usual, he wasn't overjoyed about flying around over the ocean, "looking for a damn postage stamp to land on."

Leveling off at 8,000 feet, Tex ordered the formation to tighten up and look smart. The *Saratoga* was barely visible about 20 miles off Point Loma. When approximately five miles astern of the carrier, Tex radioed its air officer and was granted permission to come aboard when ready.

The *Saratoga* was 888 feet in length, displaced 33,000 tons, and carried a crew of 1,900 men. It was under the command of Captain William F. Halsey (later Admiral "Bull" Halsey, of World War II fame), who was known for running a taut ship. Its air officer, Lt. Commander Knefler McGinnis, better known as "Sock" McGinnis, was an early aviator and he,

Fig. 13-4. Tex Rogers wearing his "sea glasses" at North Island (courtesy MGen. F.O. Rogers).

too, was a believer of discipline. What the two unsuspecting Navy officers and ship's crew could not know was that before the day was over they were to witness an amazing demonstration of how *not* to fly during carrier qualification training.

The command was given by Tex to descend in their usual airshow screeching-dive formation and, when reaching an altitude of 300 feet on the starboard side, the squadron made a beautiful tight left turn across the bow of the carrier, then zoomed up into a steep climbing turn. Tex made a break-away from the formation with his division, which immediately began spacing itself single file in the landing circle for coming aboard. The 12 remaining airplanes engaged in a few loops and slow rolls before entering the landing circle.

Captain Halsey, hearing the unusually loud propeller noise, stepped out onto the flight bridge and watched with curious interest. Sock McGinnis, trying to overlook the rather dramatic arrival of VF-9M, was heard mumbling something about the "damn Marines."

Sperry Clarke stood on the landing signal officer's platform, watching with curiosity. He remembered the squadron's attitude during fields practice and hoped the day would go smoothly.

Showing Off For The Navy

As Tex turned toward the stern of the carrier to land, his approach was too fast and slightly low. Clarke immediately signaled the necessary corrections with his paddles. When he received no response from Tex, he raised his paddles overhead in preparation for a wave-off. However, in the last split-second Tex recovered and made a nice landing, catching the number two wire. Much to Clarke's relief, the remaining pilots brought their airplanes aboard swiftly and correctly, just as they had been drilled the week before. Naturally, this eased Clarke's mind somewhat and suggested to him that perhaps he was worrying unnecessarily.

All VF-9M airplanes were taken below by elevator to the hangar deck to make room for squadron VO-7M, now preparing to come aboard. VB-6M was scheduled to qualify in the afternoon. At 1012 the last airplane landed and pilots of the two squadrons assembled in the ready room for a "welcome aboard" and a final briefing by the assistant air officer, Lt. Commander Murphy.

A flip of a coin decided that VO-7M would commence its qualifications first. At 1108 its first airplane was launched. At 1140 operations were halted by the crash of 1st Lt. E.C. Best who, in spite of his airplane ending in total loss, escaped with only minor injuries to himself.

At 1210 VF-9M began launching its airplanes. Spectators lined the catwalks, the rear gun turrets and the famous "vulture's roost," a vantage point on the island structure where aviators watch fellow pilots cope with the dangerous and sometimes fatal situations associated with carrier operations. Captain Halsey, knowing of VF-9M's reputation as a "hotshot" fighter squadron, stepped out onto the bridge and joined Sock McGinnis for a better view of the operations just getting underway. The entire ship was about to get its first lesson in the rudiments and technique of carrier landings, VF-9M style.

To speed up operations, it was decided by the air officer to launch all VF-9M airplanes, and as each pilot completed the required six landings, he was to orbit above the carrier until those in his division had finished; then the six airplanes were to return to North Island.

All airplanes were launched without any problems. For the entertainment of those watching, a few performed slow rolls after clearing the ship's bow, setting the stage for things to come.

As squadron leader, Tex was first to turn upwind for a landing. His approach was much the same as his first one in the morning and Clarke naturally gave him a wave-off signal. Tex thought his landing approach looked good, so he closed the throttle, hauled back on the control stick and caught the number one landing wire, making a perfect landing.

This rather surprised Clarke, as he didn't expect a man of Tex's caliber to ignore a command. However, it wasn't possible to dwell on it for more than a few seconds because the next airplane in line was making its approach—and some approach it was. Coming in much too high, the pilot was given a wave-off. Without hesitating, the pilot put his airplane in a steel left side-slip, while Clarke waved his paddles to no avail. He, too, made a good landing, the tail hook catching the number three wire.

Sock McGinnis began to feel that something was up as he watched the third airplane preparing to come aboard. Several hundred feet from the stern of the carrier, it commenced yawing violently, first to the left and then to the right, its pilot completely ignoring Clarke's command to reduce speed. As it crossed the stern of the carrier, its pilot quickly corrected the yawing barely in time to catch the number three landing wire. Clarke just turned and watched with disbelief.

Several other pilots came aboard performing erratic and unorthodox maneuvers, giving the spectators a good show but causing an occasional problem to the deck handlers by remaining in the arresting gear and landing area too long.

Sock Mc Ginnis was beginning to do a slow burn and called down to Clarke on the bull horn, "I want to know what in hell is going on down there. If that is an example of your teaching methods, someone is going to get killed. This is *supposed* to be a military operation, *not* a flying circus. Now get those damn Marines straightened out or you're in trouble!"

The next few airplanes came aboard obeying the LSO's commands, thus easing shipboard tensions somewhat. In the meantime, a few of the pilots were performing an airshow above the carrier, with loops, rolls, etc.

Captain Halsey was observing both shows—the one above and the one below—but for his own reasons, he chose to remain silent at this point. McGinnis, having vented his anger, was very surprised at Halsey's composure.

As operations began to smooth out, several pilots above the carrier waiting for their turn to qualify dived down into the landing pattern to replace those that had finished. A few were still smarting from the remarks made by the Navy and were waiting to get their licks in. The next four pilots coming aboard did just that!

The first one suddenly pulled up into a stall, then pushed over into a shallow dive straight for the flight deck. When he regained just enough speed for recovery he hauled back on the stick, bounced onto the flight deck and caught the number four wire. The pilot following wasn't to be outdone. A few hundred feet before reaching the carrier's stern, he quickly rolled his plane into a tight left 360 degree vertical turn. As he completed the turn he barely leveled his wings in time to land safely aboard.

The next airplane coming up on the carrier's stern was piloted by Captain B. C. "Boke" Batterton. Because of a problem with the arresting cables, the airplane that just landed from the vertical turn had not been moved forward out of the landing area. The bewildered Clarke, knowing that a crash was imminent if Batterton also ignored his wave-off, frantically commenced waving his paddles. This set the stage for the "coup de grace" of the entire operation.

In the Navy there is a golden rule that is preached day in and day out to all carrier pilots and is strictly adhered to by all who want to live long enough to become *old* carrier pilots. That rule is: Never make a right turn after receiving a landing waveoff. The carrier's island structure, which is on the right—or starboard—side of the ship, creates an enormous wake of invisible and turbulent air extending several hundred feet behind it. If a pilot, after receiving a waveoff, elected at the last second to turn right, in most instances his airplane would be only slightly above stall speed. Further, as he applied full throttle for his climb-out, the resulting torque created by the engine and propeller would produce a tremendous left roll effect at this slow speed, and he might suddenly find his airplane trying to roll in the opposite direction to the intended flight path. Now, add to this the effect of flying into the turbulent air at this moment and you have the *perfect* setup for instant death. At this point, the airplane would likely become uncontrollable, flip over on its back and most certainly crash into the carrier's island structure, the rear gun turrets, the ocean, or all three. Very few pilots have made this mistake and lived to tell about it. Clarke had devoted much time hammering this home to VF-9M pilots during the training sessions.

Batterton, now on his final approach and viewing the situation ahead with the arresting cables, had no choice but to obey the LSO's wave-off signal. However, to the horror of those aboard, instead of making the proper turn to the left, he rolled his plane into a right turn, violating the Navy's golden rule. He barely missed the rear island structure and sent all Navy personnel viewing the show from the catwalks and rear gun turrets running for their lives.

Lieutenant Torrey, following close behind and viewing the beautifully executed right turn ahead by Batterton, wasn't one to let anyone outdo *him*. Also receiving a wave-off from the LSO, he promptly repeated Batterton's performance. No one will ever know for sure if they make it because of expert piloting, lots of luck or if Someone Up There was watching over them.

McGinnis took off from the bridge to the LSO's platform below as if he'd been shot from a cannon. To say that he was furious over the happenings of the past several minutes would be the understatement of all time.

Reaching the LSO's platform, he commenced to cuss Clarke, using all of the old Navy words plus a few new ones he just invented for "allowing those crazy damn Marines to come aboard like that."

Clarke, now almost in shock, just couldn't understand why the pilots of VF-9M had done this to him. Prior to the start of this operation, he thought they were probably the best students and pilots he had ever instructed—and the events of the past hour had about proved it.

Returning to the bridge, McGinnis was entertaining thoughts of asking for court martial proceedings against a few pilots. However, he wasn't prepared for Captain Halsey's reaction.

Halsey viewed the entire episode in a much different light. At first, he couldn't believe what he was seeing, but any anger he may have felt at the start gradually gave way to laughter. To his way of thinking it was the funniest and possibly the finest bit of flying he had ever seen, not to mention the most dangerous.

Still laughing, Captain Halsey replied, "Sock, I know you're upset, but if you will just simmer down and think about what has happened here in the past hour, I'm sure you'll have to agree that it was a great piece of flying. And if they were trying to make a point of some sort, I think they have succeeded. However, I agree it was a very dangerous and wild thing to do, and I can assure you that it will *never* happen again on my ship."

Saluting, McGinnis turned and walked away. Even though his blood pressure had decreased somewhat, he had yet to see any humor in it. His thoughts were on the years of work, sweat, trial and error the Navy had invested in aircraft carrier procedures and operations, only to have them all violated in less than two hours.

Recalling those fateful days, Major General Tex Rogers said, "One of the officers on the bridge of the *Saratoga* told me later that instead of Captain Halsey getting mad, he thought our operation was the funniest thing he'd ever seen in his life. He had tears in his eyes from laughing so hard. As you may know, I was a trial to Sperry Clarke myself. I made two landings after ignoring a wave-off both times and got the hell bawled out of me, so I decided to try it their way. The result was wave-off after wave-off, so I repeated my first two performances and landed. Clarke was *furious*. Halsey called me on the radio and suggested—in the form of an order—that I should go back to the beach before I killed my damn-fool self.

I don't know what got into me. It must have been the flying over water that got to me, especially down so close. You know, I *hated* water. I just couldn't make myself let the LSO tell me how to fly. Those three landings were the total of my carrier experience during my Marine Corps career."

Brigadier General Batterton, who played no small part in the escapade, recalls: "Our carrier qualifications were, for certain, a three-ring circus. The Navy said we landed from everything including rolls and loops without scratching a single airplane. Most of us were pretty disgusted at the whole business at the time and took a dim view of the West Coast aviators always bragging that you were not a good aviator until you had operated from carriers. Dan Torrey and I took care of the Navy's golden rule when we both managed right turns after a wave-off. We sure scared hell out of the spectators sitting on the rear gun turrets and sent them racing for cover."

"Bull" Halsey Saves The Day

Near the end of VF-9M's flying antics, Col. Geiger landed aboard the carrier in his BG-1 and witnessed the two death-defying right turns by Batterton and Torrey. When he learned of the flying circus just performed, he was infuriated with Tex and his squadron. For the previous month his Marine squadrons had enjoyed a near-perfect record in the maneuvers and had made a very favorable impression on the old line West Coast Navy brass. He promised Halsey that all involved would be skinned alive. Halsey, still laughing, asked Geiger not to do anything drastic and added later over a cup of coffee:

"I was informed by your Group Operations Officer why the boys were having a little fun. I think all personnel present here today have learned a lesson and the intended message, even though very dangerous, was well put. Roy, for years your East Coast Squadrons, especially VF-9M, have enjoyed national fame. You have a good group there—the best in the business—and I don't think I would do anything to break their spirit."

"Spirit, hell," answered Geiger. "When *I* get through with them, there won't be enough left of each one to *have* a spirit!"

Geiger continued by explaining his fears of what the Commandant of the Marine Corps and the Chief of Naval Operations might do when they learned of VF-9M's clowning during a serious military operation. He knew that someone was going to be in serious trouble; namely, himself. Halsey suggested that he had nothing to worry about except talk, which proved to be true.

To this day the movie film made of these operations has never been located. All other *Saratoga* films are filed by date, but the date 3 March 1937 is missing. Even the ship's log makes no mention of it. Captain Halsey kept his word!

Chapter 14

Top Gun

Stories of the squadron's crazy flying preceded its arrival back at North Island and spread over the entire air station. By the time the last airplane had landed, the description of what had gone on was somewhat distorted from what actually did happen. However, from that day forward no one would *ever* taunt VF-9M about how good pilots had to be to fly from carriers.

That evening, a cocktail party was hosted by Lt. Col. Walter G. "Great" Farrell at his home in Coronado for Col. Geiger, his staff of Aircraft One and his squadron commanders. When Tex arrived, the evening's conversation had centered mostly on the carrier qualifications and the antics of VF-9M. He went straight to the bar for a drink. He wanted one under his belt before facing Geiger.

"I had managed to avoid Geiger until that evening, when we were invited to a cocktail party at Great Farrell's home in Coronado," said General Rogers. He had cooled down somewhat after talking with Captain Halsey; however, he was still perturbed enough to call off the airshow I planned to do at my hometown of Waco, Texas, on our way home. This really hurt. I had wired the city that we would be there for the show and they had gone all out in making preparations. No amount of talking could change his mind at the time."

At 0930 on 6 March 1937 the four squadrons of Aircraft One commenced their departure from the North Island Naval Air Station on the first leg of their return trip to Quantico. The route home was to be the same as they followed out with the first overnight stop at El Paso, Texas.

No Show in Waco

That evening, Geiger invited his staff and squadron commanders to his room for a drink. Tex again brought up the subject of the airshow at Waco. He argued the point that the whole town was turning out to give his squadron a big welcome and that he just couldn't call it off now. Recalling the incident, General Rogers said, "After he had a drink or two, he was in a good mood, so I began working on him about the airshow. He finally agreed that I could stop in Waco, but under no circumstances would he permit an airshow. His excuse was that he was afraid we might pull some more wild stuff. Of course, he was just getting back at me for our carrier performance and, too, he didn't know but that he might have to answer to the high brass about our carrier qualifications when he returned home, so I guess he was playing it very cautious.

"We arrived at the Waco airport Sunday afternoon and I could see it was jammed with people. After we landed we were almost mobbed. The people stayed all the afternoon waiting for our show. I tried to explain to the city officials that the show was off. They just couldn't understand why. The more I tried to explain, the madder I got at Geiger. It was a damn shame."

Early the following morning, the pilots of VF-9M had a surprise in store when they arrived at the Waco airport. A crowd had gathered to watch their take-off. Apparently, all was forgiven concerning the airshow. As a reward for the early morning well—wishers, Tex pulled the squadron into a very tight formation and made a low pass across the airport as the spectators waved goodby. That evening VF-9M caught up with the rest of the task force at Maxwell Field, Montgomery, Alabama.

A large crowd had gathered at Brown Field (Fig. 14-1) by late afternoon of Tuesday, 9 March, to await the arrival of the four squadrons. The Commanding General at Quantico, Brigadier General Charles H. Lyman, was on hand to officially welcome them home. They had been away for 40 days. Knowing they were tired, his speech was very short.

Following a week's leave, preparations began for the annual bombing and gunnery exercises scheduled for 2 April through 3 May at Parris Island. At 0800 on 1 April the squadron left Brown Field and arrived at Parris Island at 1400 hours after a two-hour stop at Ft. Bragg.

The following morning the fast pace began. Navy and Marine aviators would be watching and waiting to see if VF-9M could successfully defend its national title. During the next few weeks Captains Batterton, Wirsig, Harold Lee and Carson Roberts kept a close eye on flight schedules, tabulating scores and defining problem areas. If any pilot's score began to fall behind the previous year's, all pitched in to pinpoint the trouble. Crew chiefs and mechanics worked tirelessly to make sure all planes were ready for the next day's operations—even if it meant working all night. (Fig. 14-2).

The last week at Parris Island was devoted to the final scores for the official Navy record. Personnel from the offices of the Chief of Naval Operations and the Bureau of Aeronautics were on hand to record the scores. At the conclusion, they said that the scores looked very good and added further that Navy Fighting Squadron VF-5B, "The Red Rippers," based aboard the aircraft carrier *Ranger,* was leading all fighter squadrons and therefore was the one to beat. All operations ceased on 3 May and the

Fig. 14-1. Badly needed runway was added to Brown Field in 1937. Note the progress of new field under construction on opposite side of railroad tracks. Name of the new field; Turner Field, in honor of Col. Thomas C. Turner (courtesy Marine Corps).

squadron left for home the following day, arriving at Brown Field at 1330 hours.

Still on Top, as VMF-1

On 7 May it was a happy Tex Rogers (Fig. 14-3) who read an early morning dispatch from the Navy Department giving the final gunnery and bombing standings for the fiscal year within the Navy and Marine Corps. VF-9M was again "Top Gun" and had narrowly missed capturing the bombing trophy also. A squadron party was held on Saturday night to celebrate.

On 10 May an airshow was performed for Congressmen Melvin J. Mass, John M. Hauston and Robert F. Mouton, who were guests of Colonel Geiger at an informal inspection of Brown Field.

On 22 May an aerial review by all squadrons of Aircraft One and a dive-bombing demonstration by VF-9M were staged for President Roosevelt and the National Press Club.

On 2 June, at the close of the weekly staff meeting in Col. Geiger's office, the Colonel asked Tex to remain. From a stack of papers on his desk, he selected four documents, arranged them in order for his reading, and handed them to Tex.

The first document was no surprise to Tex. For sometime, he had been expecting orders for his reassignment. After all, three years of the best duty in the Marine Corps was the most anyone could hope for. The orders specified that on 1 July 1937, Major Ford O. Rogers was to be relieved as Commanding Officer of VF Squadron Nine-M. Following 10 days leave, he was to report to the Commanding General of the Senior Officers School at Quantico, Virginia, for the one-year course of study. During this period he would be attached to Headquarters Squadron One-M (HS-1M).

The second document, dated 10 May, was from the Navy Department via the Commandant of the Marine Corps. It directed that on 1 July 1937 all Marine squadrons were to be redesignated as follows. The service letter "M" (Marines) was to be moved in between the prefix letter "V" (heavier-than-air, fixed wing) and the squadron mission letter. In VF-9M's case the mission letter was "F" (Fighting). Thus, VF would become VMF. In conclusion, it specified that the squadron number must conform to the aircraft group to which it was attached. VF-9M was presently in the First Aircraft Group, or Aircraft One. Therefore, on 1 July 1937 the new designation of VF-9M would become VMF-1 (Marine Fighting Squadron One.)

New Paint, New Faces

The third document was more in the form of a memo than a directive. It stated that on 1 July 1937 all Marine Corps squadrons would be requested to paint their airplanes to conform to the Navy's standard six-color marking system used within all squadrons for identifying each of the six sections and the airplanes therein. Further, (in VF-9M's case) the squadron number (1), service letter (M), mission letter (F) and the airplane number within the squadron were to be carried on the side of the fuselage. For instance, plane Number five in the squadron would carry the following on both sides of the fuselage 1-MF-5. Actually, this marking system had been in effect since June 1931 and all Marine squadrons—with the exception of VF-9M—were already so painted and marked. Both Tex and Geiger knew this document was aimed at VF-9M because of its non-regulation show markings but no one, it seemed, had the guts to say so.

The fourth and last document was a shocker and, if carried out as specified, would most certainly spell doom for VF-9M as it was presently known. It directed that on 1 July 1937, 65 percent of the squadron's officers and personnel were to be transfered to other commands. Further, it stated that, with the exception of the squadron executive officer, engineering officer, operations officer, and gunnery officer, all replacements were to be drawn from young Second Lieutenants and Aviation Cadets direct from flight school.

Fig. 14-2. F4B-4's were washed and checked after each days flying. Line Chief, Master Sgt. Morris Kurtz, always had 18 airplanes clean, gassed and ready to go for the next day's flying (courtesy Marine Corps).

Fig. 14-3. Major Ford O. "Tex" Rogers (courtesy Marine Corps).

To Tex it looked as though the Marine's greatest squadron was in serious trouble. Both officers knew that for some time a person—or persons—unknown in the upper echelon either within the Navy or Marines—or both—was out to get the squadron; it looked as though they might succeed.

After discussing the problem at length, both officers agreed that the crisis called for action. Geiger telephoned Col. Rowell at Headquarters in Washington and said that he would technically comply with the directive—but that he intended to take full advantage of his position as the commanding officer of all East Coast squadrons. This gave him the authority to modify certain directives, when necessary, to best suit the circumstances and the good of the Marine Corps. Rowell agreed; however, he warned Geiger not to intentionally step on too many toes. He also informed him that he was free to recommend a replacement for Rogers but should do so within 48 hours.

Within hours most of the men (Fig. 14-4) knew of Tex's departure. News of this type travels fast. And, as in the case of Sanderson's departure, the men were asking the same question: "Who can possibly replace Tex Rogers as commanding officer?" All—to a man— agreed that there absolutely were no more Sandersons or Rogers in the Marine Corps. Actually, the *greatest* single loss was the transfer of Captain Wirsig, who had been with the squadron longer than any other officer. Throughout the years his knowledge and experience had been so valuable to previous commanding officers in making VF-9M the show squadron of the Marines. Indeed, he would be missed.

On 10 June VF-9M performed its final airshow under the command of Tex Rogers (Fig. 14-5). At the conclusion, he threw an informal get-together of all squadron personnel to answer any questions and

Fig. 14-4. The "*Saratoga* Aerobats" in saintly pose at Brown Field just before squadron reorganization on 1 July 1937. Left/Right sitting: C.W. Nelson; L.H. Meyer; C.A. Roberts; F.H. Wirsig; F.O. Rogers; H.R. Lee; B.C. Batterton; D.W. Torrey; W.K. Pottinger. Standing left/right: R.R. Porter; E.B. Carney; D.K. Yost; P.B. Withers; E.W. Johnston; J.F. Dobbin; A.H. Bohne; L.E. Roberts; F.R. Payne; C.C. Campbell; G.H. Knott (courtesy Marine Corps).

Fig. 14-5. Marine Bombing Squadron Six-M (VB-6M) working on formation tactics south of Quantico in 1937 (courtesy Marine Corps).

rumors. He confirmed the truth of the biggest rumor of all, that Captain "Skeeter" McKittrick was to be the new commanding officer.

A squadron party was given on 19 June in Tex's honor. It lasted until the sun was breaking over the horizon. As with most Marine parties, the drinks seemed to flow endlessly and long after food had vanished. The theme song for the evening was "For He's a Jolly Good Fellow," and numerous variations of it were heard throughout the evening. Tex Rogers was without doubt the best-liked officer in Marine Aviation at that time.

Chapter 15

The McKittrick Era

At 1000 hours on the morning of 1 July 1937, a formal inspection of VF-9M was conducted by Colonel Geiger and his guests, Major General J. C. Breckenridge, Commanding General at Quantico, and Colonel Ross E. Rowell, Director of Marine aviation. At the conclusion of the inspection, all personnel were assembled in formation on the apron in front of VF-9M's two hangars, and Col. Rowell read aloud the directive officially changing the designation of the squadron from VF-9M to VMF-1.

After a brief speech by Gen. Breckenridge on the history of VF-9M and its long record of accomplishments, Col. Geiger stepped forward and read the orders that officially transferred command from Maj. Ford O. Rogers to Capt. William L. McKittrick. In accepting command, McKittrick closed the ceremonies by issuing his first official order as commanding officer: "Leave is hereby granted to all squadron personnel until 5 July."

McKittrick came to the squadron well experienced both as a pilot and squadron commander. While commanding squadrons VO-6M and VO-7M, he had flown many airshows with Sanderson and Rogers, so he knew that end of the business equally well. In fact, when Col. Geiger recommended him, he said, "He is the only *logical* choice."

"Mac" Takes Command

Born in 1897 at Pelzer, South Carolina, Capt. McKittrick enlisted in the Marine Corps on 10 March 1918. He became a student Naval Aviator on 1 July 1922 and was awarded his wings on 15 February 1923. After serving a stint in Nicaragua, he was assigned to Quantico where, over the next few years, he served in several squadrons and did a tour of duty at Marine Headquarters in Washington. Returning to Quantico, he commanded squadrons VO-6M and VO-7M, then joined the staff of Aircraft One as group operations and training officer.

Fig. 15-1. Capt. William L. McKittrick, (center) Commanding Officer of VMF-1, with two of his squadron officers. Capt. William O. Brice, Executive Officer (left) and Capt. Harold R. Lee, Armament and Navigation Officer (courtesy Marine Corps).

McKittrick held the first meeting with his four staff officers on 5 July. Two of them, Captains William O. Brice and James M. "Moe" Daly, had just joined the squadron—Brice as the new executive officer; Daly, the new gunnery officer. Both men were former squadron members and brought with them a wealth of experience so badly needed at that time. The other two staff officers—Captains Batterton, engineering officer, and Roberts, operations officer—had been with the squadron for the previous two years and knew its operations well.

The staff meeting went very well. It resulted in an agreement to modify and increase operational and training schedules deemed necessary for the squadron to retain its standing. As McKittrick pointed out, he could not recruit seasoned and experienced pilots, which was an advantage enjoyed by his predecessors.

Probably the most important result of this first meeting was an order by McKittrick that he wanted implemented immediately. He wanted to inject more of a military bearing into the squadron. He especially wanted to dispell the "Flying Country Club" image. Unlike Tex Rogers, who was a big easy-going, unmilitary, one-of-the-boys type, McKittrick (Fig. 15-1) believed in the military way of doing things. After all, this was a military squadron and the top one at that!

The coming weeks brought many changes. Daily flights were increased to include all phases of military flying for the new arrivals. However, it was to be sometime before the squadron would recover from the "raid" of its personnal.

One change to McKittrick's liking was his nickname. Everyone now seemed to call him "Mac." It was during his younger years that someone had bestowed the name "Skeeter" as fitting his rather short statue and skinny build. As one offficer remarked "'Mac' seemed more dignified for a squadron commander."

At a meeting of his staff on 12 August, Col. Gieger announced that Bombing Squadron One (VMB-1), commanded by Captain Schilt, would represent the Marines at the National Air Races in Cleveland, starting on 3 September (Fig. 15-2). It was a big disappointment for Mac. He had hoped that somehow it wouldn't happen, but conceded it was the right decision under the circumstances. In no way was his squadron ready to take on the assignment.

Instead of yielding to despair, Mac sought and received approval to depart for Parris Island on 1 September for six weeks of bombing and gunnery practice. The new men needed this training to sharpen their skills

Fig. 15-2. Personal plane of Col. Ross E. "Rusty" Rowell, Director of Marine Aviation, in colorful red, white and blue markings at the 1937 Cleveland Air Races. This F4B-3 was completely rebuilt with spare parts at Brown Field in 1935, including new F4B-4 fuselage (courtesy Marine Corps).

and reflexes; but most of all it was needed for building confidence in their flying ability and in themselves. When a man can master these things, he is on his way to becoming a Marine Aviator.

Mac had other reasons for wanting to get away so soon. During the past few weeks it had become apparent that he might have problems with several of the young second lieutenants and cadets. All in their early twenties, they were perfect specimens of manhood and full of energy. To them, life was one big playground. Mac knew he had to put that energy to good use and do it soon.

"Pappy" Boyington, Young Rebel

Two young men that seemed to stand out almost immediately were Aviation Cadets Freeman W. Williams and Gregory Boyington (later "Pappy" Boyington, of WW II fame). From the moment they arrived on base, one or the other seemed to be involved in trouble of some sort. During their first week in the squadron they decided that a little fun was in order. Each climbed into an F4B-4 sitting on the line and went full bore to 10,000 feet, where they proceeded to dogfight and chase each other all over the sky.

After an hour of fun and games, both realized they were almost out of fuel. Williams just barely made it back to the field, his engine quitting as he landed. Boyington's luck was not that good. His engine quit while still some distance away, and, not having sufficient altitude to glide his airplane to the field, he was forced to land on the rifle range at Quantico (Fig. 15-3). Both men were severely reprimanded, charged with making an unauthorized flight that endangered lives and government property, and confined to their quarters for several days.

On 1 September, VMF-1 departed Brown Field with 19 F4B-4's for Parris Island. The following day, support personnel and equipment moved there by truck and private automobile, arriving on the third for the six-weeks of bombing and gunnery.

The first two days were taken up with pre-practice preparation. The new pilots were flown locally in the Utility Squadron's Grumman J2F-1 to become familiar with the local terrain. Intensive training got underway on Tuesday, 7 September. Previously, the custom was to perform gunnery and bombing during the morning hours, with the afternoons used for free time. Not so *this* trip. When possible, afternoons were taken up with perfecting all types of formation flying—much to the enjoyment of the local residents.

For many days heavy rains and wet field conditions plagued operations; however, Mac allowed nothing to stand in the way of completing the daily flight schedules. He purposely set a fast pace for the benefit of the new pilots.

As the training period came to a close, he was proud of the overall performance of the squadron. His confidence in the new pilots' flying ability had increased several fold and he felt that, with a little more time

Fig. 15-3. Lucky Number 13 after deadstick landing on the Quantico Rifle Range by Aviation Cadet Gregory "Rats" Boyington (Later "Pappy" Boyington of WW-II fame) (courtesy Marine Corps).

Fig. 15-4. Aircraft of squadrons VMS-1, VMJ-1 and VMB-1 lined up for inspection on Brown Field, 9 November 1937 (courtesy Marine Corps).

and barring a major setback, they had the potential for upholding the traditions of VF-9M. And through it all, no one worked more diligently than the wonderful crew chiefs.

Flying operations ceased on 13 October and Mac ordered take-off for home at 0800 the following morning. That evening he called on Brigadier General Douglas C. McDougal, the commanding officer of Parris Island, and extended his thanks for the splendid cooperation received during their stay. He especially praised the Public Works Department, which bore the brunt of their visit.

Their return home lacked the Rogers-era fanfare. Colonel Geiger was the only 'brass' on hand to greet them and the Quantico Press carried only a small mention the following day: *"Marine Fighting Squadron One arrived home yesterday at 3:30 P.M. from Parris Island, South Carolina, where it completed six weeks of bombing and gunnery practice. The squadron's new Commanding Officer, Captain William L. McKittrick, is confident the squadron will attain the high degree of excellence, proficiency and popularity enjoyed by its predecessor."*

New Pilots, New Planes

On 15 October, Mac met with Colonel Geiger to report on the squadron's Parris Island activities. It was evident that the Colonel was not pleased; however, Mac assured him he had the makings of a good squadron. At this time, Geiger brought Mac up to date on what had happened during his absence. First, the *bad* news. Sometime after the first of the year, eight or possibly 10 additional new Aviation Cadets were scheduled to join the squadron. Mac started to complain, but quickly changed his mind. He knew Geiger had enough problems without listening to his complaints. The *good* news was a letter from the Chief of the Bureau of Aeronautics, Rear Admiral Arthur B. Cook, that confirmed a rumor of several weeks. It said in part that VMF-1 was scheduled to receive a full squadron of new Grumman F3F-2 airplanes plus spares. Delivery was to commence on or about the first of March 1938. It was indeed good news. The F4B-4's were becoming weary and required more and more hours of maintenance to keep them operating.

Before leaving, Geiger read another letter from the Bureau. It asked for a progress report on the compliance of a directive dated 1 July that specified all Marine aircraft to be painted and marked in accordance with Navy Regulations (Fig. 15-4). Both officers had a good laugh and Geiger remarked that he would take care of it.

On 19 November, VMF-1 performed an airshow at Quantico. This was Mac's first show since becoming commanding officer. The show went

Fig. 15-5. Senior Officers at Brown Field for the inspection on 9 November 1937. Left/right: Col. Rowell; Col. Geiger; Lt. Col. Francis P. Mulcahy; Lt. Col. Field Harris (courtesy Marine Corps).

Fig. 15-6. Aircraft One Squadron Commanders on 24 November 1937. Left/right: Majors William J. Wallace, VMJ-1; Lester N. Medaris, VMS-1; Captains Christian F. Schilt, VMB-1; William L. McKittrick, VMF-1 (courtesy Marine Corps).

well and Colonel Geiger and his guests from Washington expressed great satisfaction with the performance. The following day, Mac was informed that the entire Air Group at Quantico was to take part in the Miami Air Races and his squadron was to be the feature attraction (Fig. 15-5, 15-6). This called for a celebration and that evening, after he consumed a few drinks, Mac could be heard singing his favorite song: "For I'm a Jolly Rebel."

It was a beautiful morning on 1 December as the four squadrons of Aircraft One prepared for take off to the All-American Air Maneuvers in Miami. Utility Squadron One, (VMJ-1) commanded by Maj. William J. Wallace, was the first to depart with its three large transports. At 0800 Scouting Squadron One (VMS-1), commanded by Maj. Lester N. Medaris, departed with its 12 Vought 03U-6 Scout bombers, followed 10 minutes later by Bombing Squadron One (VMB-1), with its 12 Great Lakes BG-1 dive bombers commanded by Capt. Schilt.

Promptly at 0830 Mac gave the take off command for VMF-1, with its 19 Boeing F4B-4 fighters. Takeoff was by sections and the assigned altitude was 3,000 feet. The four squadrons, under the command of Col.

Geiger, were to proceed independently and report to the command transport at one-half hour intervals.

Heroes of Miami

For several days, the older pilots had subjected the newcomers to many tall tales of their previous Miami visits, and excitement was running high. The city of Miami didn't let them down. Each night there were parties and dances and plenty of girls to liven things up. Mac warned his men to watch their conduct, especially the young hellraisers, but he didn't expect it to do any good.

The All-American Air Maneuvers for 1937 opened at noon on Friday, the third of December, with an official welcome by the Mayor of Miami. All of the aviation greats were on hand and the best racing pilots in the country were there to vie for the many prizes offered.

Capacity crowds cheered the Marines' segment of the show. Major Medaris' squadron provided an excellent demonstration of formation flying and Captain Schilt's daring exhibition of close-dive bombing kept the audience spellbound. Each day VMF-1 closed the Marine's contribution with its tight 18-plane formations and several aerial antics perfected by Sanderson and Rogers that included the Squadron Line Reversement, the

Fig. 15-7. Miami, Florida, Naval Reserve Air Station, at Opa-Locka (courtesy U.S. Navy).

Snake Dance and the now-famous Squirrel Cage. On the last day all 42 of the three squadron's airplanes passed in review. It was the largest Marine formation ever presented at a Miami airshow. Said a local radio station newscaster: "As usual, the flying Marines so enhanced the air maneuvers with their thrilling aerial show that description is beyond words."

The Marines were having a wonderful time in Miami. Colonel Geiger postponed departure until Tuesday, 7 December. This gave the fun lovers an extra day and night to pursue their favorite hobbies: booze and women.

By 0730 on Tuesday morning the Air Station at Opa-Locka (Fig. 15-7) had come alive with activity. Crew chiefs helped by station personnel were busily engaged in preparing all airplanes for take-off. Pilot briefing, scheduled for 0800, had to be delayed until the stragglers arrived. For a time it seemed doubtful if several pilots were going to show at all. Many arrived in cars driven by girl friends, who stayed on to see them off.

At the briefing, Bill Brice, the squadron executive officer, said to Mac, "All of our pilots are here in *some* form or another. Looks like a few have seen better days." And that they had, however none would admit to feeling badly. In fact, after a cup of coffee both Williams and Boyington agreed they were ready for *another* night on the town!

Even so, Mac was very proud of all his boys. None had caused any serious trouble. Of course there were the usual reports of a few wild beach parties and swimming in the nude with girl friends, but nothing that caused any real concern to the city officials.

At 0900 hours VMF-1 took-off from Opa-Locka in division formation for home. The last plane landed at Brown Field at dusk.

On 13 December, Geiger told Mac to have his squadron ready to depart for San Juan on or about 23 January to take part in the United States Navy Fleet Landing exercise Number 4. Line Chief Sap Kurtz immediately ordered all crew chiefs to submit detailed reports on their aircraft, including recommendations as to the need for overhaul before start of the operation.

At noon on 24 December the squadron closed down operations for the Christmas holidays. In looking back over the past six months, Mac wasn't too proud of the squadron's achievements; however, reflecting on the obstacles placed in his way at that time, and since, he thought the year could be salvaged. Next year was sure to be better.

The year 1938 opened with a busy schedule. VMF-1, along with other squadrons from Quantico, participated in the Navy Fleet Landing Exercises in the Caribbean, departing on 23 January for San Juan and returning seven weeks later on 12 March. Much to Mac's satisfaction, his squadron was praised by the Navy for its excellence performance in the fleet problems and later received a commendation from the Chief of Naval Operations.

Word reached the squadron in San Juan that delivery of the new Grumman F3F-2 airplanes (Fig. 15-8) was to commence on the first of March. Most of the pilots could hardly wait to get home (Fig. 15-9).

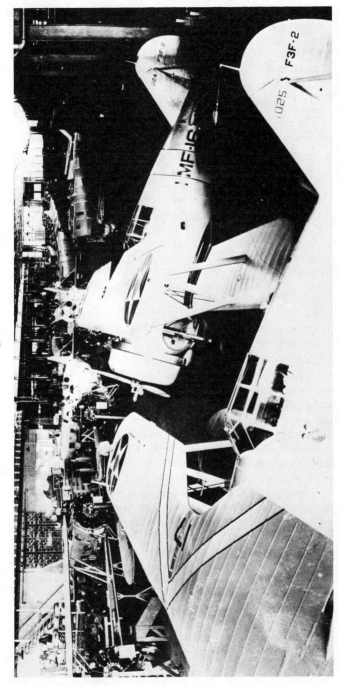

Fig. 15-8. New Grumman F3F-2 Fighters slated for VMF-1 under construction at the factory in February 1938. Note Navy regulation squadron squadron markings (courtesy National Archives).

Fig. 15-9. Col. Geiger and his crew chief John Donato, at their arrival home from the 1938 maneuvers in the Caribbean (courtesy U.S. Navy).

A large crowd greeted VMF-1's return on 12 March, and after initial greetings, many pilots rushed over to the VF hangar to get a look at the new planes, 10 of which had been delivered.

The new Grumman F3F-2's were the most advanced fighters then being delivered to the Navy and Marines. In addition to a 60 MPH speed advantage over the F4B-4's, they had controllable-pitch, constant-speed propellers, retractable landing gear and enclosed cockpits. The older pilots especially liked the enclosed cockpits. After years of flying through rain and blistering cold weather, it was a welcome addition. The planes were highly maneuverable and could dive at speeds in excess of 400 MPH.

Someone in the Navy Bureau of Aeronautics had obviously remembered the turmoil over the painting of the F4B-4's in nonregulation markings. By stipulating in the contract to the Grumman Airplane Co. that the correct painting and markings must be applied to the new airplanes *before leaving the factory,* they had outsmarted VMF-1. Colonel Geiger and Mac had a good laugh over that.

Chapter 16

End of an Era

First thing Monday morning, pilots and crew chiefs reported for a four-hour briefing by Grumman engineers on the maintenance and operation of the new planes. Following lunch, pilots began their flying checkout. A total of five take-offs and landings were required for qualification. At the end of the week all pilots were checked out and familiarization and practice in air work began.

By 23 March a full squadron of F3F-2's (Fig. 16-1) had been delivered by Capt. Charles Fike and his crew from Service Squadron One. In April, six spare planes were received, giving VMF-1 a total of 24.

In the last week of March, section and division tactics were added to the training syllabus. Out of necessity, several maneuvers required some modification to accommodate the greater speed of the Grummans (Fig. 16-2). To speed up the transition, Mac ordered that the daily flying hours be increased. He was anxious for the squadron to become fully operational as soon as possible.

F3F-Last of the Biplane Fighters

Pilots loved everything about the new Grummans except the retractable landing gear. From the start, some mechanical and human trouble had been experienced in this area (Fig. 16-3). The crew chiefs took care of the mechanical failures and Mac took care of the human portion. He ordered that a sentry with a big red flag be stationed at the end of the runway to remind the pilots to crank down the landing gear. A few days of this embarrassment ended all wheels-up landings. Within a short time check lists for take-offs and landings were placed in all cockpits.

On 21 March 11 new pilots joined the squadron, boosting its strength to 31—a 55 percent increase. Seven were cadets fresh from Pensacola. Colonel Geiger summoned Mac to his office and announced their arrival. At the time, Mac was unaware that the cadets had been refused by Maj. Madaris and Capt. Schilt for their squadrons. This left Mac to be the goat.

Remembering those days, Major General McKittrick said, "My pilots were working hard and flying long hours to qualify themselves as quickly as possible in the new planes and crew chiefs were learning all about their operation and maintenance. I sure as hell didn't need any green kids at this time—no matter *how* good they might be. However, it was my luck for two more hellraisers to be among the new cadets. The men in question were Aviation Cadets Thomas M. "Mob" Mobley and Burnette A. "Jeep" Kempson. These two kids were real characters. I found out later each had been warned during primary flight training at Pensacola that they would be damn lucky to make it through. After arriving at Quantico, both figured it was only a matter of time until they were washed out of my squadron and even made bets who would be first. Consequently, they proceeded to enjoy themselves and managed to be in some kind of trouble most of the time. It ran all the way from practical jokes to insulting generals. These two, along with Freeman Williams and Gregory Boyington, sure as hell gave me some gray hair. However, one thing I'll have to say about those kids: *They sure as hell could fly!*"

"Mind Your Own Business!"

When asked about some of the stories related to his cadet days, Colonel Kempson, (USMC, ret), said, "I guess there were some instances when I must have been a problem to my superior officers. When I, along with several other cadets, arrived at Quantico we had no idea that we would end up in a fighting squadron. At first no one wanted us, so we thought for sure they would send us back to Pensacola. When we found out we were assigned to a fighting squadron, we couldn't believe it. I guess McKittrick couldn't, either. I don't believe he was too happy about it.

"Tom Mobley and I became friends with Gregory Boyington and Freeman Williams. Soon we were known throughout the Marine base as 'Peck's Bad Boys.' One night we were on our way to becoming drunk in the Quantico Officer's Club. We had been warned about being too loud and were asked to leave. It was decided that I would do the driving. I went after the car and drove up to the front entrance and blew the horn. When they failed to appear as promised, I laid on the horn several more times.

"An elderly gent in civilian clothes came over to my car and asked me not to blow the horn as it was very annoying at that time of night.

"Not knowing who he was, I told him to run along and mind his own business. I began blowing the horn again. The old gent asked if I knew who he was and I told him I didn't give a damn. He then identified himself as General Bradman and said if I would just go along home everything would be okay.

"I told him I was a Colonel, and would go home when I damn pleased. Suddenly, I sobered up after saying those words. After all, I thought, the old gent could be a general and lowly cadets like myself don't talk to *anyone* like that, let alone a General.

Fig. 16-1. 1-MF-14 on Brown Field shortly after delivery from factory. Pilot: Aviation Cadet George W. Nevils. In cockpit: crew chief Ivy W. Crownover (courtesy Marine Corps).

Fig. 16-2. 1-MF-2 at Brown Field in July 1938. Pilot: 1st Lt. Edward E. "Barbells" Authier (courtesy BGen. W.H. Stiles).

"I yanked my old car into gear and roared off like I was shot from a cannon, leaving my buddies behind in the club.

"The next morning I was sure hoping the general hadn't found out who I was. When I arrived at Squadron Operations, Bill Brice said I was to report to Colonel Geiger's office on the double. I knew what was going to happen when I arrived there.

"Talk about a severe reprimand! After raking me over the coals for about 10 minutes, Geiger ordered that I report to General Bradman's office and apologize to him. I had been in trouble before, but not with a General. I suddenly realized that I liked the Marine Corps and didn't want to get kicked out this way.

"Surprisingly, when I arrived at the General's office in Quantico and identified myself as Aviation Cadet Kempson, the general's aide said I could go in. After standing at attention for a few moments, the General said to stand at ease and state my business. After forcing myself to tell of my miserable conduct, I then formally apologized for my actions the preceding night.

"After what seemed like hours, the General said, 'Son, I can well remember when I was a young Second Lieutenant. I used to get drunk and raise a lot of hell. I also got into some trouble too. There comes a time when a man must learn to control his drinking, otherwise, it can lead to serious trouble. I'm confident that you have the makings of a fine Marine

Fig. 16-3. Excellent one-wheel landing on Brown Field 19 July 1938. Pinion gear on right retracting strut jammed (courtesy Marine Corps).

Fig. 16-4. "Vee of Vees" formation south of Quantico on 16 July 1938. VMF-1 flew full formations everyday—weather permitting (courtesy U.S. Navy).

Officer and I know you will not let this sort of thing happen again. I accept your apology and as far as I'm concerned, the incident is closed. You are dismissed!'

"I gave the General a snappy salute and didn't waste any time vacating the premises just in case he changed his mind.

"When I reported back to Colonel Geiger and repeated what the General had said, Geiger looked surprised and advised me to watch my step, as I might not be so lucky the next time. When I returned to my squadron and told McKittrick what happened, he just smiled and from that day on, he called my Colonel."

The squadron report for the month of May showed considerable improvement over the preceeding two months in all catagories. Camera gunnery and bombing scores had surpassed predictions and tactical formations of all types were bordering on excellent (Fig. 16-4). Much to Mac's surprise, the cadets were shaping up even though they had been neglected in some phases of training because of the excessive number of pilots on the roster.

However, unknown to Mac, a decision had been made at Headquarters to again raid the squadron of many of its experienced men. Geiger knew what was going on but was unable to stop the transfers. Not one to give up easily, "Bull" Geiger, as he was sometimes called, tried to outflank the so-called decision makers and use his influence. As Marine Aviator Number Five, he had been in aviation since 1917, knew most of the Navy brass in the Bureau, and was on a first-name basis with many congressmen.

Mac finally learned what was going on, but was confident that Geiger could halt any attempt to downgrade the squadron. However, when orders arrived on 1 June transferring 13 officers plus several top enlisted men to new billets, Mac became somewhat perturbed. All transfers were effective as of 1 July.

Mac charged out the door for Geiger's office with the remark, "Dammit all, if *anyone* has to go, why not the cadets?"

During the walk to Geiger's office, he lost some of his steam and decided it best to get answers before speaking his mind. Geiger was not suprised at Mac's sudden appearance and guessed his reason for coming. He explained what had transpired over the past few weeks and gave assurance to Mac that equally qualified replacements were forthcoming. Geiger then added, "Never feel bad about becoming upset over anything that affects your squadron. I want my squadron commanders to fight for what they believe in and not be willy-nilly. Before the day is over, you will receive a complete list of both departing and replacement personnel. And, by the way, if I were you, I'd buy a pair of oak leaves for my collar. Your promotion to rank of Major has been confirmed as of 1 July. Congratulations!"

It goes without saying that Mac left Geiger's office displaying a big grin on his face.

As promised, the personnel officer from Aircraft One delivered the list of departing officers and those scheduled to arrive as replacements. It read as follows:

Officers departing on 1 July 1938:

Captains: *William O. Brice, Executive Officer*
Carson A. Roberts, Operations Officer
Boeker C. Batterton, Engineering Officer
Edward B. Carney, Personnel Officer
Lyle H. Meyer, Marine Reserve
Carl H. Nelson, Marine Reserve

First Lieutenants:
William M. Hudson, Buildings, grounds and Mess Officer
Kenneth D. Kirby, Photo & assistant Navigation Officer

Second Lieutenants: (Transfered to Basic School)

Howard F. Bowker	*Fred R. Emerson*
Gregory Boyington	*Freeman W. Williams*
Frank W. Davis	

Bill Brice read the list and remarked to Mac: "At least *one* good thing has come out of the better. You are getting rid of two hellraisers!"

The new officer replacements scheduled to report aboard on 1 July 1939 were:

Captains:

Thomas B. White, Executive Officer   Harold W. Bauer, Engineering Officer
Edward L. Pugh, Operations Officer   Luther S. Moore, Personnel Officer
First Lieutenants: Marshall A. Tyler, Gunnery Officer
Second Lieutenants:
Joseph N. Renner, Parachute Officer
Herbert H. Williamson, Welfare Officer
Pelham B. Withers, Buildings & Grounds Officer
Donald K. Yost, Navigator
Aviation Cadets: Joe B. Mauldin
Leon A. Ranchynoski

"Whimpy" Withers and "Twinkle Toes" Yost had previously been in the squadron under Rogers and had taken part in the carrier qualification fiasco on the West Coast the previous year. They were reassigned to the squadron after graduating from Basic School in Philadelphia.

On 1 August the personnel and aircraft of VMF-1 were as follows:

Personnel	*Aircraft*
15 Officers (pilots)	20 Grumman F3F-2 Fighters
3 NAP's (pilots)	1 Vought SB2U-1 (utility hack)
11 Aviation Cadets (pilots)	1 Vought SU-3 (utility hack)
29 total pilots	22 total
56 Enlisted men (all categories)	
85 Squadron total	

Ed Pugh Returns

The new Operations Officer, Captain Pugh, was an outstanding addition to the squadron (Fig. 16-5). As will be remembered, he had been with Sanderson and Rogers for several years and was an expert in conducting the type of training required. Harold Bauer, Sam Moore and Marshall Tyler were also excellent men to have aboard and would prove their worth many times over.

The task of reorganizing the squadron's flight operations commenced immediately. The plan, drawn up by Pugh, was designed to fully utilize the manpower with the available aircraft and supporting equipment. Night flying was also included. Further, to test the mobility of the squadron and meet the new night flying requirements imposed by the Bureau of Aeronautics, he gained approval from Col. Geiger to plan and schedule the squadron's first night cross-country flight.

By the middle of July the squadron was averaging 100 flight hours daily. This imposed a heavy burden on the mechanics and crew chiefs. Had it not been for the six spare airplanes on the station, it would have been impossible to support this schedule for long. The maintenance required for the Grummans was more complicated than for the Boeing F4B-4's.

A program to determine the most economical power setting for cruise on the Grummans began the first week of August. Harold Bauer, the engineering officer, asked the question "If we have to, how long can we fly on the total fuel capacity of the F3F-2's?" In other words, what was the optimum combinations of throttle, mixture control and propeller settings for flying the longest distance on the least amount of fuel? In daily test flights each pilot was instructed to use different combinations of the three. In a few days a power curve was established that proved of value in future long-distance flights.

On 2 August, a press release announced that VMF-1 would represent the Marines at the National Air Races in Cleveland. This was a coveted assignment and Mac was extremely pleased. It would be his first appearance at Cleveland as Commanding officer of a fighting squadron and he wanted to look as good as his predecessors.

The following day all squadrons of Aircraft One staged an aerial parade at Brown Field for the Commandant and his guests. Concluding the program was a special demonstration by VMF-1 that brought warm praise from all in attendance. The show proved to be a good warm-up for the races the following month.

On 10 August, VMF-1 made its first tactical night cross-country flight. Eighteen Grumman F3F-2's took off at 1930 hours for Jacksonville and returned to Brown Field the following morning at 0700, having flown all night. The success of the night flight was an outstanding tribute to all personnel associated with the operation, especially Ed Pugh, who planned it and was in charge throughout.

An item in the Navy Bureau of Aeronautics *Newsletter,* Number 81, said: *"Often, in the past, Fighting Squadron One has been known as the*

Fig. 16-5. Maj. McKittrick (center) with six of his outstanding squadron officers. Left/right: Capt. Luther S. "Sad Sam" Moore; Capt. James M. "Moe" Daly; Capt. Thomas B. "TB" White; Capt. Edward L. "Pug" Pugh; Capt. Harold W. "Indian Joe" Bauer; 1st Lt. Marshall A. "Zack" Tyler (courtesy Col. L.S. Moore).

'Dawn to Dusk' squadron. As a result of recent operations, all pilots are beginning to feel that such a title is a misnomer. In addition to regular scheduled daily flights, night flying has been added to the schedule. On 10 August an extended night flight from Brown Field to Jacksonville, Florida, and return (about 1,400 miles) was made in 9 hours and 12 minutes flying time with two fuel stops enroute, thus demonstrating the mobility of the squadron as a unit. All in all, the past few weeks has been a busy time and one pilot aptly remarked after several nights of flying: 'think I'll go home for a few minutes.'"

Preparation for the National Air Races really brought Brown Field alive in the last week of August. The squadron was flying well and the old "esprit de corps" had returned. Further, morale was at its highest level in months.

The toughest decision now facing Mac was the final selection of pilots for the show. He intended to take two spare airplanes—or a total of 20, which meant that nine pilots would stay home.

Surrendering the "Sword"

To Cadet Jeep Kempson it didn't make any difference; he was unable to go anyway. He was in trouble again and, as Geiger had promised, he

Fig. 16-6. McKittrick's number "1" at the 1938 Cleveland Air Races. Squadron dive-bombed Cleveland's water front in mock attack to open the giant air show (courtesy Warren D. Shipp).

wouldn't get off so easy "the next time." When asked what happened, Kempson, now a retired colonel, said:

"Ah hell, I was framed! I was driving through Quantico on my way to Brown Field. I noticed a car behind me but I didn't pay it any attention.. Shortly after I arrived at the field, Mac said I was to report to Colonel Geiger's office on the double.

"I was turned in by 'Handlebar Hank' Evans, (Major W. T. Evans) for exceeding the speed limit by five miles per hour. Geiger said I was under house arrest and confined to my quarters for three days. Further, I must hand over my sword! Hell, cadets didn't *have* swords! We couldn't afford them.

"Geiger said it was customary to turn in something and I must do so. Out of desperation I suggested the hunting knife in my survival kit. He said to get it and return on the double. After I left, Geiger had a big laugh and called Mac to inform him of what happened. They decided to have some fun and when I returned, there were about 10 people in his office, including the senior officers from my squadron, to witness the surrendering of my hunting knife. All had a big laugh at my expense and, believe me, it was some time before I lived *that* one down."

At 0800 on 2 September, VMF-1 with 20 Grumman F3F-2's (Fig. 16-6 through 16-8) lifted off Brown Field for the National Air Races at Cleveland, scheduled for 3 through 5 September. Two Douglas R2D-1 transports commanded by Major Stanley E. Ridderhof carried all support personnel and equipment.

222

VMF-1 Dive Bombs Cleveland

At Cleveland, the arrival of the Marines was awaited by Clifford Henderson, promoter of the National Air Races, representatives of radio station WTAM, and the press. To publicize the races, it had been arranged for VFM-1 to stage a mock attack on the city's Lake Erie Harbor. On Thursday the Cleveland Press carried the following story:

MARINE FIGHTING SQUADRON
TO BOMB PIER AT EAST 9TH STREET

Devildogs to thunder down east 9th street tomorrow at noon in diving maneuver to open the 1938 National Air Races at the Municipal Airport.

18 fighting planes of Fighting Squadron One, commanded by Major William L. McKittrick, from the Fleet Marine Force, Quantico, Virginia, will nose earthward in bombing dives—throttles wide open—and leave the city pier in theoretical smoking ruins. Through special arrangements, radio station WTAM will broadcast Major McKittrick's orders as they are given before and during the mock attack, thus enabling its listeners to eavesdrop on the conversation of a military maneuver.

The radio station prepared a short script for Mac. It was designed to clarify for the vast listening audience each military order given during the attack. On Friday morning thousands of people lined the water front area

Fig. 16-7. 1-MF-6 at Cleveland on 5 September 1938. Pilot: 2nd Lt. Pelham B. "Wimpy" Withers (courtesy Warren D. Shipp).

Fig. 16-8. 2nd Lt. Donold K. "Twinkle Toes" Yost was pilot of 1-MF-15 at the 1938 Cleveland Air Races (courtesy Warren D. Shipp).

Fig. 16-9. 18 Grumman F3F-2 Fighters of Squadron VMF-1 lined up at Brown Field for review (courtesy BGen. F.H. Wirsig).

for a first-hand view of the show. The demonstration was a huge success and resulted in sell-out crowds each day.

The usual pomp and ceremony signaled the opening of the giant airshow, where new speed records were destined to be set. The Marine's competition for military honors was an Army Squadron of Seversky P-35 fighters from Selfridge Field, Michigan.

The Marines' segment of the show began at 1325 before the largest opening-day crowd ever. Mac lead his squadron in a tight 18-plane formation takeoff and the crowd immediately sensed it was to witness a dramatic show. For the next twenty-five minutes, roaring engines and screaming power dives filled the sky as VMF-1 performed a giant figure eight. The planes barely missed one another as they crossed in the center. They followed this maneuver with a precision dive-bombing demonstration using three plane sections. The show concluded with people staring in disbelief at the Squirrel Cage and their beautiful landing in formation. From the announcer came the remark: "As usual the Marines can always be counted on to give a superior and flawless performance and provide extra thrills not found elsewhere."

On Tuesday, while winging their way home, Mac's thoughts were on the praise they had received at Cleveland. Just like the old days of Sandy and Tex. In fact, Major Sandy Sanderson, who for the first time had witnessed the show as a spectator, gave his old alma-mater warm praise.

Coming from *him*, it had to be a great compliment. Suddenly Mac felt contentment, and for the first time he knew that the squadron (Fig. 16-9) had once again arrived.

Epilogue

The 1938 National Air Races brought to a close further large-scale shows by VMF-1. For sometime, talks had been underway in Washington about the situation in Europe. With Hitler on the march, many of our nation's leaders and the Congress were becoming jittery. As a result, Secretary of War Harry Woodring concluded that this country could no longer afford time and money on non-military activities. It was time for military aviation to get down to serious business.

In line with this thinking, on 16 September Colonel Rowell arrived at Quantico from Washington for a meeting with Geiger and his staff. Marine Aviation was to drastically curb demonstrations not essential for military training. In other words, the glamour days were over! With this decision, a great era in Marine Aviation—never to be duplicated—ended.

The decision came as a surprise to no one in the upper echelon. Marine Aviation had accomplished most of the goals set forth by Colonel Turner. After his untimely death, the fighter for recognition had been carried on by Rowell and Geiger, with assistance from many sources including the Navy. Through their persistance, Marine Aviation became firmly established within the Navy Bureau of Aeronautics as a separate division. This assured its participation in all Navy Fleet Exercises and ended the Navy's practice of passing down its unwanted airplanes to the Marines. Further, Marine Squadrons were permitted to operate aboard the Navy's aircraft carriers as equals. And last but not least, they made themselves indispensable to the Navy through their development and perfecting of close air support, a technique widely used today. Indeed, they had come a long way.

On 1 July 1939, Major Thomas J. Walker became the commanding officer of VMF-1. From this date until the start of WW-II the squadron was on a full war-time schedule, participating in Naval exercises and almost-daily bombing and gunnery practice. In 1940 it went aboard aircraft carriers *USS Ranger* and *USS Wasp* for qualifications and extensive training with the Fleet.

By July 1941 the threat of war had Marine Aviation on a greatly expanding program that called for two Aircraft Wings, each composed of Groups which, in turn, were comprised of Squadrons of all types. Thus on 1 July 1941, VMF-1 was redesignated VMF-111. (First Wing, First Air Group and the First Fighting Squadron within that group). This designation elevated it to the highest echelon in Marine Aviation. It was from this squadron that the Corps greatest aviation leaders emerged during WW-II, and the Marine's leading Aces can be counted among its alumni. A fine tribute to its endeavors.

As for aerobatic teams, today we have the "Blue Angels" representing Navy and Marine Aviation. They are an extension of the VF-9M era and do an outstanding job. However, many Aviation historians and others associated with the aviation of that period believe that no demonstration team has *ever* surpassed VF-9M's all-around qualities and showmanship and daring, especially with the use of 18 airplanes. And, unlike today's demonstration teams, they were required to carry a full military work load.

There is no accurate way to measure the impact that VF-9M made on the public, but it is a known fact that it provided the inspiration for thousands of young men (including the author), to become aviators. There is scarcely a man in Marine Aviation today that has not heard of VF-9M and the great Sandy Sanderson. He is and always will be a legendary figure about whom future generations of aviators will talk.

About the Author

Jess Barrow became an aviation enthusiast at the age of nine, when he was given a ride in a Curtiss "Robin" flown by the famous "Reg" Robbins, a barnstormer of the 1920-1930 era. However, what really convinced him to become an aviator was his attendance at the 1934 National Air Races at Cleveland, Ohio, where he watched in awe at Marine Fighting Squadron Nine, the Marine Corps' "crack" show squadron perform its famous "Squirrel Cage." In 1935-1936 he worked as a mechanic's helper at the old Stickney Airport at Toledo, Ohio, in exchange for flying lessons. Graduating from the Toledo School of Aeronautics, he joined the Navy in World War II and at the close of the war was serving at the Joint Intelligence Center at Admiral Nimitz's Headquarters in the Pacific.

In 1956 he left his job as a Designer for an auto parts manufacturer to become Chief Pilot for a Michigan Corporation, a position he left in 1963 to join The Ford Motor Co, as a Design Engineer. He remained in the Naval Reserve until 1951, when he joined the Coast Guard Reserve. He has more than 10,000 flying hours logged.

Jess is an editorial consultant for the *Journal*, a publication of the prestigious American Aviation Historical Society and is listed in the World Almanac book of "Buffs" as a leading authority on U.S. Navy, Marine Corps and Coast Guard Aviation History. His articles have appeared in leading aviation publications. He resides in Dearborn Heights, Michigan.

Glossary

V- Heavier-Than-Air.

Squadron designations are formed by combining "V", the symbol for heavier-than-air (Z-for lighter-than-air), with one or more mission letters followed by a dash and number. The "V" was not painted on aircraft, but was used on all discriptions and communications. For example, VF-5 means heavier-than-air Fighting Squadron Five, Navy. If its a Marine Squadron the letter "M" is added after the squadron number. Thus, VF-5M means heavier-than-air Fighting Squadron Five, Marines. Following are the mission letters commonly used in the 1920-1930 era.

VF- Fighting Squadron	**VJ**- Utility Squadron
VB- Bombing Squadron	**VP**- Patrol Squadron
VO- Observation Squadron	**VT**- Torpedo Squadron
VS- Scouting Squadron	**VN**- Training Squadron
VR- Transport Squadron	**VX**- Experimental Squadron

On 1 July 1937 the Squadron Designation system for the Marine Corps was changed. The service letter "M" (Marines) was moved in between the "V" and the mission letter. Thus in a Marine Fighter Squadron VF became VMF or in the cse of a Marine Bombing Squadron VB became VMB, etc.

Abbreviations

NAP- Naval Aviation Pilot (enlisted)	**l.w.**- left wing
NAS- Naval Air Station	**r.w.**- right wing
C.O.- Commanding Officer	

Appendix A

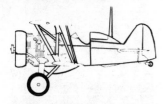

Aircraft Assigned to VF-9M

MAKE	MODEL	SERIAL No.	SQUAD. No.	REMARKS
I. Initial Aircraft of VF-2, 1925-1928				
Squadron Airplanes of 15 Septemer 1925				
Vought	*VE-7	A-5673	2-F-1	Operating condition
		A-5680	2-F-2	Under repair
		A-5959	2-F-3	Operating condition
		A-5969	2-F-4	Under repair
	VE-7-SF	A-5692	2-F-5	Built as single-seat fighter. Oper
	VE-9	A-6471	2-F-6	Operating condition
Martin	MT	A-5719	none	Two-engine bomber
Squadron Airplanes as of 1 July 1926				
Vought	VE-7	A-5673	2-F-1	
		A-5969	2-F-2	
		A-5959	2-F-3	
		A-5699	2-F-4	
				All operating
Boeing	FB-1	A-6888	2-F-5	
		A-6891	2-F-6	
		A-6892	2-F-7	
Martin	MT	A-5719	2-F-8	
Squadron Airplanes as of 1 Jan. 1927				
Vought	VE-7	A-5673	2-F-1	
		A-5969	2-F-2	Under repair
		A-5959	2-F-3	
		A-5699	2-F-4	
		A-5960	2-F-5	Under repair
Boeing	NB-2	A-6778	2-F-6	
		A-6779	2-F-7	
Consoli-dated	NY-1	A-7192	2-F-8	
		A-7193	2-F-9	
Squadron Airplanes as of 1 October 1927				
Curtiss	F6C-4	A-7394	9-F-1	
		A-7395	9-F-2	Operating at NAS Anacostia
		A-7396	9-F-3	
		A-7397	9-F-4	
Vought	VE-7	A-5673	9-F-5	
		A-5696	9-F-6	
		A-5960	9-F-7	Under repair
Martin	MT	A-5716	none	Two-engine bomber
Squadron Airplanes as of 1 May 1928				
Curtiss	F6C-4	A-7394	9-F-1	
		A-7396	9-F-2	
		A-7397	9-F-3	
				All airplanes operating
Curtiss	F6C-1	A-6969	9-F-4	
		A-6971	9-F-5	
		A-6972	9-F-6	
Consoli-dated	NY-1	A-7192	9-F-7	

II CURTISS F7C-1 AIRPLANES ASSIGNED TO VF-5M

Serial No.	Squad. No.	Date received	Date stricken	Total hours	Remarks
7657	5-F-1	12-28-28			See data below
7658	5-F-2	12-31-28			See data below
7659	5-F-3	12-28-28	9-30-29	135	crashed (motor failure) 8-19-29
7660	5-F-4	12-30-28			See data below
7661	5-F-5	12-31-28			See data below
7662	5-F-6	12-31-28			See data below
7663	5-F-7	1-4-29			See data below
7664	5-F-8	1-3-29	3-31-30	284.3	crashed at Quantico 2-20-30. Lt. Wolfe killed.
7665	5-F-9	1-3-29	3-31-30	238.5	crashed at Quantico 2-20-30. Lt. Ostertag killed.
7667	5-F-3	4-2-30			See data below
7669	5-F-8	4-2-30	6-30-30	281.6	crashed at Quantico 6-11-30. Lt. Chappell killed.
7653	spare	7-22-31	5-28-32	527.6	crashed on 5-15-32
7654	9-F-12	6-17-31	2-28-33	562.7	worn out in service.
7655	9-F-1	1-12-31	10-31-31	329.9	crashed at Cleveland Air Races 8-30-31. Lt. Sanderson, pilot
7656	spare	8-26-31	11-30-31	304.	crashed at Royalton, Ohio 8-28-31. Lt. Adams, pilot.
7657	9-F-2		4-30-32	778.5	shipped to NAF for static tests 1-12-32
7658	9-F-3		12-28-31	815.4	crashed at New Bern, N.C. 11-21-31. Lt. J.D. Nott, killed.
7660	9-F-4		3-31-33	607.9	crashed at Quantico 1-28-33. Given to rindge Tech. school
7661	9-F-5		10-31-33	934.4	crashed at Anacostia 9-27-33. Last F7C-1 in service.
7662	9-F-6		2-28-33	774.6	worn out in service.
7663	9-F-7		10-31-31	742.5	crashed at Cleveland Air Races 8-30-31. Lt. Brice, pilot.
7666	9-F-8	6-10-31	2-8-33	768.6	worn out in service.
7667	9-F-9		11-29-32	715.2	worn out in service.
7668	9-F-10	6-10-31	8-31-33	895.4	worn out in service.
7670	9-F-11	6-10-31	8-31-33	756.8	worn out in service.

III BOEING F4B-4 AIRCRAFT ASSIGNED TO VF-9M

SERIAL No.	SQUAD. No.	TAIL COLOR	DATE REC'D	REMARKS
9010	0	red	9-16-32	To Pensacola 3-16-38
9011	1	white	9-16-32	To Pensacola 7-17-37
9012	2	blue	9-16-32	To Anacostia 8-29-33
9013	3	red	9-23-32	To Pensacola 3-16-38
9014	4	white	9-22-32	To Pensacola 8-5-38
9015	5	blue	9-10-32	Crashed at Miami Air Races 1-6-33
9016	15	red	7-13-33	To Pensacola 3-16-38
9017	16	white	7-13-33	To Pensacola 11-4-37
9035	17	blue	7-13-33	To Pensacola 7-17-37
9036	18	red	7-13-33	To Pensacola 3-16-38
9037	19	red	7-13-33	To Pensacola 3-16-38
9038	20	red	7-13-33	In ground accident 11-17-33. See 9719.
9230	10	white	12-10-32	To Pensacola 3-16-38
9231	11	blue	12-10-32	To Pensacola 3-16-38
9232	12	red	12-10-32	To Anacostia 8-27-33
9233	13	white	12-10-32	To Pensacola 3-16-38
9234	14	blue	11-30-32	To Pensacola 3-16-38
9235	5	blue	12-10-32	Replaced 9015. To Pensacola 3-16-38
9236	6	red	12-10-32	To Pensacola 3-16-38
9237	7	white	12-10-32	To Pensacola 3-16-38
9238	8	blue	12-10-32	To Pensacola 7-17-37
9239	9	red	12-10-32	Crashed at sea off Virginia Beach, Va. 4-12-34
9240	2	blue	7-14-33	Replaced 9012. To Pensacola 3-16-38
9241	21	white	7-14-33	Only F4B-4 Remaining. In NASM, Washington.
9242	22	white	7-14-33	To Pensacola 3-16-38
9243	23	white	7-14-33	To Pensacola 7-17-37
9244	24	white	7-14-33	To Pensacola 3-16-38
9245	12	red	7-14-33	Replaced 9232. To Pensacola 3-16-38
9719	20	red	6-1-34	Rebuilt 9038. New serial number assigned on 6-9-34 through error. To Pensacola 3-16-38

Note: Total number of F-4B-4 aircraft assigned to VF-9M was 28.

IV GRUMMAN F3F-2 AIRCRAFT ASSIGNED TO MARINE SQUADRON VMF-1

Serial No.	Squad No.	Date Received	Remarks
1009	1-MF-1	3-1-38	Transferred to NAS Miami on 5-26-41
1010	1-MF-2	3-1-38	Transferred to NAS Miami on 5-26-41
1011	1-MF-3	3-1-38	Crashed to destruction at Culebra, P.R. 2-15-40
1012	1-MF-4	3-4-38	Trans. to NAS Miami on 5-26-41
1013	1-MF-5	3-4-38	Trans. to NAS Miami on 6-4-41
1014	1-MF-6	3-4-38	Trans. to N.A.F. on 7-28-41
1015	1-MF-7	3-7-38	Trans. to NAS Miami on 6-10-41
1016	1-MF-8	3-9-38	Trans. to NAS Miami on 5-26-41
1017	1-MF-9	3-9-38	Crashed to destruction at Guantanamo Bay, 10-15-40
1018	1-MF-10	3-9-38	Trans. To NAS Miami on 6-4-41
1019	1-MF-11	3-11-38	Trans. to NAS Miami on 5-26-41
1020	1-MF-12	3-18-38	Trans. to NAS Miami on 5-26-41
1021	1-MF-13	3-19-38	Crashed at Guantanamo Bay 3-3-41
1022	1-MF-14	3-18-38	Trans. to NAS Miami on 5-26-41
1023	1-MF-15	3-18-38	Crashed at Guantanamo Bay 1-13-41. Major Damage
1024	1-MF-16	3-23-38	Trans. to NAS Miami on 6-4-41
1025	1-MF-17	3-23-38	Trans. to NAS Miami on 6-4-41
1026	1-MF-18	3-23-38	Trans. to NAS Miami on 5-26-41
1040	spare	4-22-38	Rotated through squadron. To Corpus Christi 11-17-41
1041	spare	4-22-38	Rotated through squadron. To NAS Miami 6-4-41
1042	spare	4-22-38	Rotated thru Sqd. To NAS Corpus Christi 11-17-41
1043	1-MF-9	4-22-38	Replaced 1017. Crashed at Quantico 1-4-40
1044	BAD-1*	4-29-38	Group Commander's airplane. To NAS Miami 6-4-41
1045	1-MF-3	4-29-38	Replaced 1011. Crashed to destruction at Gtmo Bay
1046	1-MF-3	4-29-38	Replaced 1045. To NAS Miami 6-4-41 11-28-40
1047	1-MF-5	6-10-38	To NAS Jacksonville. 5-26-41.

* BAD-1 = Base Air Detachment. (formerly VMJ-1)
NAS = Naval Air Station

V. MISCELLANEOUS SQUADRON AIRPLANES
(1 January 1928—31 December 1938)

Make	Model	Serial No.	Received	Remarks
Boeing	02B-1	A-6908	9-1-28	squadron utility plane
Ford	JR-2	A-8273	6-21-29	3-engine transport. To West Coast 3-23-31
Ford	JR-3	A-8599	5-21-30	3-engine transport. To Nicaragua 8-19-30
Curtiss	XOC-3	A-7672	10-8-30	squadron Utility. (F8C-1 with exp. engine)
Curtiss	RC-1	A-8846	4-17-31	squadron transport. To west coast 7-5-33
Sikorsky	RS-3	A-8922	1-15-33	squadron transport.
Martin	T4M-1	A-7633	12-5-32	converted to mosquito duster at Quantico.
Pitcairn	XOP-1	A-8977	11-15-31	Autogiro. Military Eval. Crashed 1-18-32
Loening	OL-9	A-8740	11-30-33	squadron utility plane.
Vought	SU-2	A-9121	8-?-35	squadron utility plane. To VMS-3 2-13-36
Vought	03U-6	0005	2-1-36	loaned from VO-7M for instrument flying. returned 9-1-36
Vought	SU-3	A-9137	9-4-36	Squadron utility plane.
Vought	SB2U-1	0769	9-1-38	Squadron utility plane. To NAS Anacostia 11-16-39

Appendix B

Squadron Commanders From 1 September, 1925 to 28 February, 1942

Squadron's first designation: VF-2

1st Lt. Lawson H.M. Sanderson	1 Sept. 1925 to 1 Nov. 1926
1st Lt. Jay D. Swartwout	1 Nov. 1926 to 6 Jan. 1927
Chief Marine Gunner Elmo Reagan	6 Jan. 1927 to 2 March 1927
Capt. William T. Evans	28 March 1927 to 7 June 1927
1st Lt. Vernon M. Guymon	7 June 1927 to 3 Oct. 1927

On 1 July 1927 squadron designation changed to VF-9M

1st Lt. George H. Towner	6 Oct. 1927 to 21 Jan. 1928
1st Lt. William O. Brice	21 Jan. 1928 to 8 Oct. 1928

On 1 July 1928 squadron designation changed to VF-5M

1st Lt. William R. Hughes	9 Oct. 1928 to 28 Dec. 1928
1st Lt. Horace D. Palmer	28 Dec. 1928 to 26 April 1929
1st Lt. Hayne D. Boyden	11 May 1929 to 27 Nov. 1929
1st Lt. Christian F. Schilt	1 Dec. 1929 to 15 June 1930
1st Lt. Lawson H.M. Sanderson	15 June 1930 to 9 Sept. 1931

On 1 August 1930 squadron designation changed to VF-9M

1st Lt. Clayton C. Jerome	9 Sept. 1931 to 15 June 1932
1st Lt. Lawson H.M. Sanderson	15 June 1932 to 1 July 1934
Capt. Ford O. Rogers	1 July 1934 to 1 July 1937

On 1 July 1937 squadron designation changed to VMF-1

Capt. William L. McKittrick	1 July 1937 to 1 July 1939
Major Thomas J. Walker	14 July 1939 to 28 Feb. 1942

On 1 July 1941 squadron designation changed to VMF-111

Appendix C

Directors Of Marine
Corps Aviation (To Start Of WW-II)

Major Alfred A. Cunningham	17 Nov. 1919—12 Dec. 1920
Lt. Col Thomas C. Turner	13 Dec. 1920—2 March 1925
Major Edward H. Brainard	3 March 1925—9 May 1929
Col. Thomas C. Turner	10 May 1929—28 Oct. 1931
Major Roy S. Geiger	6 Nov. 1931—29 May 1935
Col. Ross E. Rowell	30 May 1935—10 March 1939
BGen. Ralph J. Mitchell	11 March 1939—29 March 1943

Note: On 6 April 1936 the title of the senior Marine Aviator attached to Headquarters, Marine Corps, was changed from Officer-in-Charge of Marine Aviation, to Director of Marine Aviation.

Index

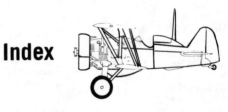

WWII:Marine Fighting Squadron Nine (VF-9M)

by Jess C. Barrow

A handful of leathernecks—against almost unbeatable odds—managed to keep the Marine air arm alive during the complacent 1920s and 1930s . . . a feat that was little appreciated until those first terrible days of WWII. Here is the enthraling account of Squadron Nine, the men who called themselves the "Rojas Diablos" (Red Devils), plus a detailed technical look at the Marine biplanes of that helmet-and-goggle era.

You'll learn the true story of men who did their best to rally public support for Marine air power in the period following WWI: "the war that was to end all wars". Men who thrilled crowds at air shows with their daring aerial acrobatics . . . men who also fought bravely in Haiti and Nicaragua, trained pilots, and developed close air support tactics to aid the Marines on the gound. Men who built a heritage of courage and competance that would be of critical importance when America entered WWII.

The planes they flew were little more than hand-me-downs already written off by the Navy . . . aircraft sometimes patched together with scrap parts and ingenuity. At one point in the '20s, the air strength of the entire Marine Corps had dwindled to less than 45 pilots! Yet, they established traditions that would distinguish the Squadron when WWII erupted.

Based on personal interviews with men who were involved, as well as official records. Includes more than 120 authentic photos of the era, plus a complete record of VF-9M activities with dates, squadron markings, and a record of all aircraft flown during the period—plus a list of serial numbers and what really happened to each and every plane!

Certain to be fascinating reading for any aviation enthusiast, and a valuable reference source for military historians!

Author Jess C. Barrow is a 10,000-hour pilot and reserve Naval officer, and is currently an editorial consultant for the American Aviation Historical Society.